From the Pennines
to the Highlands

Hamish Brown

From the Pennines to the Highlands

*A walking route through the Scottish Borders
From Byrness to Milngavie by Border Towns and the
River Tweed, by Cheviot, Moorfoot and Pentland
Hills, Canal Banks and Roman Wall.*

Hamish Brown
Lochar Publishing, Moffat, Scotland

© Hamish Brown 1992

Published by Lochar Publishing Ltd, Moffat DG10 9ED.

British Library Cataloguing in Publication data available on request from the British Library.

ISBN 1-874027-37-4

Designed and typeset in Monotype Plantin on Apple *Macintosh* computers by Adrian Tyler, Glasgow.

Printed in Great Britain by BPCC Wheatons Ltd, Exeter

For Peggy, who shared discoveries,
Keith, who first walked the route through
and Storm, on his last adventuring.

... never mock the stranger or the poor – the black ox has not trod on your foot yet – you know not what lands you may travel in, or what clothes you may wear before you die.

SIR WALTER SCOTT (*Fortunes of Nigel*)

Among the rocks we went and still looked up
to sun and cloud and listened to the wind.

JOHN VEITCH (quoted on his monument in Peebles High Street)

Above all do not lose your desire to walk: every day I walk myself into a state of well-being and walk away from every illness; I have walked myself into my best thoughts and I know of no thought so burdensome that one cannot walk away from it... Thus if one just keeps on walking, everything will be all right.

KIERKEGAARD (in a letter)

This grand show is eternal. It is always sunrise somewhere; the dew is never all dried at once; a shower is forever falling; vapour is ever rising. Eternal sunrise, eternal sunset, eternal dawn and gloaming, on sea and continents and islands, each in its turn, as the round earth rolls.

JOHN MUIR

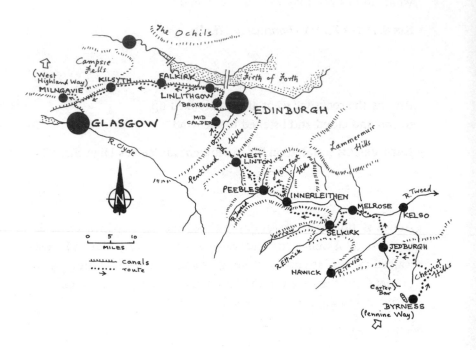

CONTENTS

DAY FIVE
MELROSE TO SELKIRK

DAY SIX
SELKIRK TO INNERLEITHEN

DAY SEVEN
INNERLEITHEN TO PEEBLES

DAY EIGHT
PEEBLES TO WEST LINTON

DAY NINE
WEST LINTON TO CALDERS / BROXBURN / EDINBURGH

DAY TEN
BROXBURN TO LINLITHGOW

DAY ELEVEN
LINLITHGOW TO FALKIRK

DAY TWELVE
FALKIRK TO CASTLECARY — KILSYTH AREA

DAY THIRTEEN
KILSYTH TO MILNGAVIE

APPENDICES

MAPS

Introduction

Introductions are traditionally the last part of a book to be written. This is no exception and if everything seems to flow naturally this is the outcome of two years of sporadic field work with no more flow to it than the completion of a giant jigsaw puzzle by a busy family. From the initial tentative route proposals on maps at home, to the testing of these on the spot, to rough notes made 'on the hoof', to piecing the text together (a jigsaw indeed!), to typing, checking proofs – and all the hundreds of photographs taken over so many erratic visits – out of all this comes a walk, logically and clearly running from A to B, from *Pennine Way* to *West Highland Way*, yet another 'gap' filled towards having described routes all the way from Land's End to John o' Groats. Indeed, with the authorities seemingly more active in producing their long-promised Fort William – Inverness line the only 'gap' left will be from Inverness to John o' Groats itself.

I'd rate the Pennines to Highlands Walk high (or even highest) in all round quality and interest among all the portions of that royal gangrel's end-to-end route. While losing nothing of the quality of hill-walking the Cheviots, Eildons, Minchmoor, Moorfoots, Meldons and Pentlands will surprise those who thought only the Scottish Highlands had hills in them; the last few days, using canal banks and Antonine Wall, will also surprise with the richness of the scenery while almost every day there are places of historical, cultural and recreational interest, something all too lacking on the Southern Upland Way (or Pennine Way) – 'It seems to avoid all the interesting places' I was told on Minchmoor. Questioning two lads who checked-out this route for their main impressions one said 'Skylarks singing and curlews reeling every day', the other said 'Good eating. I've put on weight'.

This Pennines to Highlands walk is also a superb entity in itself, for itself, and I'd challenge Scots walkers especially to make its acquaintance: the majority of the Scottish population lives within a short distance of the walk yet I'm sure are largely ignorant of their own heritage. That is as much confession as accusation – serendipity days along this route saw my annual tally of Munros reach an all-time low. Yet we don't take in Hawick, Kelso or

Galashiels on our walk, a sad but unavoidable lack, yet such is the richness of the Borders that we still have Jedburgh, Melrose, Selkirk, Innerleithen and Peebles.

As a lad I was puzzled by not finding Roxburgh Castle in my wanderings (my first extended cycle tour was in the Borders) for the name was well known from reading Scott's *Tales of a Grandfather*. Hadn't Edward I hung Bruce's sister Mary in a cage from its walls for four years? Hadn't James II died when a cannon blew up at a siege in 1460? Roxburgh Castle and town were utterly destroyed and nothing so brought home the wild history of this region to that curious young traveller. Jedburgh, Melrose, Selkirk, Innerleithen and Peebles are historical as well as geographical milestones.

From the Union Canal to the Teviot on my *Groats End Walk* I largely followed the same line as evolved for this route. With a decade between I'd largely forgotten the earlier walk so it was interesting to re-read my original comments. Little had changed on the hills I am glad to say but services have improved greatly in the towns and valleys. The Borders are aware they have much to offer and are doing something about it – and the same goes for the Union Canal, and the Forth and Clyde Canal, both increasingly important recreational delights.

Don't underestimate this walk. There may be easy days and many interesting distractions but one still has to put in the miles. Take time before, and during the trip to read up, plan – and pray. Borders weather is typically British and ranges from the unstable to the erratic. Be prepared for wet and be prepared for heat. Carry adequate liquid whatever the weather; there are few natural, safe water sources. Day food/nibbles should not be a problem but think ahead and keep topped-up, especially for the Scottish Sunday shut-down. Ask your host to pass on any forecast, or catch one on TV, or telephone the rip-off Weathercall service: 0898-500-422, as far as Falkirk, 0898-500-421 for the last two days. Thirteen days is plenty of time for the weather to change. As the old proverb puts it: the bee with honey in its mouth still has a sting in its tail.

In this guide the word *path* is used to denote a route only available to walkers (cyclists, ponies etc), *track* implies a rough or unsurfaced route which will be used mainly by forestry, farm or estate vehicles, *road* will generally mean a public, tarred route suitable for all vehicles. It is worth remembering that a 'Private Road' sign may only be valid against vehicles. Often such are pedestrian rights-of-way. Practically all of this route is on rights-of-way, open uplands or prepared walking routes. But all land is a resource which is being used commercially and we have an obligation to treat it with respect, observing the Country Code. On our route this means special care in not leaving litter, shutting gates behind us, and not walking with a dog – all points of importance in prime sheep country. The Borders have a tradition of friendly relations with farmers and shepherds. The canal days are good for dogs but they cover only a small part of the whole walk.

The Border hills are largely made of hardened sea-sands and mud, which gives them their characteristic rounded shapes from millenniums of weathering. Within this are areas of volcanic activity which stand as knobblier country or solitary upthrusts, like the Eildons. The Tweed has cut a deep course through this mixture, a course that zigzags as it runs up against stronger or weaker rocks. The north-east flow is deflected to south-east at the Meldons, where the Lyne Water joins it. The rivers Eddleston (Peebles), Leithen (Innerleithen), Gala (Galashiels) and Leader all join it from the north. Only when clear of the hills does the Tweed resume its north-east flow to the North Sea. This geography had a tremendous influence on history, the Border hills being almost as insurmountable a barrier as the Highlands. The Romans' barrier from Forth to Clyde was only a brief challenge, and when the Romans left the old barrier was re-established. The kingdom of Strathclyde was a far cry from Northumbria!

As we will keep meeting Roman sites a brief note of their presence in Scotland may be helpful. Most people, Scots as well as English, presume Hadrian's Wall was the ultimate boundary of the Roman Empire. The boundary was seldom static in reality. Caesar had first raided England in 55 BC and the real invasion began in AD 4.

It was the governor Agricola who first entered Scotland, AD 79, with the optimistic hope of adding it to the Roman Empire. One of the major routes he used was Dere Street, which we will tramp on our first two days. Trimontium (Newstead) on the Tweed became the great Borders base and, along the narrow waist of Scotland Agricola built a line of forts, quelled Galloway and headed up to the north-east to win the great battle of Mons Graupius, the site of which is still tantalisingly unknown. His fleet reached Orkney. He was then recalled to Rome. Early the next century Rome withdrew from Scotland back onto the Tyne–Solway line, and a decade later the Emperor Hadrian decided a definite defence line was needed and built the wall that bears his name.

His successor, a decade later decided to reinvade Scotland, which was undertaken, in AD 140 by the Governor Urbicus and so, a couple of years later, we had Antonine's Wall which followed the line of Agricola's forts.

Indeed several of the new forts lie on top of the early Agricola defences. We will walk parts of the wall on our last two days. The wall was held for a decade then there was another withdrawal, another brief re-establishment and, about AD 165, Antonine's Wall was finally abandoned for good. Rome's waxing and waning fortunes led to their eventual departure from British shores, but that is another story.

Some people are apt to scorn the idea of walking a described route (they probably have never done such so are in a weak position for arguing) but surely the rich variety of the outdoor pleasures all walkers enjoy should make us tolerant of one another's favoured pastime. I'd put in a plea for variety in one's own activity. *Just* to be collecting Munros or Corbetts is as narrow and unimaginative as just to be walking Long Distance Footpaths. The bigger the spread of ideas and opportunities the better; taking some of the pressures off the over-popular.

A walk like this is welcomed by those with little or no opportunity to enjoy working out a personal route for a holiday tramp. If one's dream of walking the country end-to-end has to rely on the descriptions of others, this is no worse than climbers following descriptions in a rock guide book. Nor does one need to have this larger concept. As I discovered on the *Summits of Somerset,* on Offa's Dyke and again during this walk, these are grand routes in their own right.

Most B & Bs, and many sites, are only open from Easter to the end of September, others close in October and only a quarter perhaps stay open all year. July and August are busy months so accommodation can be hard to find. High summer is often hot and humid (and flies on the hills can be annoying) so the best times for walking are spring and autumn.

The walk is laid out as a thirteen-day route but the extra days at Jedburgh and Melrose could be omitted while, better still, would be to fill a two-week holiday by adding days in Edinburgh and Glasgow. The idea is to have an all-round, happy experience, not a crippling rat race of non-stop walking. This fascinating cross-section of southern Scotland deserves better than that – and, I trust, so do you. Times are not given for stages: weather, conditions underfoot, individual fitness (or lack of it), interests along the way, will all make this a variable factor.

Don't underestimate this walk. Most of the days are of modest length but the very first gives the longest and hardest day so it is essential to have boots well broken-in and limbs hardened to tough walking *before commencing.* Set off as early as possible. Border B & Bs are better than most at providing breakfast early. Keep asking for such and make use of all the hours of each day. *Che va piano, va longano, e va lontana.* (He who goes slowly, goes for long, and goes far.)

It is a good thing to book ahead, even if just a phone call the night before, to ensure one's accommodation. Some places, Melrose for instance, are always heavily booked, others like Selkirk are under-used, other places have a limited and scattered accommodation provision. One answer to this is simply to get a bus, taxi or train to reach overnight shelter and return to the route next day. Thus, if Melrose is fully booked, just go to Selkirk for the night or, if Falkirk cannot provide a B & B, train back to Linlithgow.

When walking the route through as a final test we found ourselves coinciding with Peebles' *Beltane Festival* which meant heavy local bookings. We arranged to stay a second night in Innerleithen and simply caught a bus back from Peebles and ordered a taxi to return to our route early on a Sunday. There is usually a solution to problems. Trouble finding a B & B at Broxburn? Go into Edinburgh – and have a day there anyway to see the Roman room in the Museum. I've tried to indicate all the possible alternatives and have listed appropriate information. Check on the availability of evening meals when booking ahead. All information changes of course so I'd welcome up-to-date information on any alterations or amendments. (See note at the end of the book.)

Telephone numbers are given if possible for all accommodation or places to visit. The outsiders' dialling code is usually given at the start of the practical sections and the local numbers are always introduced with a dash, as '-72980'. (Six figures inside brackets are grid references!)

From West Linton onwards accommodation is much more scattered, and there is much less of it, so careful planning is advised. Jedburgh, Melrose, Selkirk, Peebles and Linlithgow have *Tourist Information Centres*, reflecting their importance. They are friendly and knowledgeable and stock town maps and other publications and can also book accommodation.

When phoning ahead don't forget to ask for the full name and address of the planned accommodation – and how to find it. Space means I have to give minimal descriptions when there are, say, thirty B & Bs in one place. Many B & Bs have no single rooms so a solo trip has this difficulty built into it. Two is probably the most practical and economic number for the journey. In July and August booking ahead is essential as there are nights when every bed seems to be taken. One can simply book ahead from one day to the next to maintain some freedom, or one can book every night of the walk which completely destroys any freedom to change, yet also acts as a very real spur. It is very much a matter of personal choice. I'm always glad to hear of *good* new accommodation options. I must have found most while exploring. Some I found are *not* mentioned because they were quite inadequate!

The International Festival swamps all Edinburgh accommodation for the last two weeks in August and the first week in September, and there are a number of Common Ridings, Fairs and Festivals which can make local demands. Where these are always at a regular spot in the calendar I've mentioned them.

Camping is an option which has some drawbacks. The country throughout is fairly agricultural, so casual wild camping is not easy, and there are several nights where no sites are available. The switch-back nature of the route is not the best for heavy load carrying – unlike say a coast-to-coast across Scotland – and with so many places to visit the heavy pack becomes a bit of a nuisance. Without a tent one also makes greater contact with local people, so all in all, I'd rather recommend leaving the tent behind – even if it means saving up for a bit longer before making a Pennines to Highlands tramp. The camp sites are all well-appointed, being very much geared for tourists, but I found them very welcoming to hikers. Fees however tend to be high, a small backpacking tent may be charged the same fee as a palatial family unit!

While mentioning money make sure you have enough. All the Border towns have banks, but it may not be your particular one, or you may arrive after hours or when there's a local holiday. Most B & Bs are happy to accept cheques with a banker's card, hotels are happy with credit cards, and a Post Office Savings Book is often useful.

The walk requires five *Landranger* (OSLR) maps (as the essential minimum), fifteen *Pathfinder* (OSPF) maps (for the more curious) and two Bartholomew (Bart) maps (for a good overall picture). These are listed at the start of each day's walk and also under *Appendix 4: Facts and Figures, Maps Covering the Route* (which see for the abbreviations used). The maps make up quite a bulk and weight, so splitting them and posting ahead (along with films or any personal needs) is a good idea. They are best sent to B & Bs if pre-arranged (post offices have half days, or close five minutes before you reach them). Include some packaging and stamps to return maps, films and even unfriendly stockings. The landlady will usually post a package for you if there isn't a large letter box handy. Ask about anything local. There are often special events which you may not hear about otherwise. I find walkers are given a much warmer welcome than ordinary tourists! Where it helps to pinpoint a feature a six-figure grid reference may be given; always in brackets, e.g. (329016).

Heights are given in metres as that is what the maps show and to translate is inaccurate and meaningless really. However, as most walkers still think in miles, distances are given in miles.

I'm always loathe to give times and distances as these can be very subjective, and also a lazy substitute for doing some homework. As a compromise some *Facts and Figures* are listed at the end. The walk entails roughly 170 miles (250 kilometres) of walking and 4,560 metres (14,800 feet) of ascent.

Various friends tried out parts of the final route and two of us also 'walked it through'. Keith followed my text to test its clarity, which was a useful device for bringing him down to my slower pace. We did it in two separate sorties, for practical reasons, but let me plead again that the walk is a *fun* activity. If the weather turns diabolical, go home and come again, or modify the route, or lie-up. Enjoy it at the time as well as in the dreaming, fore and aft.

You won't be able to see everything mentioned in the text, but that could be an excuse for returning. I found the canals so interesting that I've now decided to explore the two end sections, in Edinburgh and Glasgow, so a described walk can be produced linking those two cities following the canals. Maybe you can try *that* next!

As we left West Linton for the Pentlands I overheard two senior citizens commenting on us.

'Look Wullie, hikers!'
'Ooh aye, lucky lads.'

That's what I thought too, so, to misappropriate and misquote an exhortation, 'On your hike!'

While every possible care has been taken to ensure the accuracy of this guide the author does not accept responsibility regarding the information or its interpretation by readers! Signposts vanish, brambles grow, housing schemes obliterate paths, accommodation changes, so to counter this any information sent in will be welcomed, and passed on in the update sheet. Regretfully I cannot enter into correspondence on points raised, but they will be given respectful consideration! On undertaking any outdoor venture we choose to meet its vagaries; it would be dull otherwise. The Pennines to Highlands is certainly not dull.

HAMISH M BROWN
KINGHORN

Acknowledgements

MANY people helped with this book and I would like to thank them all, whether listed below or not, for many were simply met at the time and cheerfully answered questions, or put me in touch with other people and/or information. The human contacts were one of the great pleasures of working out the route, reading-up on all manner of topics, searching for old photographs and putting it all together. Jigsaws are usually more fun when tackled by more than one person. Thanks then to some of the main helpers: the staff at the Almondell Country Park Visitor Centre; Keith Anderson, who walked the route through with me; Jeannie and Allan Black, and Kay Fyfe for hospitality and testing the Cockleroy description; the Borders Regional Library Headquarters staff, Selkirk for help with information; British Waterways Board and Helen Robotham, the Union Canal Ranger; Dr Rosemary Evans, Director of the Woodland Centre, near Jedburgh; Sheila Gallimore for always typing my hieroglyphic scribbles so efficiently; Kinghorn and Kirkcaldy library staff for supplying many books, and the National Library of Edinburgh for bibliographical details; the staff at Kilsyth Library; Kirkcaldy Instant Printing, for endless photocopying; Linlithgow Union Canal Society (LUCS), and Mel and Judy Gray; Mrs McMichael for old pictures of Broxburn; the National Trust for Scotland; the custodians at the Scottish Monuments sites, always helpful; the Scottish Rights of Way Society Ltd for information; The Southern Reporter and Gordon Lockie, Selkirk, for the Common Riding photographs; Peggy Steele-Perkins who shared in the research in the field; Strathkelvin District Council; Kirkintilloch Museum and Kirkintilloch William Patrick Library staff who helped with publication and historical photographs; Tourist Information Office staff at Jedburgh, Melrose, Selkirk, Peebles and Linlithgow; D. R . Wilson, Curator, the University of Cambridge Committee for Aerial Photography, for the pictures; and the Warden of Byrness Youth Hostel for local information. Pictures not acknowledged are the author's (Hamish Brown; Scottish Photographic).

Preliminaries

TRAVEL TO BYRNESS

Probably the most practical travel arrangement is to head to Edinburgh
and then use the Edinburgh–Newcastle-upon-Tyne bus which follows the
A68 through Redesdale. Newcastle is the nearest railway station but may
not be such an economical starting point as would be available with a
return fare to Edinburgh. At the end of the walk it is very easy to travel
Glasgow–Edinburgh by bus or train, making a return fare to Edinburgh a
likely best buy. Dealing with the bus company may be a less happy
experience.

When I came to test the transport to the starting point at Byrness I
ran into a situation with all the delights of wet concrete. The enquiry office
in Edinburgh (over several calls) denied there was any bus to Byrness!
They admitted there was a service from Edinburgh to Newcastle by the
A68, but then claimed the bus had no stops between Jedburgh and
Otterburn. It was only when I went in person to Edinburgh and made a
nuisance of myself that the correct picture slowly came into focus. *There
are clear footnotes to the timetable listing additional stops that are permitted.
Byrness is one of these.*

From what I gather locally in Byrness this lack of helpfulness from
the bus companies is quite usual. Some drivers will try not to stop, others
won't stop for passengers waiting at Byrness – a rather sorry story – which
I spell out clearly so you, the customer, can, if need be, inform the bus
information office of the true situation, and so obtain the vital ticket for the
trip. (You will be charged at the fare to Otterburn as a last twist of the
knife.) Having said that, our Geordie driver was as friendly and helpful as
could be, even if half an hour late in starting.

The journey takes about two hours. *Scottish City Link* had
departures at 07.55 and 09.55 only, but *National Express* had departures at
08.00, 12.00 and 16.00. (From Newcastle Galagate Coach Station 091-
261-6077 departures were 10.00, 14.00 and 18.00.) Check and double

check the times though, and leave plenty of time to buy a ticket at St Andrew Square booking office which can often be very busy. Make sure you find out the stance from which the bus departs. The St Andrew Square bus station is just five minutes walk from Waverley railway station. *Bus Enquiry Office* 031-556-8464 but, be warned, over two days I tried phoning fifteen times (line engaged) and three times (ringing but no reply) before I was answered, which is a disgraceful service by any standards, and not very practical if you need information quickly. Walking from the Pennines to the Highlands is easy after all that.

To reach the bus station from Waverley, leave the station by the windy Waverley steps, which climb up between the old North British Hotel (now the Balmoral) to reach Princes Street. Cross Princes Street and turn left, then turn right at the first street (St Andrew Street) which leads to St Andrew Square. Keep on in the same line, passing some grandiose bank buildings (worth going in to see the main halls), and you come on the bus station. The most uncertain part of the walk will be over when the bus draws out and heads for the Border!

A night at Byrness is advisable. Keith and I were forced to use the 08.00 from Edinburgh, and by the time we'd checked various points locally we only set off from Byrness at 11.00. We walked hard, in excellent conditions, with only two real pauses (Chew Green to eat, Towford to paddle), yet still only reached Jedburgh at 19.00. The first day is the longest and hardest of the trip, even by the easier, shorter alternative. Most walkers will need the full day so use the evening bus and stay overnight at Byrness. From many home starts this works out conveniently, as it will take a day to reach Edinburgh and then bus to Byrness.

PRACTICAL INFORMATION: BYRNESS

All telephone numbers have the Otterburn code, which is 0830-
Accommodation at Byrness is adequate but rather scattered and the following are listed in a rough order of nearness to the start of the Pennine Way path as it heads up onto the Cheviot hills.

ACCOMMODATION: Byrness Hotel, -20231, stands above the A68 opposite the church/ cafe/petrol station. Forest Lodge, -20589 also stands above the A68 about 200 yards further along (towards Scotland), up a road marked 'Access Only', or reached by a pedestrian short cut which is the start of the Pennine Way route.

Byrness Village, 350 yards further up the A68 on the left, is a hamlet of forestry houses with several B & Bs, youth hostel and post office. The Youth Hostel, -20222, is 7 Otterburn Green, Byrness, Newcastle-upon-Tyne NE19 1TS, open March-October. (Closed Wednesdays, except July/August.) Near the youth hostel is a B & B at 10 Otterburn Green, -20604, and in the south side of the village is 4 South Green -20653.

Heading southwards from the church (about ⅔ mile is The Cottage, Low Byrness, -20648. It lies on the north side of the A68 (779015) just before the camp site entrance, which lies south of the A68 where the Rede is joined by the Cottonshope Burn. Across the burn one of the houses of Cottonshopeburnfoot Farm offers B & B, -20248, the entrance being a good ¼ mile further along the A68 from the camp site drive. The same entrance (initially) leads to Blakehopeburnhaugh Farm, D, B & B, -20267, on the Forest Drive. A Forestry Commission roadside board indicates these.

If staying at these long-lettered places one can walk up the Cottonshope Road (leaves the A68 opposite the camp site entrance) then, as soon as the forest is passed, turn up, left, to reach the Pennine Way route on top of Byrness Hill. This is pleasanter, and no doubt safer, than walking along the A68, or following the valley-wandering bit of Pennine Way. (If walking to the church/cafe area the Pennine Way path is preferable to the A68.) Don't wander up the Cottonshope valley beyond the forest. The road goes into an artillery range which occupies all the land east of the Pennine Way until Chew Green is reached.

CAMPING: No site and not really practical as land is all under farm or forestry use.

MEALS: Ensure B & B choice can provide an evening meal, being on the Pennine Way many do provide this service. There is a small roadside cafe, popular with both motorists and walkers.

BYRNESS, HISTORICAL

The church, built in 1756, is a grey, stone-roofed building with a small belfry and an overgrown graveyard, quite an atmospheric setting. The interior is simple but attractive, with tiled floors, and a window and plaque commemorating the 'Men, women and children' killed during the construction of the Catcleugh Reservoir dam (1891–1904). I counted sixty–four names, which seems a sad tally. The window shows the navvies at work. It looks very modern but is dated 1903. The change in constructional methods is reflected too. The fairly modest Catcleugh dam kept a thousand people labouring for fifteen years. No JCBs in those days! The keys to the church are kept in the cafe beside the petrol station and are available when the cafe is open.

Redesdale was regarded as 'the wildest and fiercest of all Border battlegrounds' and saw innumerable raids on both sides of Carter Bar. Carter Bar itself was the scene of a 1575 skirmish, described in the ballad, 'The Raid of Redeswyre', when the English Warden of the Middle Marches and the Keeper of Liddisdale met 'on business' but words grew heated and finally blows were exchanged. At a crucial moment another group rode up yelling 'Jeddart's here!', and the English fell back, not realising this was just the Jedburgh contingent arriving late for the meeting! In July the Jeddart lads still ride out to Carter Bar as the climax of the Riding Week.

Sometimes the raiding parties were armies as when Percy and Douglas clashed outside Otterburn in 1388. Even the battle has gone down in rival ballads and, as in the battle, I feel the raiders had the best of it. Simply compare the opening lines: 'It fell about the Lammas tide' and 'God prosper long our noble King'. (The English, *Chevy Chase* version is almost twice as long!)

The Earl of Douglas had led a large party into Northumberland and Durham as a diversionary raid while a larger army attacked in the west, an offence mounted as revenge for the ravages of Richard II, who burned Dryburgh, Melrose and Newbattle Abbeys, amongst other cruel deeds. Newcastle, a walled town, resisted but Douglas bore off the banner of Sir Henry Percy (Hotspur) after unseating him in single combat, so when the Scots headed home with their booty Percy gathered a force and set off in pursuit. The Scots waited for them at Otterburn and the northern army piled into them at once so the battle was largely fought in dusky summer night. It seems to have been a particularly grim encounter. Douglas was killed and Percy captured. The proud Percy is said to have refused to surrender to anyone of lower status and eventually yielded his sword to a bush, beyond which lay the dead body of the battle's victor. Of such stuff are Border ballads made. Douglas's vision of doom is unforgettable.

> But I hae dream'd a dreary dream,
> Beyond the Isle of Sky;
> I saw a dead man win a fight,
> And I think that man was I.

There is a slight irony in the area still having a military presence, much of the land north-east of the A68 being a modern artillery range whose activities can roll mock thunder over the Cheviot crests.

A BORDERS/EAST COAST SPECIALITY, THE 'READING FIGURE' ON GRAVESTONES

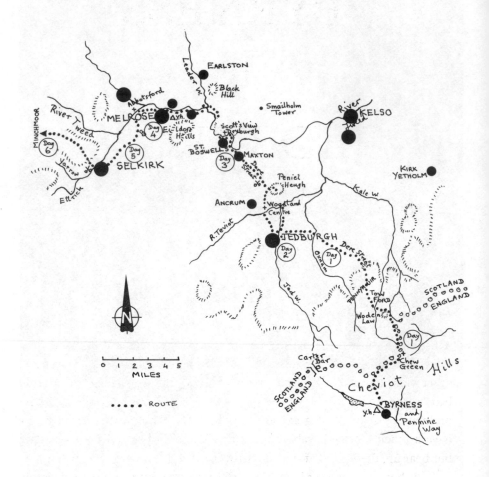

BYRNESS

to

JEDBURGH

Bart 41 OSLR 80, 74
OSPF 498 (NT 60/70), 486 (NT 61/71), 474 (NT 62/72)

ONTO THE CHEVIOTS

This is the longest and hardest day of the walk, so set off early and don't linger too long, however delectable it may be on the tops, by streams or other viewpoints. The first half offers excellent hill-walking, soft underfoot but, after Pennymuir, you may be on tarred roads with big-dipper undulations – hard going at the end of the day. Those who started fit will have a much more enjoyable experience. The unfit will feel the day's darg, but bear up, there's an off-day tomorrow.

About seventy yards up the A68 from the church a footpath angles off, right, the start of the Pennine Way's ascent to the Cheviot Hills. It runs along above the A68 to meet a small tarred road at a bend. Forest Lodge lies sharp right and the road bend leads to the gates of Byrness Cottage. Left of this house's entrance (with a Pennine Way sign post showing where) is a gate in the beech hedge which leads one up a field to bypass Byrness Cottage. Exit by a gate, cross an old track, and the route then climbs straight up Byrness Hill, as steep a haul as we'll meet anywhere on our whole walk.

There are one or two forest roads to be crossed but the route is always clear, steep and, if wet, a bit slippery. Once out of the forest there are superb views to Upper Redesdale. Real Wainwright stuff! (He calls it 'splendid'.)

A short scramble then leads up to the bare dome of Byrness Hill. The 'fire tower' on maps no longer exists; there is just the concrete base of the once conservatory-like outpost and the older stump of a stone tower, reminiscent of Irish Round Tower, remains.

The route heads northwards over Saughy Crag, Houx Hill, Windy Crag, Ravens Knowe (the day's highest point), Yard Shank and Ogre Hill, quite a peal of names, but the crags are all minor and off the route which wends along very gently on good, grassy going, well-tracked and not suffering from Cheviot's 'extraordinary capacity for storing water'. In mist careful navigation may be needed as there is a proliferation of paths, trod in all directions over the years by sheep and/or humans. The vast forest to the west (left) can hardly fail to keep the direction generally and, off Ogre Hill, the forest ends in a marked apex at Coquet Head. Under bad conditions the path down to Nether Hindhope is probably a wiser route than following the crest of the Border summits beyond Chew Green. This escape route is described below.

From Ogre Hill there is a drop to Coquet Head, so both it and the hills beyond are well seen. The Pennine Way drops down to the infant stream, then mounts the slope beyond, briefly, before turning to the right and flanking down to Chew Green, a rather illogical route which is the least

CATCLEUGH RESERVOIR AND UPPER REDESDALE FROM THE CLIMB UP TO BYRNESS HILL

observed. Most people either simply drop to the Coquet and follow its bank down to the Roman camp or continue up the slopes on the other side and follow the crest to Brownhart Law. This last option misses out Chew Green, a showpiece antiquity, and my suggested alternative is not to drop down at all, but turn east (right) from Ogre Hill along a track on the flat top of Harden Edge. Like Carter Bar this was often the meeting place of the Marcher Wardens, and drovers were to use it in later centuries. Some cattle could journey from as far away as Skye, right on to London. If only the winds could speak.

The Cheviot Hills are still mainly used for sheep grazing, with the large, hornless Cheviot breed on the lower slopes and the Roman-nosed, Viking-horned, black-faced breed on the tops. The Cheviot sheep and Highland Clearances are sadly linked but there are few Cheviots in the Highlands now. They were not hardy enough so cross-breeds or black-faced predominate – even on the muckle Cheviot. There is a recent story of a tourist lad in a Border pub who made a disparaging remark about the then Prime Minister, comparing her face unfavourably with that of a Cheviot's. He was at once ejected from the pub, and, when he said he was surprised to find this was Thatcher country, was told, 'It is not. It's sheep country though.'

Now it is the military who come up the Coquet, a tarred road turning

CHEW GREEN, THE ROMAN CAMP ON THE CHEVIOT HILLS
(PHOTO: CAMBRIDGE UNIVERSITY COLLECTION; COPYRIGHT RESERVED)

off and heading south-east on the line of Gamel's Path, as Dere Street southwards may be named. If there is firing taking place there will be plenty of red flags flying. The army assure me they do not fire in the direction of the Pennine Way/Coquet Head. We now join Dere Street.

DERE STREET

Pick up this ancient track, heading alongside the north-eastern side of the Roman camp. There are marker posts but these may not be intervisible. The Pennine Way officially turns off after a while, and drops to cross the tiny Chew Sike stream, to contour round and up as a narrow green track (Roman), which then leads to a modern farm track up to a gate just below Brownhart Law.

The track swings off to the right, but we keep on, along the Border fence, passing, as we do, the site of a Roman Signal station (not much to see on the ground) which linked with Rubers Law and Eildon North Hill. In the days when we had counties seven could be seen from here. This is one of the highest points of our day's walk and the 500 metre mark will seldom be surpassed elsewhere. A good place for a pause. See how many of these Border names you can spot on the map: Scathy Holes, Carlin Tooth, Butter Bog, Hawklawtongues, Note o' the Gate, Hephills Nob, Yearning Law, Bloodrush Edge, The Hearts Toe, Blindburn, Wormscleuch, Deadwater Moor.

After walking along the fence for a while, over Black Halls, we part company with the Pennine Way – and Northumberland. The fence, from being on our left, makes a kink (gate across our track), to continue along on our right. We go through the gate, the Pennine Way (sign) skirts off right. Blackhall Hill beckons.

There is some confusion about the route of Dere Street, and the Landranger map shows just one of the two possibilities. Unfortunately, it selects the one least clear on the ground, and least likely to have been used by marching soldiers. This veers off to cross the saddle leading to Gaisty Law, then traverses across the head of Blackie Hope, on a sort of terrace between screes, and so on towards Woden Law. The path breaks off the clear fence track as a mere sheep trod, just before a gate in the fence, after six or seven minutes walking from where we left the Pennine Way. This is an alternative only worth taking on a clear day, or on a return visit. Blackhall Hill is perhaps the finest viewpoint of the whole walk so its summit should not be missed.

The real line of Dere Street keeps along the Border line, then curls round and down the far side of Blackhall Hill – a much gentler and more logical route. Both paths are shown on the Pathfinder map. There is one fence with a gap joining our march fence, then, 100 yards on, we come to a gate on the neck of Blackhall Hill as the fence turns to run up to the summit. Go through the gate and turn left to the top. Dere Street goes on to, logically, angle round and down, below the knobbly summit. The highest point is a perfectly round, well-preserved prehistoric cairn. And what a viewpoint. Away to the east is the muckle Cheviot, behind lies the empty quarter of Northumberland, below, along the northern skirts of the hills, lies an extraordinary proliferation of bumps of all sizes and shapes which gives the area from here to the A68 an inimitable character all of its own. West is the upthrust of Rubers Law and we can see the Eildons and other ranges beckoning. It really is a magic spot. *Redgauntlet* country of course.

I once sat on top on a solitary birthday ascent, listening to Mahler's 5th Symphony (swotting it up for an Edinburgh Festival performance soon after) and if I was also tucking into almond cake and relishing the situation I paid for it later; before reaching Tow Ford the heavens opened – and that was the end of the 'super summer' of 1989. Nothing can take away the content. As an old Highlander said to Ratcliffe Barrett, 'You can never win

WODEN LAW WITH THE PREHISTORIC FORT AND THE ROMANS' PRACTICE SIEGE-WORKS
(PHOTO: CAMBRIDGE UNIVERSITY COLLECTION; COPYRIGHT RESERVED)

close to the spirit of the hills till you climb high, all your lone, where there is no one else to break the thrum.'

The encircling ramparts of the fort on Woden Law can clearly be seen, and in front of them are Roman training siegeworks. With camps at Chew Green and across Tow Ford I suppose it was as good a place as any to practice, but I'm just glad I wasn't a Roman soldier. Perhaps our weather was a bit drier in those centuries. The setting here is straight out of *Puck of Pook's Hill* , the stories of which were very much inspired by Roman-day Cheviots.

Leaving our high seat it is worth going down the fence a bit in order to see over into the head of Blackie Hope. The crumbly red rock lines the headwall with screes, and we can see the traversing path circling round below us. This west prow is rocky so go carefully, down by the fence, or as soon as the gate on a fence joining ours becomes visible, angle over towards the gate, threading through the crags. Dere Street has merely circled the top of the hill and we pick it up again at this gate. At the col to Hunthall Hill the traverse path joins in (gate), and our green road angles on down delightfully, circuiting above Twise Hope, so one can really stretch the legs and walk 'arm in arm with the breeze' as Tom Rix wrote in a Cheviot poem. We cross some of the earthworks, almost un-noticed, but the last line is quite

THE VIEW UP TO BLACK HALL AFTER PASSING ROUND THE WODEN LAW

distinctive. There is a circular sheep shelter down right, a feature which is very much a Borders speciality.

We come to, and skirt, a walled-off field (with a stand of hardy deciduous trees, Streethouse Wood, below it), and as we approach a sheep fank (fold) with an ugly blockhouse of a stone building, the track veers left to begin its drop to the infant Kale Water. There is a gate/stile and then we head down with military determination between Woden Law and Hangingshaw Hill. The solitary building among the trees acts as a marker to aim for. (Once a schoolhouse it is now an outdoor centre.) Don't be led off on a track which goes over to a clump of trees on the left. Keep straight down, through a gate, and so to the minor, fenceless road. Cows as well as sheep roam this ranch-like area, and one of the cows is probably a bull built on the lines of a battleship.

A 'No through road' sign marks the road, to the left, for Upper Hindhope, whose most distant waters rise on the same col as do the waters of the Coquet, the easier or foul weather route for us. There is also a stray railway van – but we've met this local oddity already, on the Pennine Way. Carry straight on down the minor road to the Tow Ford (*two-ford*), which is a real ford, but there is a sturdy footbridge as well. This is the juvenile Kale Water, one of the historic Border waters, the opposite number to the English Coquet. Could it have been of here W H Ogilvie wrote of his true March Burn:

> *The playground of the swallow,*
> *The heron's banquet-hall,*
> *Just a gleam the wild ducks follow*
> *When the evening shadows fall.*
> *Just a strip of sunny water*
> *That a man may step across,*
> *Just a little laughing daughter*
> *Of the mist-cloud and the moss.*

COQUET HEAD – TOW FORD ALTERNATIVE

If mist, clouds or storm make the high route less attractive, or one feels such a long, hard day to start is best trimmed of a vital couple of hours, there is an easier, shorter alternative from Coquet Head. This runs by Whiteside Hill to Nether Hindhope Farm which lies just over two miles up the Kale Water from Tow Ford. In mist the fences can aid navigation.

After coming off Ogre Hill and crossing the fence that comes along the

Coquet, keep following the fence ahead to where it bends left. Here the Pennine Way turns right, but we keep left, along the fence still, till the fence off Brownhart Law joins ours. From here take the path down to pass Whiteside Hill, running parallel with Hindhope Burn, and then bearing off left across the neck before Hindhope Hill, descending a spur to a wood above Corse Slack where a track is picked up which leads down to the farm.

TOW FORD – PENNYMUIR – WHITTON EDGE

From Tow Ford our minor road swings up, along under the site of a Roman temporary marching camp (the earth ramparts can just be made out but, as with Chew Green, one really wants to view such sites from 500 feet overhead, which is a bit difficult to organise). We come to a T-junction, Pennymuir (once the site of large sheep fairs), which is really a cross-roads for Dere Street, goes straight ahead, not very visible initially, but giving us a happy hour of tarmac-avoidance. Dere Street, from Tow Ford to St Boswells, is being resurrected as a proper walkers' route, and the stile here is one indication of work done, but there are problems, like crossing the Teviot, and the route north of the Teviot has no indication of being salvaged and made available, and much elsewhere tends to be muddy or overgrown.

From Pennymuir, the stile leads us past a hall (wooden building) then we walk along a path beside a wood, a bit *rashy* but, as soon as we begin to gain height, the going becomes excellent, often green road or clear farm track. The *agger*, or embankment, of the Roman road is often plainly seen. Just before the end of the wood there is an old well, now in sorry state. When I stood up on the first stile last time a startled roe buck exploded from the other side of the wall and went bouncing along between wall and trees. I don't know who had the bigger fright.

Just right of the first cairn shown on the map is a dumpy standing stone, dark and polished by the skarting of sheep. By the 332 spot is quite a good trestle cairn, but its circle of stones is rather inaccessible over the walls. The Five Stanes circle on the other hand is easily seen. This bare upland dome gives grand walking, seldom without a breeze (no trees you'll notice) and, of course, wide horizons. The Eildons jink in and out of view. It will take a few days to lose them.

Sir Walter Scott knew the Border line and Dere Street. In *Guy Mannering* there is the observation: 'The march rins on the tap o' the hill where wind and water shears' and, in a letter he writes to a friend in the autumn of 1792, 'Having bewildered myself among the Cheviot Hills it was nearly nightfall before I got to the village of Hownam...'

Beyond the Five Stanes (the remains of a prehistoric circle) our Roman Road becomes more of a drovers' road in character as it runs along between walls and/or fences. Recently there was a battle to stop commercial planting up onto Philogar Hill. The developers said they would only come up to within 100 yards of Dere Street, a distance which would have ensured the loss of the big view when the trees grew, an aspect seldom considered by greedy exploiters. The loss here would have been great. We don't have much poetry based on sitka plantations, we do have it of this landscape:

> *Grey recumbent tomb of the dead in desert places,*
> *Standing-stones on the vacant wine-red moor,*
> *Hills of sheep, and the home of the silent vanished races,*
> *And winds austere and pure.*

Stevenson's magic description does not need to be spruced up!

Rashy Knowe, Heathery Shin, Coldside, Cadgers Knowe, Hen Banks and Bloodylaws Hill are some of the resonant names hereabouts. The 335 metre hill on our left is Cunzierton Hill. The rings of its prehistoric fort are clear. Every bump of the lower Cheviots seems to be an old fort, often obviously so with the rings of encircling ramparts still visible.

These rings round many of the prominent hills in the area have given rise to legends of serpents being coiled round them as the origin of these

DERE STREET AT ITS BEST – NEARING WHITTON EDGE AFTER THE MOORLAND WALK FROM PENNYMUIR

DERE STREET'S UNMISTAKABLE 'ROMAN' LINE CROSSING THE COUNTRY EAST OF JEDBURGH (PHOTO: CAMBRIDGE UNIVERSITY COLLECTION; COPYRIGHT RESERVED)

markings. A legend persists at Linton (to the north-east, near Morebattle) of a Laidely Worme which was killed by a specifically real person, John de Somerille of Lariston, who was knighted by William the Lion and lies buried in Linton churchyard. He succeeded by using a long lance with a burning peat on its tip which was thrust down the serpent's throat. No grass grew on the mound because the beast's breath was so abominably bad.

We drop a bit then undulate up between walls to a minor road at Whitton Edge, with a couple of tattered oaks beyond. The panoramic view is still grand. The whole northern skyline is hills, impossible to tell apart. Cheviot is nearer, bolder, and more familiar. Off to the right is the bold, solitary Hownam Law which has a huge fort on top. As soon as we turn left (west) along the road which has, temporarily, hijacked Dere Street we are looking south-west to the upthrust of distant Maiden Paps and Rubers Law, which sometimes is taken for the Eildons, or sometimes just leaves people wondering what on earth it is. The Romans had a signal station on top of the hill, linking Eildon summit and the Cheviot crest at Brownhart Law.

In a lonely cottage under Rubers Law lay the home of John Leyden, one of the most remarkable of all Border figures. He was born in Denholm (off the A68) where there is a monument. Very poor, he still managed to acquire an education. The minister taught him Greek and Latin so he obtained a place at Edinburgh University where he learnt Oriental languages, French, German, Spanish, Italian, Hebrew and Icelandic! A stickit minister he became a medical doctor, which took him to India where he was a professor of Hindustani, assay master of the mint, a commissioner and a judge, besides doing research in geology and natural history. He went to Java with Lord Minto (another Borderer), having learnt Malay and other languages, but died of a fever, still only thirty-six years old, and master of more tongues than he'd had years. He joins Scott and Hogg as poet and keen collector of ancient lore and ballads.

The Eildons and the monument on Peniel Heugh come into view again as our road begins to lose height rapidly. The road is lined with a surprisingly fine variety of trees, with oak and ash predominating. After descending the road levels for a bit, and then puts in a little kicking descent and ascent (tummy-leaving in a car!) to come up to a T-junction. The junction is really a cross roads like Pennymuir for the line of Dere Street heads on from the junction, a rather jungly Roman Road now. The house at the junction has the name Shotheids, the road to the right is signposted 'Morebattle 6', the road to the left 'Oxnam 1 ½'. This latter is a road-only alternative to the Dere Street continuation if conditions are muddy or wet, or the route is just too overgrown for pleasant assaulting without nettle-proof breeches. In hot conditions, however, the road walking with its big dipper characteristics, is pretty wearisome coming at the end of the day. You'll just have to choose!

SHOTHEIDS – JEDBURGH

The Roman Road from Shotheids runs remarkably straight for almost two miles, dropping to a hollow then a slight rise to pass between plantations, Hillhead (left), Sourlees (right), before running down steeply beside the latter to come out at a minor road between Cappuck Farm and Crailinghall.

Cappuck was the site of a small Roman Fort, excavated in 1911–12. It stood directly above the ford on the Oxnam Water. The burn has eroded away the bank so a corner of the fort has disappeared.

We've had farm track down to the road but it becomes a mud slide on down to the Oxnam (pronounced *Ousnam*), a forgotten ford but now with a sturdy new footbridge twenty yards upstream. Dere Street crosses the flat valley bottom and starts to pull up again steadily. Where it crosses a small tarred road we turn left for Jedburgh, and our night's lodgings. Dere Street continues with Roman disregard for deviations or contour lines to Jedfoot Bridge and the Teviot.

Our small road climbs steadily for just over a mile. Opposite the Overwells track once stood a house called Pity Me. Nearing the top of the brae we have beech hedges and a variety of trees (chestnut, lime, ash, oak, etc), and when we dip for the descent there are Scots pine plantations: Belvidere Wood, Crouchie Wood and Justice Wood. This is definitely a kindlier finish than the alternative road-walk from Shotheids. At the next junction the two routes join each other so we'll return to Shotheids to describe the alternative. There is still no sign of Jedburgh!

SHOTHEIDS – PLEASANTS ALTERNATIVE

Walk down the road signed for 'Oxnam 1 ½' then turn off first right (as do the telegraph poles) to descend past Harden Mains and more steeply down to prosperous-looking Millheugh beside a nice bridge over the stream. Turn right at the junction and dip again to Pleasants (another small road goes off to Crailinghall) which has done its best to live up to its name. You just don't see farms or houses in the countryside here which are not looked after with pride and care, often with attractive gardens. Not so pleasant is our pull up the hill ahead. Any side roads are ignored. And finally we leave OSLR 80.

Jedburgh remains as hidden as ever, even when we begin the last descent to it.

Beech hedges line the route and through the gaps we glimpse the ever-present Eildons. There is a junction signposted 'Jedburgh 1 ¼' where those who kept along Dere Street join in. We pass an ornate gatehouse (Wildcat Gate, as the OS have rendered Walky Yett) and then suddenly are confronted by big boxes on the hillside: the harsh geometrics of an industrial estate which, I suppose, is blessedly hidden from the town. Not long past this the road curves left (Oxnam Road) but, in the corner, a little secretive track keeps straight on. Take this, the original old route, which becomes little more than a path as it drops steeply down, to join a tarred path which bears left, still down, to reach the Jed Water beside the Well House.

The Well House bears the date 1934 over the door, a reminder of the times (not so long ago) when drinking water was not something always 'on tap'. Turning down Old Bridge End (left of the Well House) we pass a shop as we approach the perfect little Canongate Bridge over the Jed. Look at the bridge from all angles, it's an early gem, a rarity dating back to the sixteenth century when it was the main approach to the town. Just upstream is the Colic Well which, with the Katie Well (at Well House), were two of the town's main water sources. The houses upstream (east bank) are reached by going *under* the bridge and they are defended by a massive flood gate and embankment. (Sheltered housing in more ways than one.) There is also a ford upstream of the bridge. Once across turn left rounding a house known as the Piper's House. There is the figure of a piper perched on the crowstep gable and it could be the ancient home of the town's hereditary pipers, the Hasties. Over the door are the initials AA and IA with the date 1601. An underpass (A68 overhead) takes us right into the historic town centre. I hope the first day has gone well and you do not feel like Strabo who commented, 'When they saw the men of Rome walking for the pleasure of Walking they thought they must be mad'.

PRACTICAL INFORMATION: JEDBURGH

Tourist Information Office, Murray's Green, 0835-63435/63688.
Telephone code for Jedburgh numbers is 0835-

ACCOMMODATION: Jedburgh has quite a list of B & B options and several hotels, but booking is advised in the peak tourist season.

Coming into Jedburgh if, instead of turning off down the lane, one keeps to the main road (Oxnam Road) there are several B & Bs on the way in. The first, Strowan, -62248 does B & B but the next, Kenmore Guest House,

-62369, also does dinner and has a bar and is a very tempting option. Below it, first left, then first left again is Hillview, -62956.

Central accommodation: 7 Queen Street, -62482; 48 Castlegate -62504; 64 Castlegate -62466; 77 Castlegate -62557; 75 Castlegate -63353; 67 Castlegate -62728; 30 High Street -62604; Froylehurst, The Friars -62477; Willow Court, The Friars -63702; Olivet, Lanton Road -63823; Jedburgh Arms, 1 Abbey Place -62467; The Spread Eagle Hotel, 20 High Street -62870, which claims to be Scotland's oldest hotel, is reasonably priced. At double B & B prices are Glenbank House Hotel, Castlegate -62258, and Royal Hotel, Canongate -63152.

On the Ancrum route out (Sharplaw Road) the last house, left, is Mayfield -63696, and on The Friars is Glenfriars Hotel -62000. On the Jedfoot Bridge route out there are several B & Bs along the Bongate (A68): Nos 55 -63259; 81 -62630; 91 -63206; 124 -62480; and 11 Old Bongate -63817. High to the east is 1 Hartrigge Crescent -62738.

There are quite a few rural possibilities which could be reached by taxi if the above proves insufficient: Larkhall Farm -62155 one mile west on the B6358; on the A68 (south) are Ferniehirst Mill Lodge -63279; Hundalee House -63011; The Spinney, Langlee -63525; Jedforest Hotel -4274; Camptown -4252; on the A68 (north) is Harrietsfield -3327; in or near Ancrum are Craigellachie -3562; Ancrum Craig -3280; to the north-east are Crailing Old School -5382, and Nisbet Mill Farm -5228.

CAMPING: Elliot Park -63393 lies over the bridge just beyond the 30mph sign on the A68 heading north (657218).

TAXIS: -63700, -63208.

MEALS: Some B & Bs will also do evening meals, but there are several restaurants in the town centre, the hotels do meals and there are bar meals a-plenty. Half-day is Thursday.

The Jethart Callant's Festival occupies the first two weeks of July. There are daily rideouts, games (dating back to 1853) and other activities to stir the blood.

Day Two

JEDBURGH DAY

BART 41 OSLR 74
OSPF 474 (NT 62/72)

EXPLORING JEDBURGH

A day off at this stage is quite welcome as it splits two of the longest days of the trip. 'Clean-gleaming' Jedburgh is worth exploring and it is an easy-going, restful place for a lazier day. A town map from the Tourist Information Office will prove useful, and you may also find leaflets to a Town Trail which is an easy way of ensuring sites are visited efficiently.

Allow an hour to explore Jedburgh Abbey, the most complete church among the Border abbeys, which still dominates the town. It was founded, under the patronage of David I, by the Augustinians and soon grew to importance on both sides of the border. Jedburgh Castle was popular with the

JEDBURGH ABBEY, STILL IMPRESSIVE DESPITE THE RAVAGING OF CENTURIES

43

kings and Alexander III married Yolande de Dreux in the growing abbey. Unfortunately his death led to centuries of conflict. The abbey was burnt or sacked at least nine times. Edward I thought nothing of stripping lead off the roof. Violent assaults occurred in 1410, 1416 and 1464, Surrey fired it in 1523, and during the Rough Wooing of 1544–5 there were only eight canons left, with the Reformation having little effect. The nave was used as the Parish church until 1875.

Enter by the Visitor Centre, an old house with a very modern interior. Here, as for Dryburgh and Melrose, there are excellent guide booklets so I'll not go into details. A circular walk is suggested for Jedburgh. One is struck by the massiveness of the church which is emphasised by the almost total destruction of the monastic buildings. Stone was always looted for other buildings and I suppose the secular would be more naturally pillaged first, especially as the church did remain a place of worship. On the stairway in the Visitor Centre is a pre-abbey-date incised stone which was found built into the abbey – so they did it too.

The abbey took a century to build. The Romanesque choir was the earliest part and is a rare survival of that period. The Gothic nave followed, showing much of architectural development as the twelfth century closed. (The striking rose window is sixteenth century.) This religious upsurge was

THE BEAUTIFUL FIFTEENTH-CENTURY ROSE WINDOW IN JEDBURGH ABBEY

Europe-wide, and such buildings are a testimony to its power. The church gained great lands and civil power and became all too strong in politics. Numbers of those seeking a religious life fell, there was a great deal of corruption, which led, inevitably, to the Reformation, itself a strange mixture of religious zeal and power-grabbing. The Home family gained greatly by the privatisation of Jedburgh's lands.

If Jedburgh Abbey still presents extensive ruins the castle has completely gone, having been rebuilt many times over the turbulent years of 'Jeddart Justice' and the ploying of the 'Jeddart axe'. A castellated gaol was built on the site in 1823 and this building, still dominating the length of the town's main street, is now a museum showing local life – and nineteenth-century prison conditions! Open 10.00–17.00 weekdays, 13.00–17.00 Sundays, -63254. The monks of the Abbey made a special effort to produce good pears, the 'Jethart Pears' and you can also track down 'Jethart Snails' – a brown mint sweet in the shape of a snail!

A story lingers on about Alexander III. He was banqueting in the castle shortly after marrying for a second time when a skeletal figure appeared among the masked revellers and approached the King. This rather spoilt the evening's entertainment. Alexander III later crossed the Queen's Ferry over the Forth on a stormy night determined to reach Yolande at Kinghorn. In the storm he and his horse went over the cliffs above Pettycur Bay. His heir, the Maid of Norway, died before reaching Scotland and the bloody interference of Edward I followed – and all history since. It is one of the great IF events of history.

A lesser IF was the visit of Mary Queen of Scots. She was by then interested in Bothwell and made a fifty mile ride to and from his castle, at Hermitage, where the earl lay after being injured in a typical Border fracas. The day's effort led to a near-mortal illness and in her unhappy later years the queen sometimes sighed 'Would I had died at Jeddart'. Poor Mary was a butterfly in a spider's web, yet she, blindly one feels, contributed to her own downfall by her disastrous marriage to Darnley, a mean, nasty pervert, and then to the chancer Bothwell. She was only twenty-three when she stayed at Jedburgh.

Queen Mary's House is interesting and is the only one of six Jedburgh *bastels* (fortified houses) to survive. They were built when Jedburgh Castle was demolished. Both Jedburgh and Roxburgh castles were utterly destroyed as the only way to stop their constantly being the focus of Anglo-Scots fighting. Jedburgh still went up in flames, several times, so little has survived. The house has a *pend* (passage) entrance and a left-turning staircase, having been a

Ker-owned building. (Mary paid Lady Ferniehurst £40 rent!) The house has been laid out as an interpretive centre and there are objects associated with Mary on display, including her death mask. Open daily 10.00–17.00, -63331.

Prince Charles Edward Stewart also stayed in Jedburgh in 1745 on his march into England, perhaps the happiest days of his rash venture. His house lies off the attractive Castlegate, as the upper half of the High Street is called. The Prince marched on foot all day, every day, laying the foundations of a loyalty among ordinary soldiers which was sadly lacking among his officers. They went on to Carlisle but, at Derby, with London in a panic, the quarelling army turned back for Scotland and the inevitable massacre of Culloden and all that was to follow.

Sir Walter Scott made his first appearance in court at Jedburgh in 1793 and later sat as sheriff. He entertained the Wordsworths in a house in The Bow. Burns was made a Freeman of Jedburgh. The most romantic associations are still those of Mary Queen of Scots. Sir James Barrie, who was also made a Freeman, opened Queen Mary's House in 1929.

The Market Place in the centre of the town is a delightful spot to relax in. The new houses down the Canongate are an example to all developers as to how to build modern buildings to blend into a historical setting. The town divides into Uppies and Doonies (those born uphill of the Cross, those born downhill of the Cross), the two sides each February competing in the historic game of Hand Ba' when a beribboned ball, by means fair or foul, is taken to the rival's end. Numbers of players are not limited and shutters go up on the shops in self-defence! This wild game supposedly originated when a rogue had his head cut off – and the townspeople made grim sport with it. The town was made a Royal Burgh by William the Lion and the site of the market cross is marked by a plaque set in the ground. The fountain marks Queen Victoria's Jubilee. There are plenty of eating places or one can take a picnic down beside the river. The classic view of the abbey is from across the water from the picnic/car park area south of the river.

JEDBURGH

to

MELROSE

Bart 41 OSLR 74, 73
OSPF 474 (NT 62/72), 462 (NT 63/73), 461 (NT 43/53)

A DAY of considerable variety, and quite a long one calling for another early start. There are some refreshment stops available however, and the walking changes from road, to hill, to road, to river bank, to road, all with rich landscape views and notable tree interest. The Woodland Visitor Centre and Dryburgh Abbey are special sites en route.

TRANS-TEVIOT

The local authority has been reviving Dere Street as a walkers' route, but the Teviot was a big gap in their plans as there was no public bridge across the river between the A68 and Nisbet. An old pedestrian suspension bridge used to cross to Mounteviot House but this had long been closed (as unsafe), but in 1991 it was rebuilt and hopefully, by now, there will be a marked linking path from Dere Street at Jedfoot Bridge leading down to this new bridge, round Mounteviot House, and on to the Woodland Centre – which certainly should not be missed.

For this route head out of Jedburgh along the A68 northwards, the Bongate, to just before the A68 crosses Jed Water. Turn off right on a little road which wends up a dell, then forks. Take the left fork and simply follow it all the way down to the A698, which crosses the Jed Water by a bridge opened in 1970. This is Jedfoot Bridge. Dere Street joins our route, as a good farm track (opposite a sheepfold), just before the A698 junction. It was not possible to walk from here down to the new bridge when this guide was completed but the marked path should be available by now and would be worth following. If in doubt check with the Jedburgh Tourist Office the night before, or telephone the Woodland Centre 08353-306.

When we walked the route through we, perforce, took another route which was interesting enough that it is now given as an alternative. It followed what was the old Jedburgh road northwards (before the A68 was thought of), a pleasant right-of-way which the Landranger map no longer condescends to show. Head down the High Street.

Left of the drive in to the Bank of Scotland is a 'loupin-on stane' (a mounting block), which was a boon to Sir Walter Scott on his legal or social visits to Jedburgh for his childhood lameness made loupin onto a horse none too easy. Across the road is the British Legion Hall.

The High Street swings right to join the A68 but we keep on, towards the fire station, whose tower stands up like a piece of modern architecture. Just before it is the corner Railway Tavern where we turn left onto the Pleasance (there is no name visible), and along past the buildings of the Jedburgh Grammar School. The road swings right at the Episcopal Church and is clearly named Sharplaw Road. Sharplaw is the farm at the top of our steep ascent. Mayfield (B & B) is the last building on the left, as we pull up out of the town. Beyond Sharplaw the road dips to the Harden Burn only to

*THE WATERLOO MONUMENT ON PENIEL HEUGH, ONE OF THE
MOST VISIBLE BORDER MONUMENTS*

climb even higher to Monklaw Farm.

Monklaw lies off left at an angled crossroads. The tarred road bends downwards to the right for Bonjedward but straight on into the trees is our track (the old Jedburgh–Edinburgh road) which then loses all the height gained as it contours round and down to Ancrum Bridge; perfect walking.

On leaving the tarred road at the Monklaw crossroads the track leads to a gate into a field but there is no need to go through this as, just to the right, there is a track along through fine beech trees. Continue through to a gate on the far side of the wood (sycamore plantings on the left) which gives a sudden view of the Eildons – and Peniel Heugh looking nice and near at last. We wander through some rich parkland with mature specimen trees, initially following the edge of a wood, in the first field between fences, in the next just along the wood's edge, then on, in the same line, across an open area to a gate on the far side. This leads into a narrow woody dell and, beyond this, we cross more open ground towards a protruding corner of woodland. The buzz and flow of the A68 obtrudes off right.

The edge of the wood is followed to the corner of the field where a gate leads into what appears to be someone's back garden. It is! The right-of-way runs down their lawn, past their door and out the gate onto the A698. Have consideration for those living there and pass quietly. There are lots of gates all down this rural section; ensure you close them all please.

Go through the gates opposite on the old tarmac approach to Ancrum Bridge, which is fenced off against vehicles. There's a stylish house, right, and looking away ahead, left, we glimpse Ancrum village which, sadly we have no time to explore. Despite the ravages of war there is a thirteenth-century cross on the green, and several prehistoric sites. A famous person not quite like others has Ancrum connections – Beatrix Potter. From the age of five she and her family spent many summer holidays in Scotland, and her brother, Bertram, farmed at Ancrum beside the Ale Water (his grave is in the local cemetery).

Ancrum Bridge is in need of love and attention. Part of the parapet has collapsed and trees are rooting in the masonry. As it is a classic example of an early bridge (Ancrum Bridge is one of the oldest recorded bridges in Scotland) with angular refuges and spiky finials it is well worth preserving. Like its full description? 'A 3-span, segmental-arched bridge, of dressed stone construction with rusticated voussoirs and a dentilated string course. The triangular cutwaters are extended up to form pedestrian refuges.' (There are basically two arches, the third being an emergency arch to take floodwater along the flat left bank.) The A68 bridge just downstream is a graceful, wide-arched, stone structure and dates from early this century. (They don't build aesthetic bridges like that in these days of straight steel and crude concrete.)

Skirt Ancrum AFC ground and, opposite the 'grandstand' there is a gate which leads us onto the most dangerous minutes of the trip, walking along the A68. On the right there is a gatehouse, and the rough road there leads to the Woodland Centre, which lies left at a junction. Take this way in rather than going along the risky A68. The centre, based on the old Harestanes Farm, is open Easter-October, 10.30–17.30, 08353–306.

WOODLAND CENTRE–PENIEL HEUGH–MAXTON

The Centre is sited in the old sawmill buildings (once water-driven) and has been beautifully designed (in natural wood, naturally) to hold several displays: one concerns maps, another profiles the plant-hunting explorers (a near-Scottish monopoly one feels) and I can recommend the Whittle book (see bibliography) as further reading on these hardy types. Their travels in far ranges make mere mountaineering look a soft option. Perhaps the best known of these Scottish explorers was David Douglas. His fame is partly due to having a lovely fir named after him, and also his unhappy end – trampled to death by a bull in a pit trap in Hawaii. He first introduced a wide range of well-known plants: Camassia, Garrya elliptica, lupins, flowering currant, noble fir, Douglas fir, sugar pine and Sitka spruce, which, while lovely as a solitary showpiece is generally obnoxious in the serried ranks of today's insensitive commercial plantings. (See bibliography; Morwood.) The Centre also offers displays on various woods, explains the growing of timber, has a working sawmill, wooden crafts, a natural history bookshop and a tea room with scrumptious home baking. An excellent place to take the kids later on, but we had better turn to our walk again. Obtain the pack with a map and description of the Wellington Walk which we follow. I'll leave it to describe the route and its interesting features. You may also like to visit the pinery with its magnificent mature trees.

The path goes up through the woodlands west of the minor road to Maxton and then swings round across it to take us up Peniel Heugh. The walk's name is appropriate for we end at the Waterloo Monument and, en route, have passed an avenue of Wellingtonias (sequoias), a species introduced in 1852, the year Wellington died, and planted in many estates in Britain.

The view from the monument is probably the widest we'll have on our walk for we can see back 'to where the filmy Cheviot hung along the southern sky' (Roger Quin), and on ahead to Minchmoor and the Moorfoot Hills. Walk over a bit to see the rampart-circles visible on the iron age fort (658262).

The monument looks like a black lighthouse that has lost its way. A plaque declares: 'To the Duke of Wellington and the British Army William Ker, VI Marquis of Lothian, and his tenantry dedicate this monument. XXX June MDCCCXV' – which is 1815, the year of Waterloo. Building started within a fortnight of the battle but the partially completed tower collapsed and it was not really completed till later. The rocket-like tower is 150 feet in height and weighs over 3,000 tons. There are 228 steps spiralling up to the wooden summit balcony. Eventually it is hoped to rebuild this structure so the tower can be climbed in safety. The monument is astonishingly visible over a wide area for all the hill is only 237 metres in height.

The Lothian Estates are owned by the Marquis of Lothian but the family name is Kerr, one of long fame (or notoriety) in this area of the Borders. Ferniehurst Castle, just off the A68 south of Jedburgh is a Kerr tower. For many years it was leased to the Scottish Youth Hostel Association and as a teenager I slept in a haunted tower room, rather hoping to be visited by the 'green lady'.

Monteviot has a connection with one of the most poignant Border songs, 'The Flowers of the Forest' for its author, Jean Elliot, died there, in what was her brother's home, and he had almost casually suggested she should write a song about Flodden, saddest of all national disasters. There are many versions of the song but this one is perhaps the best loved.

> *I've heard them lilting, at the ewe-milking,*
> *Lasses a' lilting, before dawn of day.*
> *But now they are moaning on ilka green loaning;*
> *The flowers of the forest are a' wede awae.*

At present Dere Street north of the Teviot is hardly walkable but the authorities are working on it and I'll pass on any up-to-date information. Walking on a path would be more enjoyable than the tarred road, however minor, down to Maxton. Any change here will probably lead walkers to the A68 (about 596295) so the option then would be to break off at Forest Lodge, or the minor road beyond, and walk down to Maxton.

Leaving Peniel Heugh: from the monument descend to the north-west, in line slightly left of the red-tinted whaleback-shaped hill (Black Hill) and, when the forest edge appears, pick out the stile, at the only area of slatted fencing in an otherwise unbroken wall. It is marked with green-paint and a path, which becomes a track, leads down to reach the minor road where we turn right to walk north to the Tweed.

Another road merges with ours but, apart from a few wriggles, our road runs very determinedly to Maxton on the A699. Look back for the best views of the monument. At the highest point of the road we can see, left, the dome of Baron's Folly, a summer house erected by a local laird and merchant called Rutherford, who had been given this courtesy title by the Russians for his activities as their agent during the war against the Turks in 1770. Beyond the folly lies Lilliard's Edge, site of the Battle of Ancrum.

Ancrum Moor was one of many bloody episodes of the 'Rough Wooing' when Henry VIII tried to force the Scots to have Mary (the future Queen of Scots) and his son Edward united in marriage. In 1544 the Earl of Hertford had devastated the Lothians, and in 1545 the English warden of the Middle March was given his go-ahead to seize what he liked. The Earl of Angus, who was likely to suffer most, was further enraged when his Douglas family tombs were desecrated and Melrose Abbey burnt. Angus's force was repulsed from one attack and could only snap at the heels of the larger English army. The regent Arran joined Angus but still the English forces outnumbered them by more than five to one. However a force of Lindsays and Scotts of Buccleuch arrived, the odds were reduced to two to one and Aungus determined on action.

All the horses were sent off, ridden by boys and grooms, in an

THE PREHISTORIC FORT ON PENIEL HEUGH, STILL VISIBLE AFTER MANY CENTURIES

altogether successful feint. The English forces rushed up to the high ground north-west of Peniel Heugh where they found an army waiting for them. Blown as they were they had no option but to charge on against the long spears of the Scottish foot. The Scots won but the outcome was an even angrier Henry VIII (shades of Edward 1) who was furious that the Scots should fight for their freedom. After all, Angus was even his brother-in-law.

The sad outcome though was the return of Hertford who so ravaged the Borderland that much was never rebuilt, including the five great abbeys. In 1547 he came back as Lord Protector, Henry having died, and the Scots made complete asses of themselves at the Battle of Pinkie, fleeing before the battle had really been joined. Resilience, no doubt bred of long practice, saw them slowly regain all that had been lost and two years later the last English soldier had been driven from the Borders. By ironic twists it was to be the hapless Mary's son who would come to the throne of England and so unite the kingdoms.

The battle of Ancrum Moor is popularly remembered however because of Maid Lilliard, a Maxton woman who joined in the fray, after seeing her lover slain, and eventually fell mortally wounded and was buried on the spot, which became known as Lilliard's Edge. Some books deny the site's very existence but I've seen it, and photographed the monument on its crest (a superb viewpoint). The inscription on the grave is a quaint gem:

Fair Maiden Lilliard lies under this stane;
Little was her stature but muckle was her fame.
Upon the English loons she laid mony thumps
An when her legs were cuttit off she fought upon her stumps.

Muirhouselaw is the major landmark on our route: a large house, pleasant gardens and farm buildings, all very trim. Just before Maxton there are signs of the old North British railway line to Berwick – one old level-crossing gate and an obvious railway cottage which was once the station. The line was axed in 1968. A branch line once ran up to Jedburgh.

Turn left at the A699. Maxton is an unspoilt, pleasant hamlet, with part of an old cross in a street off the main road. Maxton is one of quite a few Borders place names which have become personal names. (Not far west is Maxpoffle, but so far I've not met a Mr or Ms Maxpoffle.) We turn right down a lane signposted for 'Maxton Church' where we pick up the discreet yellow arrows of a public footpath. St Cuthbert's church is attractive in its simple way, and rather like some of the Telford Highland churches with four doors and windows on the side, and a small bell-lantern on the gable – but

Telford would not have added the round window in the centre; his budget was too tight. The original church was founded in the twelfth century, but rebuilt several times. There's a 1609 Dutch bell in the lantern belfry.

THE TWEED TO DRYBURGH

The River Tweed, from here up to Abbotsford, offers rich golden miles. The markers direct us round the church onto a woodland path which we follow down (a flight of stairs!) to a burn, which is crossed, then we cross a track to climb up again along the top edge of the woods (below Benrig House) as far as a brick wall and another flight of steps down to actually reach the River Tweed. (Do I hear an 'At last!'?) Riverside walking leads to the Mertoun Bridge. There is an attractive plantation (poplars) on the other bank, behind which runs the lade, from a one-time mill further upstream, fed by a cauld (weir) across the Tweed, an obstruction I can recall from a canoe journey down the river. This can be seen from the bridge, which we have to climb up to and then drop down the other side. Take care! It may only be a B road but the traffic can bomb through b. fast. There is a toll house set in the embanked approach to the bridge with the watching-window and door on the upper storey.

The Tweed is a really big river at this stage, big in width and water

LILLIARD'S STONE (AND BLOODTHIRSTY RHYME) **DOES STILL EXIST. IT IS SITED RIGHT ON** *DERE STREET AS IT CROSSES LILLIARD'S EDGE*

volume. The Tweed is ninety-seven miles long, making it one of our major rivers. Its fame as a fishing river is constantly under threat but salmon are just one species in its waters. There are at least sixteen different fish and the whole river is granted Site of Special Scientific Interest (SSSI) status because of its rich diversity. It always strikes me as a gentle giant of a river, an aspect which was noted by Ratcliffe Barnett who wrote, 'The Highlander, like his rivers, is full of impulse and passion, but Ettrick, Yarrow and Tweed, like the Border breed, are full of quiet restraint, silent with a strength which seldom lifts up its voice...'

The name Tweed is very old and, like most short river names, cannot be given any meaning now. The cloth, named tweed, was the result of a mistake by a London merchant who received an order of *tweel* (*twill*) and read it as tweed then astutely realised this was a more marketable name.

We come on St Boswell's Golf Course. Keep along the landward edge (track) or tight by the river so as not to distract the players. From the club house a small road leads into the town. The main street is attractive and an old well has a religious text on it about drinking. There is a date of 1724 above one doorway. The name St Boswell's comes from St Boisil, a monk from Old Melrose who founded a settlement. The huge village green has a Fair each July, once a main stock-selling point and still attracting travelling people. The old hawkers were called *muggers*!

It might be wiser however to push on to Dryburgh without losing precious time. Paths wend on along the high riverbank from the golf course, squeezed between town and river, to descent into the dell of the West Burn which is followed down again to reach the banks of the Tweed. The path by the river runs through woodland rich enough to be a SSSI, walking which delighted me on my *Groats End Walk*. Keep an eye open for tree creepers. Round a last bend we come on a sturdy suspension bridge which we cross to reach Dryburgh, a mere hamlet, most of which is visible from the bridge. The gravel reach of shore here was a useful landing spot when a group of us canoed the Tweed in 1969. We didn't like the red cliffs just downstream. They had sharp ledges sticking out under water, real canvas-rippers.

Before walking downstream, scramble up the bank straight ahead (after crossing) and, on the left, there is a folly, sorry, a 'Temple of the Muses'. Perched in the depths of a cedar grove it is the sort of spot for an incident from a John Buchan novel. The Temple was erected by one of Sir Walter Scott's contemporaries, the eccentric Erskine, Earl of Buchan whose works will keep popping up along our route. A bust of the poet Thomson stood in the temple and while the earl was reading a poem he'd written (before unveiling the monument) a local lad stole into the screened-off temple and placed an old hat on its head! The peroration's climactic 'Lo! the man!' had the audience hooting with glee.

The earl also erected a figure of Inigo Jones within the ruins of Dryburgh Abbey. What connection there was nobody could discover and eventually the piece was quietly removed from sight. The most astonishing statue the earl was responsible for we'll come on shortly.

The road twists up, passing ornamental gates on the left (which simply lead into a high walled field!) to reach a junction. On the left is a small post office, on the right the entrance drive to the Dryburgh Abbey Hotel, which is worth a visit either for its good bar meals or a welcome pot of tea. It offers relatively well-priced accommodation if you are feeling very weary. From the hotel, whatever you do, walk over to see the abbey which stands surrounded by a wealth of majestic trees, including some huge cedars, reputedly dating back to Crusading times. There is an 800-year-old yew.

The rich sylvan setting gives Dryburgh a charm all of its own. Jedburgh impresses with its bold majesty, Melrose has a rose romanticism, Dryburgh beguiles and blesses, an intimate site.

Dryburgh was *not* founded by David I, though it is of his period. It is a Premonstratensian establishment ('white canons' as against the Augustinian 'black canons') founded in 1150 by Hugh de Morville, Constable of

MAXTON CHURCH ABOVE THE RIVER TWEED

Scotland. This was a relatively new order (1121), akin to the Augustinian, taking its name from the founding seat of Prémontré, near Laon in France. A daughter house was founded at Alnwick in 1140 and from there it came to Dryburgh.

Dryburgh Abbey had a tough history. It was burned by Edward II (1322), Richard II (1385), again in 1461, 1523, 1544 and then by Hertford in 1545. Dryburgh itself was once a town, but Hertford's army destroyed it so completely, burning and pillaging (they bore off sixty horses), that there was no will left to rebuild. Scotland, at heart, has good cause to dislike southern government, but *this* history is not taught in England of course!

The church itself is in ruinous state, but quite a few of the monastic buildings remain and there are some fine doorways, rare touches of mural painting in the Chapter House and the scratched outlines for a game of *merelles*, a Norman equivalent of noughts and crosses, no doubt the tea break entertainment of the masons.

The graves of Sir Walter Scott and Earl Haig are major attractions at the abbey. Scotts, Haigs and Erskines alone have the right to be buried within the abbey. The stone marking the grave of the Field Marshall is the simple military one used for soldiers all over Europe, a nice touch. Haigs have been at Bemersyde since the twelfth century. The estate was bought from one branch of the family and presented to the Earl after the First World War. He was one of the whisky family, and far from the sombre figure so often

LOOKING TO DRYBURGH ACROSS THE TWEED

presented. He proposed to his future wife just three days after meeting her! One of Thomas the Rhymer's sayings is regularly trotted out in reference to the Haigs.

Tide, tide, whate'er betide
Haig will be Haig at Bemersyde.

It has held good for 700 years, even if there was a panic in one generation when a son came along only after twelve girls had been born.

The Scott graves – wife, family, son-in-law as well as the bard – lie in the North Transept, the best-preserved bit of the church (a 1678 sketch shows little has changed in over 300 years), while the 11th Earl of Buchan appropriated a chamoer off the cloisters, once the library and vestry. His is the memorial pillar standing out on the lawn to the south of the gatehouse. With brief interruptions the Erskines had owned the abbey back to 1541.

DRYBURGH ABBEY – THE FINE DOOR LEADING INTO THE CLOISTERS

THE TWEED TO MELROSE

Return to the post office, and on up the steep road. As it swings right a path breaks off beside the last house on the left (white gates) and this is signed 'Public footpath to Wallace Monument'. The path rises steeply up through woodland and, near the top, doubles back to the lip of the bluff where the McGonagall of statues stands staring into the tree canopy. The monument is a huge, crude figure of delightful bad taste, erected by the aforesaid Earl of Buchan early last century.

Curious to see how many visitors it received, the earl built a 'fog-house' and installed a local poet, Jamie Barrie, as caretaker. (There were 15,000 visitors in the decade following.) Like McGonagall, he produced a volume of his poems and was obviously a character of note. His cottage had a sign outside declaring:

Small beer sold here,
Penny a bottle – not dear.

Poet and earl died within months of each other in 1829.

The earl may have had a mania for monuments but we can be grateful to him for one thing. David Steward Erskine, Earl of Buchan, was an enthusiastic antiquarian and in 1780 called a meeting at his house to propose a society to collect historical items. From this came the Society of Antiquaries and its collections, the basis of our Royal Scottish Museums of today.

The atmosphere would be improved if the trees were cut back so Wallace (or at least Wallace's visitors) could enjoy the view of the sunset over the hills of Ettrick Forest. Escape by continuing along the path (a woodland track) which comes out to the B6356 where we turn left.

On the first open stretch, away to the right, we can spot the outline of Smailholm Tower. When the infant Walter Scott was struck down by infantile paralysis he was sent to stay with his uncle and aunt at Sandy Knowe beside Smailholm Tower, one of the major influences on his life as he himself admitted. W.H. Ogilvie's poem on the tower dwells on this.

Here by the peel-tower old and grey
In the sunlit mornings a lame boy lay,
Spending his thought o'er ridge and tree
To the magic peaks of the Eildons three...
We have built him statues in street and square,
We have carved him a temple rich and rare,
But the grandest stone to his memory still
Is a grey-walled tower on the windy hill;

In 1799 Scott was staying with Scott of Harden at Mertoun House when he heard that Smailholm was to be demolished and pleaded for it to be spared. The owner agreed, on condition Walter wrote a ballad about the tower. *The Eve of St John* was the result, quite a spooky tale which appeared in *The Minstrelsy* with only a passing line on its origins!

The scattered hamlet we soon come to is part of the Bemersyde estate of the Haigs. The road swings up right then bends sharp left (a sign 'Scott's View ½' stops motorists from going straight on), and just ahead is Bemersyde Hill and, beyond, the whaleback of Black Hill which we noted back on Peniel Heugh.

THE MASSIVE STATUE OF SIR WILLIAM WALLACE ABOVE DRYBURGH

Scott's View of his 'delectable mountains' is so well known one expects the reality to be slightly disappointing but, given a day of meteorological character, it really is fantastic:

a jewelled garter of icy river
Twists around the limb of Eildon (Ken Morrice)

No wonder Scott always drew rein here to just feast on the view of river, trees and Eildons, those three crests against the saffron sky. Andrew Lang caught the brightness and sadness well:

Three crests against the saffron sky,
Beyond the purple plain,
The dear remembered melody
Of Tweed once more again.

Twilight, and Tweed, and Eildon Hill,
Fair and thrice fair you be:
You tell me that the voice is still
That should have welcomed me.

Scott always paused here and when the funeral cortege carrying his body to Dryburgh passed this spot his horse automatically stopped, as it had always done, an incident which is rather touching, though it really only illustrates the horse's general lack of intelligence! (A modern example of this nature tells of a blind rider who always walked to her horse with her guide dog, a black labrador, made a circuit of the field and stopped beside her dog again. One day the horse made half a circuit and stopped. Why? Because a black dog happened to be sitting there!)

We follow the next loop of the Tweed. Gledswood sits in its woody depths and, opposite, is the site of Old Melrose (Mailros) where Boisil founded a monastery in the seventh century. Oswald, King of Northumbria had welcomed the Celtic saint, Aidan, and one of his followers, Boisil made his way up the Tweed. Boisil took a shepherd lad, Cuthbert, under his wing and Cuthbert succeeded him as prior before travelling on to greater renown at Lindisfarne. Boniface the 'Apostle of the Rhine' also came from Mailros.

At a junction ('Scott's View' the only sign) swing left, passing the Gledswood entrance, and walking along a beech hedge, quite a tunnel of trees, to come out suddenly on another view of the Eildons and, as we swing right, downwards, a view to the Leaderfoot bridges, dominated by the graceful, high-stilted railway viaduct. Keep left when we meet another road.

SCOTT'S VIEW – THE FAMOUS VIEWPOINT ABOVE THE TWEED LOOKING TO THE EILDON HILLS

THE THREE BRIDGES – CROSSING THE RIVER TWEED: RAILWAY (FROM BELOW), OLD ROAD (PEDESTRIANS) AND MODERN A68

The angle steepens as we twist down (minor road right for Redpath) and round to the bridge over the Leader Water.

About one and half miles up the Leader, below Black Hill, which has been such a landmark to us, lies Earlston, the home of Thomas the Rhymer who was a real person, Sir Thomas of Ercildoune (Earlston), born 1220, died 1297. A mysterious person, he left many rhyming prophecies which time has fulfilled.

Having crossed the bridge, ignore the road, right, which just leads up to the A68. We go ahead, under this modern steel and concrete bridge which, I think, has a certain functional grace, to cross the utterly beautiful old Fly or Drygrange Bridge (built 1776–80 to replace the Fly ferry) which is then dominated, upstream, by the many-arched Leaderfoot viaduct. The three bridges over the Tweed are, in themselves, a contrasting, fascinating museum of bridge building. The 1865 railway bridge (nineteen arches) bore a line to meet the east coast main line at Reston, north of Berwick, but as part of an imagined *grand* Tweed route it flopped. The North British–Caledonian rivalry saw to that. Mind you it was British Rail which killed off the last Borders line, the Waverley Route from Edinburgh to Carlisle, in 1969, an attractive route which simply lacked imaginative management and investment. What a tourist asset it could have been, should have been, linking as it did with the Settle–Carlisle route. Drygrange Bridge was a product of the turnpike era of road-building when bridges had to be wider, to take carriages, and new lines were chosen to avoid hilly approaches. Now with simple horsepower, rather than horses, roads just bash over anything. The Leaderfoot Viaduct has now been 'taken into care' by Scottish Heritage and will be developed for its tourist potential.

We will not cross a more beautiful major bridge than this one. Once across turn right ('Newstead 1') to follow the road. The obvious river bank option is rather discouraged you'll notice. On the highest point of this road is a monument, in the form of a Roman altar, to the great Roman fort of Trimontium *(the three hills)*, a monument as tasteful as the Wallace one is *kitsch*. There is nothing to see on the ground but archaeologists early this century found some marvellous antiquities which are mostly on display in Edinburgh, and some day, money, planners and developers allowing, there will be a complete dig of the huge site which took up to 1,000 soldiers at a time in the period AD 79–213. It was a Melrose solicitor, Dr Curle, who excavated the site 1905–11 and set new standards for the archaeologists. One altar he found has a ringing text: 'To the god Sylvanus, for his own and his soldiers' safety, Carrius Domitianus, the centurion of the Twentieth Legion, surnamed Valiant and Victorious fulfils his vow justly and willingly'. An exhibition, leading to permanent Roman Museum, is on the cards. At present this is sited in the Ormiston Institute in Melrose but you can ask for details at the Melrose Tourist Information Office.

We drop down into Newstead. The old school on the right (now a Health Board building) is as red as I think natural stone can be. (At least it is in the rain!) Newstead reminds me of East Neuk fishing villages with a main street and diverting *wynds*. Newstead is one of the oldest places in Scotland, having been lived in for *c.* 2,000 years. Once through the village turn left onto Dean road and, almost at once, leave it, right, into what looks like a stable yard. It is a stable yard, but the discreet yellow signs and arrows of the *Eildon Walk* point this way to gain a footpath running behind the houses.

Walk along this well-made track – which was used daily by the masons building Melrose Abbey as they had digs in Newstead. Below the last house there is a gate, then the walk runs along the hillside like a bit of abandoned railway line – but the path predates railways by many centuries. Another gate leads onto a tarred path which runs past two houses to reach a road as it makes a big U-bend (Priorswalk/Priorsdene). Turn right and walk along to the equivalent place where the road begins to curve up, and branch off, right, onto another paved path; it starts at the end of the row of off-white cubist houses. The older houses, on the uphill side, have some interesting gardens.

THE CENTRE OF MELROSE, STILL WITH AN OLD MERCAT CROSS

Keep to the paved path. It puts in a wiggle and runs across a grassy area (overlooked by the sumptuous youth hostel; access top corner) to pass alongside the Abbey grounds. At the end is the National Trust for Scotland (NTS) shop, Tourist Information Centre and Priorwood Gardens complex. Across the road, by the car park, is a map of Melrose. Turning left the Market Cross/High Street is only 150 yards off. Melrose is very compact and many consider its small size makes it the most attractive of the Border towns.

Just beyond the car park is a coffee house, and next door to it is Braidwood, and across the road is Dunfermline House, both B & Bs. Marmion's Brasserie does excellent food in a friendly setting and if you turn up the next lane there is the cosy Old Smiddy Bistro. There is also a restaurant at Melrose Station, and the George and Abbotsford does excellent dinners, as do other High Street hotels, so Melrose offers a wider choice than we usually enjoy. There's a chip shop next door to the Station Hotel. A *wynd* leads through from the Old Smiddy to the High Street. Across the High Street, right, next door to the King's Arms Hotel is Orchard House (B & B) while, left, round the Market Cross (part of it is dated 1645) are the Bon Accord, Burts, George and Abbotsford, and Station Hotels. In an attractive side lane off Abbey Street, linking the Market Square and the Abbey, is Little Fordel B & B. Other accommodation lies out westwards or across the Tweed in Gattonside but if you can't find a bed quickly in the central area call into the Tourist Information Office and enlist their aid. This is all summarised below.

PRACTICAL INFORMATION: MELROSE

Tourist Information Centre, Priorwood Gardens, 089682-2555.
Telephone code for Melrose numbers is 089682-

ACCOMMODATION: Central Melrose: Melrose Youth Hostel, Priorwood, Melrose, Roxburghshire TD6 9EF, -2521, Bon Accord Hotel, -2645, King's Arms Hotel, -2143, Station Hotel, Dingleton Road, -2038, Little Fordel, Abbey Street, -2206, Braidwood, Buccleuch Street, -2488, Dunfermline House, Buccleuch Street, -2148, Orchard House, 17 High Street, -2005, 15 Prior's Walk, -2087 (top circle of first houses entering Melrose). More expensive, Burt's Hotel, -2285, George and Abbotsford, -2308.

Suburban Melrose (heading west or lying south of the road westwards): 12 Quarrydene, -3204, Torwood Lodge, High Cross Avenue, -2220, Craigard, Huntly Avenue, -2041, 42 Ormiston Terrace, -2236.

Other local accommodation: Little Broadmeadows, Waverley Road, -2739, Waverley Castle Hotel, Waverley Road, -2244, (palatial, upmarket, between Darnick and the R Tweed), Old Abbey School, Waverley Road, -2816, Bidston, Waverley Road, -2730 (half mile out B6374), Collingwood, Waverley Road, -2670 (no smoking), Wraysbury, Dean Road, Newstead, 203 (before reaching Melrose), Treetops, Gattonside, by Melrose, -3153 (hamlet across the Tweed), Friarshaugh Farm, Gattonside, -2027, Grianan, Gattonside, -2971, The Gables, Darnick, -2479 (well out but on tomorrow's route).

Accommodation in Melrose is often completely booked up and one simple remedy is to take a taxi to Selkirk for the night, then return the next day – which would allow two nights in a B & B and a day walking with minimal load. Another possibility is to try Galashiels. One could also stay at St Boswells or Newtown St Boswells, stopping earlier in the day.

St Boswell's B & Bs: 0835-22711, -22366, -22731, -22650, and 05736-343. Hotels: 0835-22243, -22261.

Galashiels: B & Bs: 0896-56255, -2649, -57276, -55270, -55224, -3073, -55854, -3068, -4257, -56437, -3437, -2641, -2987, -56437, -2517.

(There are also half a dozen expensive hotels).

Also Halidean Mill, near Scott's View, Bemersyde. 089-682-2341.

TAXIS: Melrose 089682-2892; Selkirk 0750-21827, -20354, -21061, -21478, -22489; Galashiels 0896-56796, -53935, -55584, -56227, 56789, -56565, -58444.

CAMPING: Gibson Park 089682-2969. Seasonal site on sports field. Almost in town centre. Good facilities.

MEALS: Marmion's Brasserie -2245, Old Smiddy Bistro -3171, and Melrose Station -2546, are recommended, and several hotels are popular. The George and Abbotsford is excellent value.

The Festival Week takes place in the third week in June and puts pressure on the accommodation available. Melrose's half-day is Thursday.

EILDON HILLS
and
MELROSE

Bart 41 OSLR 73
OSPF 461 (NT 43/53)

This day will pass all too quickly so don't waste any of it. The Eildons will give a classic walk and there is so much to see in Melrose that the day will vanish in no time. Dinner in one of the good restaurants can round off things nicely – not many options like this on the Pennine Way or Southern Upland Way!

CIRCUIT OF EILDON HILLS AND RIVER TWEED

The Eildon Hills occupy a very special place in ancient lore and present fact. They are such an immediately recognisable group from so many places that they lure visitors into an ascent, even if they don't normally go up hills.

The summit of the North-east top has a prehistoric fort/settlement and a Roman signal station. Tradition has it that King Arthur and his knights lie asleep in a cave on the Eildons, waiting the day when they shall rise to save Britain from catastrophe.

The Arthurian legend has been long-entrenched in the Eildons, with probably as much justification as any other place. West of Falkirk too, there was a sacred shrine, of pre-Roman vintage, which was linked with being the depository of the Holy Grail. It survived into the eighteenth century and archaeologists are trying to work the site now. That area has 150 place names with Arthurian connections, yet there is nothing in songs, ballads, etc – which suggests new races have ebbed and flowed since then. Drumelzier, further up the Tweed, is claimed as the last home and burial place of Merlin.

We'll start today in the Market Square. The old Mercat Cross with the arms of Scotland on it is dated 1645 (tastelessly painted recently). It faces across to the Ormiston Institute with its mere 100 year old clock.

Leave Market Square by the B6539 Lilliesleaf Road (Dingleton Road) which runs up past the Station Hotel, to go under what used to be the railway and is now the bypass. Unless too early in the morning it is worth going up to see what has happened to the old station. It lies up the road opposite the Station Hotel, clearly signed 'Melrose Station'.

The building itself is one of the few pre-1850 stations to survive; an A-listed building looking a bit like a Jacobean mansion, in creamy sandstone, it was the most prestigious of the stations on the late lamented Waverley Line. Abandoned from 1969 until 1985, an architect then bought and restored the station, and its rooms are now used for offices. The ground floor houses a restaurant, 089-682-2546.

Return to Dingleton Road and walk up under the bridge. There are houses on the left but about 100 yards from the bridge there is a gap in the row and clear signs indicating the Eildon Walk. (We meet these periodically but are not following that described route.) This is the start of an interesting steeplechase: a dip to the river, some steps (some steps!) and several stiles before we win clear of the fields, which go surprisingly high on the hill. We

MELROSE STATION'S RESTORED PLATFORM AND SOME OLD LUGGAGE FROM THE MUSEUM (NOW CLOSED)

keep left of the hedgerow up the first field and then right of the hedgerow for the second field, all clearly marked as 'Eildon Walk' (yellow markers). Once on the gorse-thick hillside the main Eildon Walk route contours off left. We bear up, and right to reach the saddle between Eildon North Hill and Eildon Mid Hill.

I once overtook a party of sixty-nine trailing up this route, rather a people-pollution I felt. They had a badge-bedecked leader setting the pace. Reminded me of one such who told those behind to tell those behind to 'Be sure and shut the gate'. The tail were puzzled by the garbled message that reached them: 'something to do with Hepplethwaite'.

Climb up to Eildon Mid Hill, the highest of the Eildon summits at 422 metres. There is a cairn, a viewpoint indicator and trig point on top and one of the great views of the trip is the reward for our exertions. Eildon Wester (which lies to the south!) is only about 371 metres and seldom visited. Mid Hill need not be re-climbed if the Wester is visited. From the col a path circles round, back to the col between the two big hills, on a line higher than the one shown on the Landranger map. Climb up North Hill 404 metres.

The view is every bit as grand as that from Mid Hill. The sweep of the Cheviots is particularly pleasing to those who have walked from that distant bastion to this windy outpost. North Hill is ringed by the defences of an Iron Age fort, a huge place with about 300 house foundations inside the triple walls of their defences; 300 houses in twenty acres is quite a high population density! This, the largest such fort in south Scotland, was the main base of the Selgovae tribe. They were displaced by the Romans, who established a signal station in the fort, linking up with others along Dere Street (north and south) and no doubt with Trimontium just below.

The Eildons look a bit like volcanoes, but only Little Hill (545319) is a proper volcano. The other summits were formed by underground activity, so are strictly speaking *laccoliths*, which only broke the surface after millions of years of weathering, and the grinding of the ice ages. The soil is very acid so supports plenty of heather which is why the Eildons appear so dark when seen from a distance. The lighter patches are the naked scree areas. Grouse, stonechats, whinchats, wheatears and pipits all like this environment.

Folklore credits the multi-summits as being the work of a demon, rising to the challenge to split the hill, given by Michael Scott. Michael Scott was a real twelfth-century astrologer and mathematician, but such scholarship was no doubt viewed with suspicion by the ignorant populace who turned him into the 'wizard of legend'. (How many poor women in later centuries were to be burnt as witches for knowing too much about herbs and healing.) Michael Scott was supposed to have kept the plague a prisoner (tied up in a sack!) in Glen Luce Abbey which greatly riled the devil who sent a minion to battle with Scott. The demon gave the wizard three chances to be rid of him. The first challenge was to dam the Tweed at Kelso, the second was to cleave Eildon into three, which was also accomplished but Scott finally won when he challenged the demon to make a rope out of Solway sand!

Leave the summit to head down east, then north-east to reach the top end of the thin plantation shown on the map (converging paths). This is the Eildontree Plantation which runs down the spur above the Bogle Burn. It was under the Eildon Tree that Thomas the Rhymer encountered the Queen of Elfland. Tradition has it that he really did disappear for seven years but probably for good-enough reasons which were not gone into after his return when a tale of mystery was used as a smokescreen. Tradition has it that he spent this time in the north-east of Scotland rather than Elfhame. (The area is full of his prophecies – see Tranter's *Portrait of the Borders*.)

One of his prophecies concerned a tragedy we have already touched on. Thomas was visiting the Earl of March and was asked, rather facetiously, to tell what the morrow would bring. He declared it would be a calamitous day and just when people were beginning to joke that nothing had happened the news came that Alexander III had been killed at

THE EILDON HILLS (VIEWED FROM THE SOUTH)

Kinghorn – possibly the most far-reaching accident in all Scotland's history.

Continue down left of the plantation (plenty of gorse again) to reach a stile/gate, which leads onto a track which is followed down to the A6091. Turn right for a short way then off left again (clearly signposted) on a track descending to Newstead. All the Roman camps are over on the right but Trimontium is all under the soil – a huge excavation for the future. We pass under the abandoned railway to a T-junction. Turn right (the Eildon Walk goes left), then first left, down Claymires Lane to reach the 'main' road through Newstead. There is a telephone box across the road and right of this the Eddy Road, which we follow.

Heading down Eddy Road there is a wooden shack on the left and then a small brick building. Look at the stonework of this for it is typical of many Melrose buildings made from the local many-hued sandstone. The lane becomes a track and drops down past the Newstead sewage works and two children's swings to a grassy area. Keep to the left track which soon becomes just a path, crosses a concrete pedestrian bridge over a tiny burn (the old leet from the Abbey Mill), and leads along by the bank of the Tweed. Bruce Sandison, lively fisherman-author, following this route says, 'For me, the Tweed is the Borders. I grew to love it as a boy... The Tweed has an unforgettable smell, like no other river I know: warm, friendly, inviting, promising perfect peace, absolute contentment'.

One soon comes to a stile at the start of a long grassy field which is followed round by the curving bank of the Tweed. At the end a gate leads out onto the top of a wall – which is the path continuation! This is known as The Battery and is an anti-flood barrier to stop the alluvial fields from being inundated. In flood conditions a way could be made below the wall on the left I suppose, but the normal alternative is the path, beaten out by the faint-hearted, along between wall and river.

The Battery follows the curve of the Tweed for quite a spell, then peters out. The path leads on past the Melrose sewage works and along a further embankment wall-top. At a gate a yellow arrow points left, and crossing the field-end leads to a kissing gate onto the minor road and Melrose. More interesting however is to continue on the path on the wall for the length of this small field to reach a second gate, right beside the road and, from which, the Chain Bridge is visible. Walk along to inspect it before heading back on the minor road which meets the B6361 (Annay Road) from Newstead. Turn right and a few minutes' walk leads into Melrose.

The Chain Bridge is a pedestrian suspension bridge built by local smiths in 1826 to link Gattonside with Melrose. Tradition records that people used to cross the Tweed here on stilts. The bridge was taken down (1991) for restoration work so may not be in use when you read this. A temporary bus service Gattonside operates instead.

RED MELROSE

On entering Melrose the first building, right, is the Motor Museum. Open 10.30–17.30, Easter to October, 089-682-2624. There is a collection of old cars, motor cycles and associated material that will fascinate anyone, no matter how unmechanical.

The mill shop is in a building which was once a corn mill. The lade for this was cut above the Chain Bridge and runs on below the Priorswalk to return to the Tweed at The Eddy. The monastery bakehouse once stood here at the mill.

We soon come to the abbey again: 'probably the most famous and lovely of all Scottish abbeys' Nigel Tranter writes. It is another founded by King David I in 1136. Celtic Christianity had come centuries earlier. David I was the devout son of Malcolm Canmore and his Saxon queen, Margaret, who were responsible for Roman rather than Celtic forms becoming the normal in Scotland. The abbey was established by Cistercian monks from Yorkshire's Rievaulx and was famous for its agricultural practices, the monks being skilled sheep farmers and fruit growers.

Like all the border abbeys it was vulnerable to attack and pillage, and after the 1545 Hertford rapine was never rebuilt. The heart of Robert the Bruce was buried at Melrose (his body lies in Dunfermline Abbey). Alexander II and his queen, Johanna, Michael Scott the Wizard and an assortment of Douglases are also interred here. Sir James Douglas had been taking Bruce's heart to the Holy Land when he fell fighting the Moors in Spain. The Black Knight of Liddesdale is a less noble incumbent. When his rival was appointed Sheriff of Teviotdale he grabbed the poor man and threw him into a dungeon to starve to death. He in turn was killed while out hunting. The Douglas of Otterburn fame is also buried here.

Probably because it was a ruin already, the Reformation had no effect on the abbey, and some interesting statues survive – like a cook with his ladle and a pig playing the bagpipes (a gargoyle high on the south side). You can try and find the red 1761 tombstone with the following cheery legend on it. (It lies near the floodlight illuminating the south-east corner of the abbey.)

The earth goeth on the earth,
Glistring like gold;
The earth goeth to the earth
Sooner than it wold,
The earth builds on the earth
Castles and towers;
The earth says to the earth
All shall be ours.

Scott's stone erected over his servant Tom Purdie is better known. Jedburgh's Sir David Brewster, the Victorian scientist, mostly recalled now as the inventor of the kaleidoscope, is buried here.

The fortified commendator's house is now the museum. This building was erected on the site of the Abbot's house as the home of the secular controller of the property following the dissolution of the monasteries. The carefully worked stone of the older building can be seen below the rougher addition which, also saw the addition of the gun loops. A Douglas received this plum at the Reformation. One of the earlier Abbots had been an illegitimate son of James V, as had been the Abbots of Kelso, Coldingham, Holyrood and St Andrews!

There are so many details to note that the guide booklet is nigh essential. All the abbeys are in the care of Historic Scotland and it might be

MELROSE ABBEY – THE FINEST OF THE BORDER RUINS

tempting to sign on as a 'Friend'. I always think the windows at Melrose are particularly fine (doors at Dryburgh) and the presbytery ceiling is superb. Unlike Dryburgh the church has survived better than the monastery building. At its peak it was the biggest and grandest of Border abbeys. Like Jedburgh a parish church was built inside the derelict church (1618).

Next door to the abbey lie Priorwood Gardens. The actual building houses the National Trust for Scotland shop, the Tourist Information Centre (both with local literature, maps etc) and there is a shop specialising in dried flowers, many of them home-grown, for one of the garden's specialities is the growth and study of this art which was practised as long ago as Tutankhamen's day. Over 200 different labelled plants are grown, hung to dry and then sold – the labour of a volunteer force of experts. The other speciality at Priorwood is its apple orchard which grows samples of apples from through the centuries back to Roman days. (They introduced apples and cider-making to Britain.) Priorwood is open weekdays and Sunday afternoons, 089682-2493.

Melrose does not have any bounds to ride but each June there is a festival with a 'Melrosian' chosen and various pilgrimages and visits to the abbey are ceremoniously carried out. There are horsey activities of course and a fancy dress parade which we watched in 1990 from Marmion's where we were dining – unaware it was festival week.

I am not sure whether we can truly call this an 'off day' for we will have covered quite a mileage and seen a great deal. On one occasion an athletic but aesthetic friend insisted on retiring to the top of the Eildons to watch the sunset: an early sunset, being late autumn, a sunset richly hued and fading into breathy-cold, reminding of another Will Ogilvie word picture.

Along the Ettrick hills a splendour wakes
Of red and purple; dark the shadows run
On Ruberslaw, but see! the Dunion takes
The golden sword-thrust of the setting sun!

A snowstorm drifting down the Bowmont vale
A little hour ago made Cheviot white,
And left him glistening in his silver mail;
The day's last champion in the lists with night.

Day Five

MELROSE

to

SELKIRK

Bart 41 OSLR 73
OSPF 461 (NT 43/53), 473 (NT 42/52)

A genuinely easy day. The morning will go in walking to, and exploring, Abbotsford before following a drovers' route over the hills to svelte Selkirk, a friendly town, full of monuments, in a delightful situation.

TO ABBOTSFORD

Head off along the High Street, passing Greenyards (Melrose Rugby Football Club ground) on the right. Seven-a-side rugby had its origins in this spot. Police and fire station are on the left. Into suburbia the road forks and though there is a sign for Abbotsford pointing right this is strictly the way for motorists. We bear left along High Cross Avenue ('Darnick ½' B6394). There is a Catholic church on the left, then an Episcopal church on the right, as we walk out through this opulent end of Melrose into a section of open country.

The road curves up into the attractive hamlet of Darnick, dominated by Darnick Tower, which is a private house, but you can keek through the gates at this fine example of an old Borders' peel tower, the home of the Heitons. The original was built in 1425. Hertford's expedition burned the tower in 1544, so what we see now is mostly from the 1560s. Scott was keen to buy the tower but the owner would not budge at any price. It is still lived in by the descendants of the original builders. The tower has several stones in it which obviously came from Melrose Abbey. Using old buildings of irreplaceable value seems reprehensible but it was common practice until very recent times.

The road wiggles through Darnick and heads on for the busy main roads, but we turn left, up Broomielees Road, at the last house on the left, the start of very pleasant walking, albeit with some ups and downs, but every *up* reveals a superb view and the big *down* is to Abbotsford. The first up, onto the bridge over the motorway-like Melrose bypass, is typical, giving a sighting of the Eildons on one side and over to the ugly 'Golan Heights' of Gala on the other. A pink house stands starkly ahead, part of

DARNICK TOWER NEAR MELROSE

Broomilees Farm. We pull up steadily, passing other farms on the left (Cot Green, Sunnyside and Kaeside), with the view increasing in scale all the while. Past Kaeside the road crosses a saddle (the view goes) and dips to a junction. We head left, eventually, but before then should visit Abbotsford. For this take the right fork: it rises slightly then turns sharp right to drop down steeply towards the Tweed. The B6360 is reached at a telephone box, and the Abbotsford car park and entrance are immediately on the left. An old route continues on down to a ford on the Tweed, which gave Scott the justification for changing his house's name from the unromantic Cartleyhole (he jokingly called it Clarty Hole) to the more romantic Abbotsford.

Abbotsford is not a huge mansion. It feels very homely – and of course it was a home to a real family. Scott himself was a *lad o' pairts*, but even if today his books are more praised than read his memory lingers, the memory of a good man, a very human character, a passionate man too on some things.

> *Breathes there the man, with soul so dead,*
> *Who never to himself hath said,*
> *This is my own, my native land...*

ABBOTSFORD, ONE END OF THE ENTRANCE HALL WITH A VIEW
TO SIR WALTER SCOTT'S STUDY BEYOND

I often wonder how much people really know about Scott, and how much we are in his debt. Let me quote: 'It's difficult to give an adequate sense of the structure of the man: an Edinburgh lawyer, born into an old Border family, he virtually invented the novel as we know it, played a major part in the development of the Romantic movement, revolutionised Europe's understanding of history, and did more than any of his contemporaries to make the history of Scotland both available and intelligible. He wrote poems, novels, histories, biographies; collected traditional ballads and tales; amassed a huge library of rare and important Scottish books; kept a wide and astonishingly varied circle of friends which included men of letters, poachers, princes and ploughmen – Scott was a giant of a man. Without him, the world would know little of Scotland, and Scots would know a great deal less of their own history'.

Scott was an insatiable collector of personal memorabilia and you'll see relics of Bonnie Prince Charlie, Flora Macdonald, Rob Roy, Robert Burns, Montrose, Bonnie Dundee and Napoleon, quite apart from the stones and timbers which may be from the old Tolbooth in Edinburgh or a ship of the Spanish Armada.

Abbotsford was built as and when money came in for his novels. The sums involved were substantial: £4,000–£6,000 for the advance on a novel, and the *Life of Napoleon* received £19,000.

In 1826 the dream was shattered when his publishers went bankrupt and he was faced with debts of £117,000, which he then set about clearing

FALDONSIDE, ON THE WALK FROM ABBOTSFOR TO SELKIRK

by his writing. He really wrote himself to death in the six years remaining to him, a rather pathetic end to the story. The famous Chantry bust and his death mask are both at Abbotsford: they tell the story better than words can. If you look at your Bank of Scotland £5 and £10 notes you will find the portrait of Scott thereon – an ironic choice if ever there was one! Abbotsford is open, spring to end October, 10.00–17.00 Monday to Saturday, 14.00–17.00 Sunday, 0896-2043.

DROVE ROAD TO SELKIRK

From Abbotsford, no doubt refreshed at the tea room, we turn to head up the steep hill by which we arrived. Back at the junction we turn right, another stiff pull for about a quarter of a mile, but then there is a crest from which the black Eildons are suddenly in view again, a view of the peaks which it is hard to better. This rolling high land of woods, fields and lochs lying west of the Eildons is quite unknown to tourists – to our gain. The lochan at Abbotsmoss is hidden in woodland and shortly after we turn right at a T-junction.

The road rises steadily, swings left at a wee farm and, shortly after, the tarmac runs out. The track is lined with beech trees, through which there is a remarkable view over Faldonside and its loch to the Tweed Valley. At Faldonside last century lived a Mr Boyd who achieved a certain immortality by discovering, and bringing into cultivation, two Highland plants which were previously unknown (and which have not been seen in the wild since). One was a rather dull pearlwort, but the other, *Salix x boydii*, is a curious dwarf willow, a Peter Pan tree that will never grow up. Twenty years ago this was a treasured rarity. Now you can buy one in a garden centre for £1.

A track branching off left leads to Cauldshiels Loch, a pleasant spot for a pause (path to north shore). Cauldshiels Hill, and all this area, is riddled with prehistoric forts, ditches and other features. Our route continues, Roman-straight, over a hill with a mixed wood on the right, dips, and swings left just past a big tin hay shed. There is a sheepfold and the ruin of Faldonsidemoor. From there the path pulls up as a good green lane which runs along the edge of cultivation, at times rutted, with plenty of gates, sometimes a fence or old thorns on the right, but, all the time a wall on the left.

The old drove arcs round above the wide hollow of Lindean which carries the eye on to the Tweed Valley beyond. Yair Hill is the big tree-covered dome (Ashiestiel lies beyond it) and the sharp hill left of it is the Three Brethren, from which we start our traverse of the Minchmoor Hills. Below Lindean is the junction of Tweed and Ettrick Water, just above Selkirk is the meeting of Ettrick and Yarrow and just below Abbotsford is the Gala Water confluence, thus four great rivers combine in the Selkirk–Melrose stretch. No wonder Tweed can be a formidable river at times.

As we top the rise out of the Lindean *coombe* the Selkirk TV mast becomes a focal landmark, and when we dip down and up across a minor road it is straight ahead. This steep wee uphill path joins a stables' drive to exit onto another minor road (Halfcrown Corner) with the TV mast service road going straight on. We turn right, along the minor road.

The views north are still open as we begin to lose height. In about a mile a big farm, Shawmount is reached and, left, 'Greenhead' is signposted. Turn along here, to use an old bridleway down to Selkirk rather than the minor road which becomes very steep. Greenhead itself is a big farm which also does B & B and will show visitors round so it is very tempting to stop in this delightful corner. (Greenhead Farm, by Selkirk, 0750-20737.)

At the lower side of the farmyard (right of the barn) an old bridleway heads off round Bell Hill, a route of great age yet young compared to the scattered Iron Age forts on the knobbly hill itself. After the small Dean Burn is crossed the slopes above are Selkirk's South Common; heathery moorland, with an interesting golf course. After a small group of houses our track becomes a narrow tarred road. A small rise reveals Selkirk just ahead, and then, on the left, a small road breaks off to the secretive Pot Loch. We keep straight on up into the start of the town, a street which reveals itself as Goslawdales. The Argus Centre and the High School are obvious, and High School Lane between them leads up to the A7 just above an area where there are several B & Bs. You can either head for them or simply carry on down Dovecot Park which takes the walker right into town, reaching the main street at the Congregational Church.

SOUTARS O' SELKIRK

To reach the Market Place we turn left. Selkirk has an extraordinary number of monuments and churches, some of which we can spot as we walk along. The most notable comes first, the Clapperton monument to the Battle of Flodden. It is simply inscribed, 'O Flodden Field'. While I was taking a photograph of the trooper portrayed two locals passed and I overhead 'There's a man taking a picture o' oor Fletcher'.

Flodden was catastrophic for Scotland. Because of his popularity James IV led an army such as no monarch had gathered, yet the march into England was an act of poor judgment and could have been avoided. The flower of the leading nobility as well as 10,000 men perished, leaving a year-old heir, a leaderless people and Henry VIII to rampage across the land. In this terrible period the Borders suffered repeatedly. The abbeys were wasted, towns were burnt, and crops and animals destroyed. Selkirk had sent eighty men to the king; eventually one returned, a solitary figure who trauchled in with a tattered banner. Tradition knows him as Fletcher. The re-enactment of his 'casting the colours' is at the heart of the Common Riding to this day.

Behind the statue is the bold front of the Victoria Halls, just one of many signs of Selkirk's confidence in those boom times. There's a very fine fountain at the side of the building about which I can find no information. On the street corner though is the plaque to J. B. Selkirk (really James Brown) another of the Borders' literary figures. Selkirk was his 'bonnie toon' but he could still joke:

> Wi' Ettrick water for her drink
> And Yarrow for her dreams.

Thomas Clapperton, who also had his hand in the Mungo Park statue further along, designed the plaque. Fletcher, Mungo and The Shirra could be taken for living town worthies the way they are referred to by the locals, the 'soutars of Selkirk'. Andrew Lang, most prolific of Selkirk's literary sons, is commemorated by a granite plaque to the right of the Victoria Halls at the entrance of his old home, Viewfield, now a cottage hospital. What a pity Clapperton was not commissioned to commemorate this more outlandish literary figure. Of more modern times Lavinia Derwent, forever known as the creator of *Tammy Troot*, came of a Selkirk family, and her brother was minister there for many years. Her real name was Elizabeth Dodd. But to revert to Clapperton again.

He was the son of a Galashiels photographer and won a scholarship to the Glasgow School of Art, and later went on to study in London and on the continent. The range of his work was varied – his frieze for Liberty's on Regent Street was the largest ever done for a modern building, his bust of John Buchan is famous, his Robert the Bruce statue stands proudly on the esplanade of Edinburgh Castle, his lifelike 'soldier from the trenches' of the Minto war memorial is moving, while Gala's 'reiver on horseback' (Gala's

THE STATUE ABOVE THE DOORWAY OF THE ROMAN CATHOLIC CHURCH, SELKIRK

ONE OF THE PANELS ON THE MUNGO PARK MONUMENT, SELKIRK

war memorial) is the equestrian equivalent of Fletcher – notable. Thomas Clapperton died in 1962 at the good age of eighty-two.

The big church on the left is now the Parish Church but it was long known as the Lawson Memorial Church. Set back a bit, on the right is the Roman Catholic Church. I told you there were plenty of churches. These are some of the active ones. There are as many more now empty or used for other purposes. This church has a pleasantly simple sculpture on the wall facing the street.

The Mungo Park statue stands at the Back Row–High Street junction facing the old municipal buildings, once the home of Dr Anderson, under whom he served his medical apprenticeship and whose daughter he married. Park planted the huge chestnut tree on his return from Africa. He was then in practice in Peebles, but was persuaded to go out to West Africa once again. On Mungo Park's last expedition thirty-eight Europeans went out. None came back, but it was disease, not fighting, that took the toll of life. Park's death was an accident. Two locals who were with him are also named on the monument, and so is his son who went out to West Africa later on to try and find out the full facts of his death.

The bronze panels on the monument were Clapperton's first commission and were added to Currie of Darnick's statue (now painted a dirty white, quite out of keeping) in 1906, the centenary of Park's death. They were so liked that there was another whip-round and money raised for the bronze figures which were added in 1912.

Beyond the Park statue we are on the High Street. The wedge of buildings between it and the Back Row was the original Selkirk, once enclosed by a defensive wall. The Selkirk we see though is Victorian – fine Victorian, which has been well preserved to make Selkirk the most elegant of Border towns. Walk on the left side of the road and you'll notice some attractive tiled shop entrances. Across the road above the offices of the *Southern Reporter* is the Clapperton portrait bust of water colourist Tom Scott, some of whose paintings are on view in the old Court House.

Number 28 is the Photographic Studios of R. Clapperton which has been family run since 1867 and houses plenty of historical interest as a working museum. Open: Saturday, Sunday afternoon, or by appointment, 0750-20523.

We now come to a busy area as the A7 Edinburgh–Carlisle road snakes through the centre of Selkirk. The County Hotel is a historic coaching inn. John Wesley, the Duke of Wellington, Robert Southey, James Hogg and Scott all stayed there at one time. At a gathering (perhaps here as it was in Selkirk) we have an example of Scott's powers of memory. James Hogg forgot the words of *Gilmanscleugh* when he was singing the balled and Scott (no singer!) simply recited the whole eighty-eight stanzas through without apparent effort. The monument ahead is to Sir Walter Scott and it stands before the steeple of the old court house. Scott was sheriff of Selkirkshire for thirty-two years, which comes as a surprising fact when we think of his writing output, which was all done with a quill pen and none of our modern aids. He was gifted with a phenomenal memory though, and had a huge library (including French and German works) so much of the work was done in his head and the writing was merely its out-pouring. The old tolbooth once stood where the statue now stands, but when the new courtroom was opened in 1803 it was pulled down. The courtroom is open and has various historical items on display.

Along a bit, on the corner, is a bakery/cafe which has a notable history. In the Napoleonic Wars French officers were billeted in Selkirk, and being both urban and urbane they furnished a cafe for their use. Despite changes over the decades it is still a cafe. And it sells Selkirk bannock, a round fruit loaf, first made here by Robbie Douglas in 1859. He only used the best ingredients: local butter, Turkish sultanas and no spices or extras. If the perfect ingredients weren't available no bannocks were

SELKIRK HIGH STREET AND THE MONUMENT TO SIR WALTER SCOTT

baked. Queen Victoria, given a spread at Abbotsford, refused everything else and got stuck into the bannock! They make small ones too, just right for the rucksack to eat at the Cheese Well on Minchmoor.

The Pant Well is eighteenth-century, and brought clean water in to the Mercat Cross site. The overflow was caught in a trough (*pant*) and eventually gave its name to the structure we have now. (The stonework came from the East Port.)

It is worth wandering down the A7 for 300 metres: the war memorial (Clapperton again), St Mary's Church, and the baronial sheriff court are on the left, the old jail, restored as the town's library, on the right. An underground passage linked jail and court – and still exists under the A7. Le Noyer (B & B) is just beyond. 'The town set on a hill' becomes obvious from this road, so return to the Market Place before losing too much height!

At the far end of the Market Place the Tourist Information Office is signposted and can be reached through Halliwell's Close. There is a museum in the restored eighteenth-century house which is one of the best of its kind anywhere, with everything well laid-out and clearly explained. There are impressive recreations of an old shop and home of 150 years ago and a clear display on the Battle of Philiphaugh, a site on our route tomorrow. Open office hours, Monday–Saturday, and 14.00–16.00 on Sunday. 0750-20096.

A town map and toilets are situated beside the Tourist Information Office, and if the office is shut a list of B & Bs in the window may be useful. Some B & Bs I've already mentioned. There are two main groupings as well. Descending the West Port (our route for tomorrow) leads to Heatherlie, really a separate village between the old town, up the hill, and Selkirk Bridge over the River Ettrick. There are several B & B or hotel options there. Up the A7 (Tower Road) leads to several more – some of which are below High School Lane (mentioned earlier) and a few beyond that level. They are listed below according to area.

After finding accommodation return to see the museum if you have not already done so, then turn off the Market Place by Kirk Wynd and have a look round the old kirkyard, and the now ruined Kirk o' the Forest where Wallace was proclaimed Guardian of Scotland in 1298. A church has stood here since the Dark Ages but was rebuilt time and time again. The present building was abandoned when St Mary's was built in 1861. In the Murray aisle lie some of the maternal ancestors of Franklin D. Roosevelt. J. B. Selkirk and Andrew Lang are also buried here as is Dr George Lawson, the long-serving minister, from 1771 to 1820, who was succeeded by two of his sons and one of his grandsons as parish minister. Selkirk Castle once stood nearby, a Norman *motte*, barely recognisable. Selkirk Abbey was founded by David I in 1113, but not long after moved to Kelso, nobody knows why (perhaps because of the richer agricultural possibilities), and a setting too close to the border for comfort. Hardly anything has survived at Kelso, nothing at Selkirk.

Left of the church ruins (as you come in) is my favourite gravestone – a figure, dressed in latest eighteenth-century fashion, reading a book. This type of figure is a Borders' speciality, not met with elsewhere. Coming out the gates turn right, and at the corner with the Back Row, up on the gable, you will see Johnny Soutar, a reminder of Selkirk's past. In 1694 when the population was only 715 there were forty-seven guilded cordiners (saddlers, cobblers, parchment makers, etc). The town supplied 2,000 pairs of shoes to Bonnie Prince Charlie's Jacobites – and is still awaiting payment!

The Back Row has been completely rebuilt and it won a Civic Trust Award for the late town council. Not all housing developments have to be ugly, though we try hard. Turning left into Tower Street you'll come on a famous chip shop, and so back to the High Street.

If you weren't drouthy on arrival, wandering round will have raised a thirst I'm sure, so relish a pint, along with a Border rhyme:

> *He that buys land buys stanes,*
> *He that buys beef buys banes,*
> *He that buys nuts buys shells,*
> *He that buys ale buys naethin else!*

PRACTICAL INFORMATION: SELKIRK

Tourist Information Centre, Halliwell's House. 0750-20054.
Telephone code for Selkirk numbers is 0750-

ACCOMMODATION: Selkirk is relatively well-off for accommodation and is a pleasant place to stay.

Greenhead Farm, -20737 (2 kilometres above the town, see above)

Central and down A9 (northbound): County Hotel, High Street, -21233 (Welcomes walkers. Note Cross Keys is not residential but does good bar meals, as does the Queen's Head. The Fleece does not want walkers!!), Endler, Victoria Crescent, -21305, Dinsburn, 1 Shawpark Road, -20375 (north end of main street). Le Noyer, Ettrick Terrace, -20523 (off A7, 5 min from Market Place), Oakhurst, Eltrick Terrace, -22560 (down A7), 53 The Loan, -20517 (further out on A7, garden).

Uphill, on or just off the A7 (southbound): 75 Tower Street, -21156, 3 Hillside Terrace, -22207, 34 Hillside Terrace, -20792, 36 Hillside Terrace, -21293, Ivybank, Hillside Terrace, -21270, Alwyn, Russell Place, -22044.

Downhill: (The Green, Heatherlie, Selkirk Bridge) Collingwood, The Green, -20018, 4 Heatherlie Park, -21540, Woodburn House Hotel, -20816, Heatherlie House Hotel, -21200, Endler, Victoria Crescent, -21305, Glen Hotel, -20259 (by Selkirk Bridge), Philipburn House Hotel, -20747 (over the river, up-market).

CAMPING: Victoria Park, -20897. Summer only, council-run site on the banks of the Ettrick Water, just downstream from Selkirk Bridge.

TAXIS: -21061, -22489, -21478, -20354, -21827.

MEALS: A variety of good pub and hotel meals. Popular chip shop in town centre – Tower Street).

The Common Riding is held in the second week in June each year and accommodation will be swamped with soutars from all over the world. The actual riding is always on the Friday following the second Monday in the month. Selkirk's half-day is Thursday.

CASTING THE COLOURS, HIGHLIGHT OF THE SELKIRK COMMON RIDING CELEBRATIONS

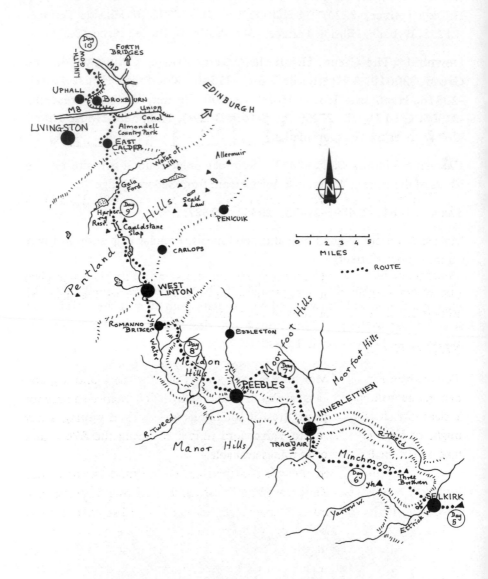

Day Six

SELKIRK

to

INNERLEITHEN

Bart 41 OSLR 73
OSPF 473 (NT 42/52), 461 (BT 43/53), 460 (NT 23/33)

Minchmoor has a ring to its name and the crossing of this hill range gives pleasurable walking, but should still leave time for a visit to Traquair and Robert Smail's unique printing works at Innerleithen.

PHILIPHAUGH

Today's route crosses Minchmoor – a route as old as time – and a grand panoramic walk if given a clear day. There is really no alternative so pray for a clear day. It is an exposed crest if conditions are bad and waiting a day might be best, or walk up to Yarrowford (minor road, not the A708) and take one of the lower/shorter routes available.

All travellers used this crest in the days before modern roads and bridges. The monks of Kelso traversed it to reach their lands at Lesmahagow beyond Lanark, Edward I took his army along it in 1296, Montrose's defeated troops fled this way from bloody Philiphaugh (see below), and of course it was used by drovers coming from Falkirk tryst to the English markets. We back-track their route during our advance to the Lowlands over the next few days: Peebles–West Linton–Cauldstane Slap... romantic to us now, but we have such easy travel on our modern roads it is hard to envisage Selkirk carriers (horse-drawn carts) taking two weeks to go to Edinburgh and back in the eighteenth century – for all of thirty-eight miles!

Don't forget to buy a Selkirk Bannock to supplement the day's rations. We called in to the 'Home Bakery' (just twenty yards down the A7 from the Market Place) and left with several goodies from this traditional sweetie shop. A local, hearing of our plans, wished us 'a dry walk across the Minch', which conjured up a distinctly odd scene to the pair of us who automatically thought of the Hebridean Minch.

As you leave the Market Place note the fine doorway of Bogie's Close with the knotted rope ornamentation and the Town's Arms, a classic example of ornate Victorian public-house architecture. On the other side of the West Port is a plaque marking where Montrose spent the night before Philiphaugh. We pass the Queen's Head and, on the right wall, as we descend (West Port becomes The Green) is a marble plaque marking where Robert Burns once spent a night in the Forest Inn (now demolished), and wrote his *Epistle to Wullie Creech* to fill a wet evening, the locals not being in sociable mood. *The Selkirk Grace* is well known:

> *Some hae meat and canna eat*
> *And some wad eat that want it;*
> *But we hae meat and we can eat,*
> *And sae the Lord be thankit!*

From the bends of the road at Heatherlie (plenty of accommodation), Selkirk's Sheriff Court and the old parish church of St Mary dominate an impressive skyline, up on the right. The road snakes on down. Carry on, across the crossroads (for Peebles, Moffat) and a last curve down past the Glen Hotel. The church opposite is now a carpet and furniture showroom, and the church below the Glen has been converted into a house. The latter is just above the bridge over the Ettrick. Two miles upstream it is joined by the Yarrow Water, two miles down it enters the Tweed.

A camp site and swimming pool lie downstream and, at the far end of the industrial estate, are the airy, modern works, showroom and cafe of Selkirk Glass. Only started in 1977 the small firm has built up an international reputation. Glass-blowing must be one of the most satisfying of spectator sports. Open 09.00–17.00, Monday–Friday for glass making; shop and cafe also open 10.00–16.30 on Saturdays, 12.00–16.00 Sunday. Tel 0750-20954.

The original bridge here was built in 1778, enlarged in 1881 and destroyed by autumn floods in 1977. The present steel and concrete functional bridge was opened in 1981. Beyond the bridge we pass Ettrickhaugh, home of the Selkirk Rugby Football Club, then fork left on the

Moffat road (A708). At the next junction (really a crossroads) head straight across to take the very minor, unsignposted road.

Before heading off into the hills we must take note of Philiphaugh, the grim battle site on the haugh between the A708 and Ettrick Water.

Philiphaugh is a battle that still stirs emotions for it marked the end of the remarkable exploits of James Graham, Marquis of Montrose and the King's Captain General in Scotland. From September 1644 Montrose had won victory after victory during a series of marches till, after the battle of Kilsyth in August 1645, he had won Scotland and seen all the King's enemies flee the country.

Naseby in June however had been a death-blow to the royalist forces in the south and, while Montrose tried to hold on to his Highlanders and enrol Borderers, preparatory to marching south, a strong force of cavalry under David Leslie marched up from Hereford. Colkitto and his Macdonalds had gone off to pillage Kintyre, many clansmen deserted at the prospect of service in the south, and the touchy Gordons decamped en masse at some supposed slight. The Borderers, who probably wished a plague on all armies, were more forthcoming with promises than men. Montrose had to withdraw before the Leslie threat.

With some casual earthworks thrown up the army settled for the night at Philiphaugh. Montrose lodged in Selkirk itself. During the night a Royalist

LOOKING UP TO SELKIRK

picket was chased off by Leslie from just three miles outside Selkirk but their news was not believed. A thick autumn mist ushered in the new day, and while the men were still eating, Leslie's horsemen, who had forded the Ettrick in the night, charged at them out of the east. The Irish bore the brunt of the fighting. Four out of five hundred died as they defended the earthworks and dykes round Philiphaugh Farm, but when taken on the flank by the remainder of Leslie's cavalry it was soon over (500 had withstood 5,000). Montrose was persuaded to flee and went over Minchmoor to win to the north. His next attempt, five years later, was to end on the scaffold. Few kings ever had a more faithful servant, few generals a more thankless king. The remnants of the Ulstermen who had only surrendered on promise of their lives were shot to a man in Newark Castle the next day, and over 300 women and children and 200 unarmed civilians were butchered, while a cleric, watching, commented that the work 'went merrily on'. All the officers were executed. In the end the head of Charles I was to roll as well. It was a bloody end but also a bloody continuing. At the Restoration it would be the turn of the Covenanters to be viciously persecuted. Philiphaugh was not forgotten.

Newark Castle lies just up the glen. A Douglas tower of 1423 it passed to the Scotts of Buccleuch. It is now a roofless ruin. The title of Newark which Leslie assumed as part of his golden handshake for Philiphaugh is from Fife, not here.

The Scotts of Buccleuch were a typical Borders' family. By the fifteenth century they were powerful enough that Sir Walter Scott aided James II in putting down the Douglas power – and thereby gained further lands hereabouts. The head of the family was to die at Flodden, a son of his, putting aside the long feud with the Kerrs, brought about the victory of Ancrum Moor. Through the seventeenth century they went from Lords to Earls then, when an heiress married the ill-fated Duke of Monmouth they were jointly made Duke and Duchess of Monmouth and Buccleuch. Monmouth lost head and title after Sedgemoor, but his wife kept hers, head and title. Ironically a grandson married a Douglas which later brought the next duke the Queensberry dukedom. He then married the heiress of the Duke of Montague, quite an accumulation of titles and wealth which makes one a bit cynical about the validity of all such rankings. I rather liked Harold Wilson's reply to the fourteenth Earl of Home, that his lineage was as old and valid, being the fourteenth Mr Wilson. He then took a peerage too, didn't he? Politics!

This accumulated wealth enabled the family to build the mansion of

Bowhill in 1708, but it was rebuilt and extended all through the nineteenth century and now houses world-famous art and furniture collections, Meissen porcelain, Aubusson tapestries and so on. The garden setting is beautiful – another place to visit on a return to the Borders. Below Bowhill is Carterhaugh which is the setting for the eerie ballad of 'Tam Lin' in which an innocent girl rescues, at great peril, the knight who has been ensnared by the Queen of the Fairies. It is a story, old as man, but the version I can recall gave me the creeps as a toddler. Enough of grim history and legend. It's time to go, in James Hogg's words:

> *Up the river and o'er the lea*
> *That's the way for Billy and me.*

MINCHMOOR

Our little tarred road does not go far into the hills. There are several houses, with Ravensheugh, on the right, hidden behind some tall trees. When the road forks bear right over the bridge and then turn left to follow the track up above the burn: the Long Philip Burn, which we keep to for several miles. After 400 yards the view opens out pleasantly to the left. There is a junction, but keep left, skirting along by the woods (this is the Corbylinn Road). Tracks go off right and then left (just above the Corby Linn), but keep on up the valley to the motorable track's end at a reservoir. Tibby Tamson's grave

THE MINCHMOOR HILLS SEEN FROM THE YARROW – ETTRICKBRIDGE ROAD

lies on the hillside beyond – of which more shortly. On Peat Hill there is the mysterious Catrail.

The Catrail is a defensive ditch of prehistoric origin which runs clearly from here to north of Galashiels, and less distinctly to the border. The most likely suggestion is that it marked some holding of the east-west Tweed passage across Scotland by peoples unknown. (Victorian maps mark it 'Picts Work'.)

A rougher track continues up the valley beyond the reservoir and we follow this. There is a short break in its line, but follow the stream bank to regain the track after seventy yards then, when it climbs up rightwards, leave it to follow a path that keeps straight on in line with the cairns of the Three Brethren (464 metres) that are now visible on the skyline ahead. The path runs clearly to this summit with its meeting of fences, trig point, a post indicating the Southern Uplands Way (SUW) and the three 'stone men' that give this viewpoint its name. Yair, Selkirk and Philiphaugh parishes meet here so each claims a cairn. If visibility is bad the track could be followed up right to the saddle leading to Peat Law, and the SUW/edge of forest followed up to the Three Brethren. Choose one particular June day and you may find this route busy with 400–500 horsemen – the hill is climbed as part of Selkirk's Riding of the Marches. The Common Riding ceremonies arose from the need to guard one's boundaries jealously, and the march

THE THREE BRETHEREN ON THE MINCHMOOR HILLS

(boundary) was regularly inspected and, at key points, cairns were erected, such as here. The view is another sweeping Border panorama. The Eildons look well and lie in a satisfying mirror-image to our earlier views of them from distant Cheviot.

Our route heads off west. The track alongside the edge of the wood gives the easiest walking. When the trees end there is a stile and we ramble on alongside a wall. After a few minutes there is a sign indicating Broadmeadows Youth Hostel, which lies down on the sunny slopes above Yarrow Water.

Broadmeadows was the first-ever youth hostel of the Scottish Youth Hostels Association and opened in 1931. Foulshiels nearby was the birthplace of Mungo Park, a much-loved man. Walking and talking, it was high on the Minchmoor road that Scott and Park took leave of each other. Park's horse stumbled and Scott took this as an ill omen. Scott was then living at Ashiestiel which he rented from a cousin and where he spent probably the happiest seven years of his life. Here he wrote the poetic epics that made his name, began *Waverley* and commuted between Borders and Edinburgh regularly, enjoying many notable friendships.

Our route is a clear path, sharing the line of the SUW, which came up from Yair and runs on to Traquair. If you enjoy this Borders to Highlands route you would find the SUW a congenial challenge as there are harder, higher and more desolate days on its 202 mile length.

This grand highway brings home how hilly and complex the Borders are – which explains quite a bit of its history. The centuries of reiving would never have occurred in a tamer landscape. Dr John Brown described the hills lying about 'like sleeping mastiffs – too plain to be grand, too ample and beautiful to be commonplace'.

Our path contours north of the dome of Broomy Law and rims a deep valley which leads the eye down and over to Clovenfords, a hamlet/pub often used by Scott and his cronies. There are plenty of SUW marker posts, stiles at all the fences and the path is always clear. We skirt the next bump (shown as 451 metres) on its south-western flank, passing along above the top edge of trees to dip steeply to a col beyond which is the sprawling bulk of Brown Knowe. The col is Four Lords Lands on the Pathfinder map. (Another ancient territorial affair?) Three fences meet on the Brown Knowe summit, 524 metres, but there is only one cairn this time. Unhappy Newark Castle can be picked out down in the Yarrow valley.

Just after we leave the summit we pass over an ancient trench cut across the crest. Called Wallace's Trench it probably predates that hero by centuries, its *raison d'être* unknown. Wallace could have had a skirmish there of course. He was known to have been in the area. If you walk down the prehistoric defence line till it meets the Minchmoor Road, out to Hangingshaw Rig then turn left there is a well which was long known as Wallace's Well. (It is Katythirsty Well on the OSPF map.) One well I've never found, as all I've read is 'midway between Yarrow and Tweed', not much to go on. A peaty surface well, it once had, may still have, a stone with 'Amos Iv and i' on it. The writer took this as surname Ivandi and amused a local shepherd asking who Amos Ivandi was. (You can look up Amos chapter 4 verse 1 yourself.)

As we near Hare Law the jaws of the forest plantings open to swallow us but, at least the old right-of-way is unplanted, unlike the situation on some other historic routes.

Minchmoor Road from Yarrowford merges with our route. The name Minchmoor has a tang to it and the name is forever tied to Dr John Brown, a literary physician (the Charles Lamb of Scottish literature) and author of the volumes *Horae Subsecivae*, a title guaranteeing their current neglect. These are essays and stories about people and places, and one chapter describes Minchmoor, and another the story *Rab and His Friends*, rightly appears in every anthology of dog stories, a classic weepy. In the chapter on Minchmoor we read of Scott's mother crossing the Minch, when a girl, 'in a coach and six, on her way to a ball at Peebles, several footmen marching on either side of the carriage to prop it up or drag it out of the moss haggs...'

Another writer touches on this end of the hills in a ballad called *The Bush Aboon Traquair*. Two verses go:

> *Will ye gang wi' me and fare*
> *To the bush aboon Traquair?*
> *Owre the High Minchmuir we'll up and awa*
> *This bonny simmer noon,*
> *While the sun shines fair aboon,*
> *And the licht sklents saftly doun on holm an' ha'.*

> *And what would ye do there*
> *At the bush aboon Traquair?*
> *A long dreich road, ye had better let it be:*
> *Save some ault scrunts o' birk*
> *I' the hillside lirk,*
> *There's nocht i' the warld for man to see.*

A lang dreich road indeed! John Campbell Shairp's Victorian ballad is one of the best of these works which cast back in feeling, or even incorporate older legends (Scott's *Thomas the Rhymer* is perhaps the best known). Principal Shairp lived at Uphall (Day 9) where his tower-house home is now the luxurious Houston House Hotel.

When I crossed Minchmoor on my *Groats End Walk* it was an unhappy experience for we ran into a plague of flies and intolerable heat. Midges may make you mad but flies by the thousands are utterly depressing. Maybe that camp was jinxed by the nearness of Tibby Tamson's grave, a spot of superstitious fear at one time. She was a religious depressive who eventually committed suicide and, being cursed of God in the eyes of the people, was carted out of town, the people stoning the cheap deal coffin till it crossed the Ettrick, and buried on the wild hillside where three lairds' lands met. What a stench lies in the bigotry of the past even though the good book declares 'the mountains shall depart, and the hills be removed; but my kindness shall not depart from thee, neither shall the covenant of my peace be removed, saith the Lord that hath mercy on thee'.

Our route is now along a pleasant green track. We traverse below Hare Law, 509 metres. A forestry road crossed the col beyond and, when the forest falls back on the left, we can abandon the marked route and turn up the heathery slopes to the Minch Moor summit cairn and trig point which, at 567 metres is the highest point of these hills, yet missed out by most walkers. The view is as extensive as ever, and tomorrow's route from Innerleithen

THE CHEESE WELL ON MINCHMOOR

over the cone of Lee Pen and the Moorfoots will most interest us. It offers a walk rather like today's. The map shows the whole area as conifer-planted but the summit dome is, thankfully, not planted, except for a stray seedling. By the path, 100 yards from the top is a stray clump of Nancy Pretty/ London Pride, a lacy, delicate, pink touch on the brown serge of heather.

Shortly after rejoining the track we come on the Cheese Well, the source of the Plora Burn. Two stones mark the well which is of ancient renown. (It was marked on Blaeu's map of 1654.) The name is assumed to come from the habit of people in times past leaving cheese there (not *in* the well as the notice suggests) as a gift to the spirits of the water. *Well*, in Scotland, primarily refers to a *spring*, a point that sometimes confuses visitors. (In some areas of Scotland even a tap is referred to as a well.) The trickle from the well drains to the Tweed eventually, and was the setting James Hogg used for his eerie poem 'Kilmeny'. The erratic Ettrick Shepherd has left several stories connected with places on our walk: *The Hunt of Eildon* and *The Witches of Traquair*. Both are in the Lochhead book on magic and witchcraft of which the Borders have more than their share. The ballads and legends seldom deal with kings and royal princes, but often tremble in the weird worlds beyond ours. The Cheese Well fits well with these.

Continue west from the Cheese Well, crossing the open band of moor that has been left along the crest down to Pipers Knowe and Plora Rig (the trees do not swamp everything as shown on the map). The path then turns down and angles into the forest for the steep descent to the Quair Water. The Broad Law hills fill the far view. There are two forestry roads crossing the track (the map only shows the lower) but, being the Southern Uplands Way, our route is carefully indicated. There is a sudden, superlative view, when the trees are finally left, to the River Tweed and the geometric thrust of Lee Pen. We circle round and down, less steeply, through pastures, the old drove road clearly defined by widely-set walls, presumably built to keep the cattle from straying into cultivated areas as they made the ascent. Our route becomes a lane with some houses and the village school off it, and soon reaches the B709.

TRAQUAIR

Traquair village centre is little more than a row of cottages with a dominating war memorial, a red sandstone cross, which stands at the road junction. We turn right onto the B709 for Innerleithen, but a small extra loop gives a large extra interest in Traquair House, really an old castle: 'ghostly, grey Traquair', as romantic and historic a place as you can find. It claims to be the oldest inhabited house in Scotland, visited by twenty-six monarchs. Take the B7062 ('Peebles 7½') from the crossroads. This runs down to cross the Quair Water by the 1770 Knowe Bridge and, in half a mile, reaches the entrance drive of Traquair.

Before going into the policies, walk on past the cottage north of the gate and there, on the right, are the Bear Gates from which one looks right down a spacious avenue to the house. This was probably the original entrance but tradition has it, and Sir Walter perpetuated the story, that the then earl entertained Prince Charles Edward at Traquair (*all* the support he got), and closed the gates behind the Prince swearing they would only be opened again when a Stewart monarch sat on the throne once more. The house certainly has plenty of royal associations. Mary Queen of Scots slept there (where did she not sleep?) with Darnley and the babe, later James VI and I, whose cradle still reposes in their bedroom.

The Wolf of Badenoch was the grim fount of the family. An illegitimate descendant bought Traquair from one of James III's favourites, at a suspiciously give-away price. The earldom came in 1633, but it was strange for a Lord High Treasurer to die destitute. The second earl unheroically spurned the fleeing Montrose after the Battle of Philiphaugh, and he had also hedged his bets by informing Leslie, the Covenanting Army's general, of the royalist dispositions. These Stuarts were Catholics

TRAQUAIR HOUSE

which perhaps explained some of the goings-on. There is a priest's room on the top floor of the tower, with a secret stair leading to it. Another story of the locked gates suggests they were locked in disgust when the owner was banned from using horse and carriage, which he had been doing illegally, being a Catholic. This petty law was often ignored but some neighbour *clyped*. A third story suggests the gates were shut by the seventh earl after the funeral of his wife, he swearing they'd stay closed till another countess would swing them open. His son died childless and the line ended with his sister (who died in her 100th year). The present owners are Maxwell-Stuarts.

Alexander I had a hunting lodge at Traquair and William the Lion signed Glasgow's burgh charter there, so its claim to be the oldest inhabited house has some merit. The original tower of 1492 once stood alone but has been added to many times. The first earl even moved the Tweed, which put a stop to fishing out the windows! The present design was complete by the late seventeenth century and later 'improvements' somehow didn't happen, so we are left with a building of considerable charm and character, even if the Wordsworths thought it gloomy: Traquair and Abbotsford are the most notable buildings of our walk. Scott used the Bear Gates at Traquair as his model for the gateway of Tully Veolan in *Waverley*. Flodden Field claimed the owner of Traquair in 1513. There are pleasant grounds to walk round if the history overwhelms. You can try navigating the maze. The old working Brew House may interest the thirsty walker (a unique *carry-oot*), there is a tea room, and several outbuildings are used as craft workshops where you can watch screen-printing, wood-turning or tying flies. Traquair is not a fossilised building but offers constantly-changing interests. Open: June–Sept 13.30–17.30, July and August 10.30–17.30. 0896-830323

Leave Traquair by the exit drive to the B709, turn left onto this road and, after five minutes, the road turns sharply left to cross the Tweed to Innerleithen. Lee Pen is the conical hill above the town, a very dominant landmark on our route for tomorrow.

IN INNERLEITHEN

We cross the Tweed on an attractive iron bridge of 1886, and so come to 'Innerleithen and St Ronan's Wells' to give the town its full title. The Wells part of the name is not ancient, but as the wells lie on the morrow's main route, description will be given then. Innerleithen suffers a bit from being too near the bigger, popular town of Peebles, but is a clean, Victorian, stone-built town which I find very friendly and attractive. St Ronan's Wells was a bonus to the town. Its more mundane wealth is due to sheep, or the wool from sheep. A Traquair blacksmith Alex Brodie went to London, made a fortune, then returned home to open the first woollen mill in 1790. The town is full of monuments but I don't think there is one to him. Robert Burns just visited (1787) and there's a plaque to him in the centre of town. There's also a pickle of churches; five of them were built by Robert Mathieson, irrespective of denomination – what you might call ecumenical economics. In the twelfth century the church was granted to the monks of Kelso by Malcolm IV and declared a sanctuary. The King's son had been drowned in Leithen Pool in the River Tweed. It was a popular royal hunting area then with deer, fox, wild boar, bear and wolf offering a varied challenge.

Just over the bridge, right, is the Toll House, dated 1830. Further along the sharp-eyed may spot a house, right, which has a station canopy for a porch and is, in fact, the station on the dismantled railway that once ran from Peebles to Galashiels. Past a sawmill, some sheds, and the Traquair Arms, and we come to the A72. St James' Catholic Church is on the corner, the Cleikum Mill opposite and, just along from it, A. & A. Caldwell, selling home-made icecream – an irresistible first stop!

Make sure you reach Innerleithen in time to visit Robert Smail's Printing Works, as intriguing a step-back in time as you are ever likely to make. These printing works were established in 1848 and stayed in the Smail family till 1985. In that time nothing, but nothing, was ever thrown out. The actual machinery is functioning again so it's a mechanical dream; the front office is like something out of Dickens; the mix of working museum and invaluable archive is unique – a really special place in the National Trust for Scotland's range of good works. The High Street premises are open 10.00–13.00 and 14.00–17.00 Monday to Saturday and 14.00–17.00 on Sunday.

July sees the St Ronan's Games and Cleikum Ceremony, the town's equivalent to Selkirk's Common Riding. The St Ronan's Club was founded in 1827 and led to the games being established with the patronage of several eminent men like Scott, his son-in-law and biographer Lockhart, William Blackwood, Christopher North and James Hogg – who was more than happy to join in the events or sing for the company after supper. St Ronan is a shadowy seventh century figure who traditionally used his crook to *cleik* (tumble) the Devil, an act which is re-enacted each year by the schoolchildren, though now the Devil is consigned to a bonfire on Caerlee Hill.

PRACTICAL INFORMATION: INNERLEITHEN

Telephone code for Innerleithen numbers is 0896-

ACCOMMODATION: Smaller Innerleithen (Tuesday half-day) may have fewer beds available than the other Border towns but quality makes up for quantity.

Coming in on the Traquair Road we pass the Traquair Arms, -830229, which is excellent and welcomes walkers. Caddon View, 14 Pirn Road, -830208, (over bridge, east end of town) is a spacious guest house; Backcroft, 33 Chapel Street, -831179, dates to 1833 and, in stage coach days, Edinburgh mails were collected from its hallway. Both these provide good evening meals. Nether Pirn, -830398, is a newer B & B.

Along the High Street are three small hotels, reasonably priced: St Ronan's Hotel, -830380, Tweedside Hotel, -830386, Corner House Hotel, -830818. There are two recommended farmhouse possibilities near Traquair: Traquair Bank, -830425 on the B7062 (323356) and Damhead Farm, -830474, just off the B709 (329341). Up the Leithen Water (B709) and set in a commanding site (328396) is the up market/*cordon bleu* The Ley, -830240, which, if used, gives access directly onto the hills beyond Lee Pen. There is a ruined tower occupied successfully by Home and Ker Tenants.

Walkerburn (Code: 089687-), just three kilometres along the River Tweed eastwards (A72) has a variety of accommodation: West Bold Farm, -615 (south of the Tweed), 2 High Cottages, -253, 13 High Cottages, -252, The George Hotel, -219 and, more expensive, the Tweed Valley Hotel, -636.

CAMPING: Riverside site in south-east corner of the town (Montgomery Street).

TAXIS: -830486, -831028 (also Peebles 0721-20329, -22594, -20832).

MEALS: Hotels, pubs and cafe.

INNERLEITHEN
to
PEEBLES

Bart 41 OSLR 73
OSPF 460 (NT 23/33), 448 (NT 24/34)

THE AUTHOR WITH LEE PEN BEHIND

The Moorfoots may be as ungrammatical a name as the Hillfoots for the towns under the Ochils, but they will give us the highest separate range of our walk entirely in Scotland (the Cheviots were on the border) not that we go over the highest point of the Moorfoots. An easy-enough day, with lovely surfaces underfoot, there will still be time to enjoy Peebles with its centuries-old motto of 'Peebles for pleasure'. An old burgher had visited Paris and was asked how it compared. He replied, 'Paris, a' thing considered, was a wonderful place – but still, Peebles for pleasure'. Cockburn, on his Circuit Journeys noted 'as quiet as the grave or as Peebles' and an old rhyme goes:

> *Glasgow for bells, Lithgow for wells*
> *Falkirk for beans and peas,*
> *Peebles for clashes and lees.*

OVER THE MOORFOOTS

Set off from Innerleithen by the B709. This is the road north from the crossroads beside the Leithen Water bridge, a crossroads with several interests. The bridge, 1914, has decorative iron lamps from that period, and the house on the south-east corner, now a pub, was once a social club. Not many pubs sport a Latin motto over the entrance. As one turns onto Leithen Road

INNERLEITHEN PARISH CHURCH – THE OLD CROSS STONE IN FRONT

('Heriot 14') there is a granite obelisk, a 1906 memorial to a local GP, and fifty yards on is the War Memorial.

This is an unusual memorial. There is a simple slab with the names of the fallen, and behind is a garden which is laid out as a miniature of the Leithen valley itself with the hills, stream and Cuddy Brig all there! The clock tower on the building behind chimes on the quarters, and a small local museum is housed in the building, the 1922 Memorial Hall.

Walk on up the B709. Beyond Bond Street (left) lies the present Parish Church, an ornate building with a tower in a trim garden setting. In front of it is the decorated shaft of an ancient cross which was discovered in the foundations of the old parish church when it was demolished in 1871. After the next street left is the white Episcopal church. The next street left is the Strand, which we take but, first, go on for fifty yards to see the 1701 bow-backed Cuddy Brig which spans the Leithen Water. This replaced an earlier wooden bridge and, in pre-turnpike days, was the eastern approach to Innerleithen. A charming spot.

Walk along the Strand. This swings left for Innerleithen again but we turn first right onto Wells Brae, for 'St Ronan's Wells', which will be found at the top of the street, on the right, an obvious blue and white pavilion, in a garden setting, with a royal coat-of-arms over the door and a Scottish flag flying. Enter by a small gate. Behind the counter on the pavilion verandah

ST RONAN'S WELL, INNERLEITHEN

there is a tap so you can have the dubious pleasure of trying the waters.

Originally there were fenced-off springs in the Doo Wood. As the water 'tasted like the smell of an ancient egg' it obviously had to be good for one, and by the late eighteenth century the wells had quite a reputation for curative powers (everything from bad eyes to bad tummies), and women believed it increased their fertility. Burns, in May 1787 recorded: 'visited Innerleithen, a famous spa'. Scott's mother and sister were often there and a letter complains they couldn't find accommodation in the town, but it was Scott himself who set the seal on the site when he published *St Ronan's Well* in 1824. The association was probably true enough but Innerleithen was not passing up such a gift. St Ronan's Wells were proclaimed far and near. Hotels went up. The town was set to rival Harrogate. Scott, Hogg and Christopher North often met at Innerleithen, and in 1827 the Border Games were established. When hydros opened at Peebles and Melrose (on the new railway links to Edinburgh) the fortunes of Innerleithen declined somewhat even if the establishment became 'By Royal Appointment'. The present pavilion, with pump room, bathrooms, waiting rooms and an aeriating and bottling plant was built in 1896. In the Second World War soldiers were billeted in the run-down buildings and eventually the site was handed over to the Town Council and restored. You can still buy clear, sparkling bottled water from St Ronan's Wells (it's not from one of the more tasty wells!). The wells themselves are simply cisterns at the top of the gardens. An annual festival was introduced in 1901 to keep old historical traditions alive and the Wells naturally play an important part in this Cleikum Ceremony.

Beside a second, *vehicular*, gate in to the Wells, and between this and

INNERLEITHEN AND THE TWEED VALLEY FROM CAERLEE HILL

the 'St Ronan's Terrrace' sign, a footpath leads off up through the trees. Take this up to a T-junction and turn left to wend along through the woodland. At one stage the path splits but soon joins up again. Shortly after, when the path swings left and drops steeply down there is a smaller footpath breaking off right. Follow this. It passes a water tank (others are lost in the jungly undergrowth) and indicates the site of the old Chapman's Well. Our path comes to a stile on the wood edge with a small tarred road and Caerlee Hill beyond. Cross this TV station service road to a path beyond which leads up to the top of the hill, a prehistoric fort site with plenty of visible grassy dykes and ditches, and a view out of all proportion to the modest altitude of the hill. Pirn Craig across the Leithen Water has a comparable fort on its shoulder, but the rest of the Leithen valley is strangely devoid of any other prehistoric forts.

The views down the Tweed, over Innerleithen to Walkerburn and up the Tweed, past Cardrona House, are a study of historical usage and, across the valley, is Minchmoor, whence we have come. There is even a last glimpse of the Eildons. Turning the opposite way we see the route ahead to Lee Pen: the track clearly heading up beside the crest wall on the long spur of hill.

We pick this route up on the saddle of Caerlee Hill where the service road puts in an 'elbow' bend and we simply follow it to Lee Pen, a good stiff ascent. The final cone has some scree but paths wend through them. *Pen* is a variant of *ben* or *ven*, meaning hill, and is the Welsh version to this day. Peebles may come from the Welsh *peblys*, a plant name. In ancient documents it is often *Peblis*, as it was in the book James I wrote.

A BORDERS SHEEP SHELTER IN THE UPPER LEITHEN VALLEY

On my John o' Groats to Land's End walk (which really sparked off the idea of a continuous route) I slept overnight on top of Lee Pen, a memorable night of great beauty. (It was as well I did not foresee the horror of the next night up beyond Minchmoor.) The day had been broiling hot but I relished being back in hill country. Most of the afternoon was spent reading down at the first water available below Black Law, with a gun barrel view down to the Tweed and Cardrona Forest. A breeze kept the flies away. We made supper and, with precious water, wandered the hour along to Lee Pen where we pitched the tent, made coffee, and sat to watch the colours run up the Glensax Hills and vanish into night. The sun woke me at 06.00. The Tweed lay in cloud and for the rest, there was range on range of tinted hills. Fabulous. I was down to Innerleithen early and sat reading in the sun, drying-off the tent, which drew a few comments. People stopped to chat. Not for the last time I mentioned how friendly the Borders people were. The dog of course acted like a magnet. 'Aw mister, can ah clap yir dug?'

A brief diversionary comment. I'm sometimes asked why I sound so anti-dog yet frequently seem to have a dog of my own with me – as I did on the Groats End Walk. I am *not* against dogs. I am against the owners of badly-trained dogs, dogs which are allowed to be a menace to livestock and obnoxious socially. So I give dire warnings. A rabbit can leap out at my dog's feet and he will completely ignore it. On entering a field of sheep he will, unbidden, come to, and walk, at heel. I judge dogs by his standard and, frankly, find most are wanting.

Beyond Lee Pen the walking is over grassy heights, basically just following the wall by Lee Burn Head, Mill Rig, Black Knowe, Clog Knowe and Black Law, 'a high and handsome ridge' as Roger Smith called it; 'Good old Moorfoot Hills' as Douglas (of Douglas Boulder fame) wrote a hundred years ago in a Scottish Mountaineering Club Journal.

Beyond the Black Knowe we are fenced-off on the left by the upper edge of Glentress Forest. The earliest plantings date back to the 1920s; but huge new areas have been planted in the last decade. The forest down on the left has various trails laid out, using the roads built in the 1930s under a government scheme for the unemployed.

The trig point on Black Law stands on a heathery dome, not buried in forest as the map suggests. Our grassy tracks turn into rougher heather-trods and we dip steeply down to a col, the old pass of the Leithen Door. The pull up beyond the col is brutally steep. A gate at the col allows a path beside the trees to be used. Higher up it is marked with a mountain bike trail marker post and we'll see several of these in the next hour so I'll not always mention them.

Dunslair Heights, 602 metres, with its tall booster tower and other erections is quite a landmark. Unfortunately the OS mapping of the summit area is not accurate. There is a clear wedge of open ground running west from the road circling the deep, east-facing *hope* (glen), and from this open area a break leads straight up to the summit. Simply cut over to use the headwall road briefly and then turn off to the gate at the break that leads to the tower.

The view is a bit restricted from the summit but we will feel very much in hill country. A bit like the Mountains of Mourne. But what names. Over the Leithen Water is Totto Hill and the Garvald Punks. There's a Lamb Law, a Wooly Law, a Hog Hill, a Collie Law and a Wolf Cleugh. And resonant names and oddities like Bareback Knowe, Wallet Knowe, Carlsman Hill, The Yoke, The Kipps, Dundreich and Milky Law. (*Law* is a Saxon word for hill, a *cleugh* is a deep-cut glen, a *hope* is a valley or valley-head, a *shaw* is a wood.)

James Hogg began his life of shepherding at Willinslee (now corrupted into Williamslee) down on the Leithen, so he would be up here often enough. With only six months of schooling behind him he began to read, and, eventually, write. Though his output was uneven, there are several poems, stories and books which are evergreen classics.

Pass left of the tower, descending north-west to the col leading to Makeness Kipps. The OS map again shows non-existent plantings. There is quite a bit of open ground to the left. At the col we turn left (cycle marker poles) onto an old right-of-way and peat road. Anciently the right-of-way crossed the col here to descend steeply to Craighope and the Leithen Water, but is now planted over and lost. We turn down south-west anyway on a clear track flanking the spur off the Makeness Kipps. Ignore the two forestry tracks crossing the old trail. After the second forest track, on the left, is the ruined Sheildgreen Tower, now just an overgrown green hump. The path descends steeply through stands of Scots pines, and swings left to reach the white building of the Shieldgreen Centre (Crookston Castle School, opened in 1975). Pass along in front of it and out by a gate/stile onto a track which is simply followed down the valley of the Soonhope Burn to Peebles. Various paths join in and there are a couple of gates, but nothing that should lead astray. Acres of fireweed in high summer, and brilliant red-berried elders add touches of colour. The last mile is lined by holiday chalets and huts (one is an old railway carriage which must have given an unusual transporting challenge) and then the stables and back entrance of Peebles Hydro are passed. This hotel alone boasts of 150 rooms so we should manage a bed in Peebles! On reaching the main road (A72) turn right and five minutes walk leads into the centre of town.

PEEBLES FOR PLEASURE

On walking along to the High Street several hotels and B & Bs are passed, and the road out on the Biggar side is equally well served, as is the Edinburgh A703 road.

The High Street has a wide range of shops of interest, from the Moffat Toffee Shop, various craft workshops to the ubiquitous woollens. At the west end there are two small bookshops, and by the Cuddy Bridge is the larger Bridgehouse Books. There are cafes, restaurants and carry-oots to suit most tastes besides good meals in several of the hotels.

Dominating the High Street is the Old Parish Church, a spacious building of some character, which has enjoyed some good modern touches and is worth seeing; there is a fine screen on entering (and note how the door handles are bronze shepherds' crooks), modern paintings are hung round the walls, a side chapel has a charming screen, and there is plenty of good woodwork.

One road swings left in front of the church to cross the Tweed (Tweed Bridge), another swings right to cross the Eddleston Water (Cuddy Bridge). Tweed Bridge has some decorative iron lamps on the parapet but is perhaps most interesting seen from the riverbank beside the modern swimming pool – the bridge is a real glut of geometrics. Peebles has one of the earliest recorded bridges in the country, and in 1632 there is a mention of 4,000 turfs being used for its parapets.

THE HISTORIC TWEED BRIDGE WITH THE PARISH CHURCH AT THE NORTH END

We tend, wrongly, to assume great antiquity for bridges. 'Roman' bridges abound; all false. The Romans built bridges but when their empire was overwhelmed stone bridge-building disappeared for 600 years. Only in the thirteenth century did bridge-building begin again. London Bridge, completed in 1209 after years of labour was to fall down, as the song commemorates, and few bridges of this date survive. Scotland didn't really start building stone bridges till the time of the early Stewart kings. Bridges are fragile and most suffered destruction and/or rebuilding. Only with Telford did some permanence seem likely, but even the best bridges can be destroyed by spates. In 1609 Peebles and Berwick were the only bridges over the Tweed, possibly giving the town its water-bright, busy but relaxed atmosphere.

Back in the High Street: in front of the Tontine Hotel is the memorial to Peebles-born Professor Veitch, one of the Victorian Border poets and an outdoors enthusiast (died 1894). There is a portrait medallion, and the pedestal is topped with a lion figure. He was an early president of the Scottish Mountaineering Club though more a walker than a climber. He caught the atmosphere of the hills more than many of his wordy contemporaries ('...a hill-enfolding glen/Where summer shadows dwell with mountain sounds'). Every day he walked, quite purposefully to keep in touch with 'pure free Nature...for something in earth or sky or cloud undevastated by the hand of man'.

The Tourist Information Office is based in part of the 1859 Chambers Institute. William Chambers was the Dick Whittington of Edinburgh. Born in Peebles in 1800 he left desperate poverty behind to try his luck in Edinburgh. With his brother he founded the publishing house W. & R. Chambers, produced encyclopaedias and ended as Lord Provost of the capital. This building was his gift to his birthplace. It houses the Tweeddale Museum which contains a collection connected with the area over the centuries, and also the 'Secret Room' with its unique display - which I'll leave a secret for you to discover.

In the Chambers Institute yard is the unusual war memorial, a domed shrine with a hint of the east about it and a colourful cross which is quite Byzantine. Mungo Park had a surgery on the south side of the High Street, and John Buchan had family ties with Peebles, the family home being the last house at the west end of the High Street. Many of his holidays were spent at Broughton where there is now a John Buchan Centre (08997-267). Buchan's father (born in Peebles) started his ministry at Broughton during a period of Revival. He had charges at Perth, Kirkcaldy and Glasgow before retiring to Peebles. One of Buchan's brothers died while on leave from India, the other was killed in the war. His sister Anna (O. Douglas as a writer) had her home in

Peebles too. It is not surprising John Buchan's fiction is full of Border settings. His affection was deep.

> So I, who love with equal mind
> The southern sun, the northern wind,
> The lilied lowland water-mead
> And the grey hills that cradle Tweed....

The Cross Keys was the prototype for the Cleikum Inn in Scott's *St Ronan's Well*. He often stayed in the inn, which dates back to the fourteenth century when the then building belonged to Arbroath Abbey, and was administered on their behalf for their own people or anyone else on their travels. Later it was a private house. The present building is eighteenth century. To the west of the town is the square graveyard tower, all that is left of old St Andrew's Church. One stone had the kindly jingle:

> Thomas Stoddart
> Lyes here interr'd
> Who liv'd and dy'd
> An honest herd.

The grave of Davey Ritchie, Scott's three and a half feet tall model for the *Black Dwarf* lies buried at Kirkton Manor, south-west of the town. Peebles folks have always been *Gutterbluids* and incomers are referred to as *Stooryfits* (dusty feet!). On the back road (B712 from Peebles to Innerleithen) lies the Royal Botanic Gardens' Dawyck Gardens, famed for the first larch grown in Scotland and other old, rare trees, besides all the usual features of a country house garden. Open April–September (072-16254) and worth a taxi ride if a tree-freak.

The most historic ruin in the town is that of the old Cross Kirk, a thirteenth-century building with a later priory, which had a shrine dedicated to St Nicholas and was the focus of pilgrimages till into the seventeenth century. There is little to see now. St Mungo's Well is reputedly named after that saint, who founded Glasgow, when he visited Peebles in the sixth century. David I built a castle here rather than an abbey, but the attraction was Ettrick Forest, the wildest area of the south, the refuge of Wallace and Bruce. Edward I conferred the forest on the Earl of Pembroke but he, on top of this thankless position, was captured at Bannockburn and had to sell some of his English estates to raise his ransom.

Not far along from the Tourist Information Office is another wynd leading to Newby Court where there are several craft shops including No 8,

Woodworks and No 9, Dunnydee which is a pottery with a difference. Duncan Hood produces works of art in a range which vividly catches the colours and textures of the Scottish landscape from which he draws inspiration. The next wynd along leads to the unique Museum of Ornamental Plasterwork: The Cornice, 0721-20212. There is a large collection of surviving master casts, and you can even don wellies and coat and have a go! Nearer the church, on the High Street, is The Bamboo Flute, a curio shop of character. If the hour strikes on the church clock give a nod to the donor of the thirty and a half hundredweight bell, a local surgeon, Maylard, who was a pre-war President of the Scottish Mountaineering Club and a keen local walker.

Peebles has its festival time in the third week of June though it is called The Beltane Festival. Beltane dates back to the Celtic custom of May Day bonfires on hilltops, celebrating the victory of light over darkness, of new life out of deadness and so on. (Samhaim, 1 November, was the counterpart as winter dark began to grip and still has echoes in our plastic Hallowe'en ideas.) Festivals like these were outlawed at the Reformation, but this one was revived for Queen Victoria's jubilee: a week-long celebration with a riding of the marches and the crowning of a Beltane Queen.

In the north-west corner of Peebles lies Rosetta House (camp site, q.v.), a name which may cause some curiosity. Rosetta House is a Georgian mansion, erected in 1807 by Thomas Young, a military surgeon who had been on the Abercromby expedition to Egypt which captured Alexandria in 1801 – and secured the Rosetta Stone. Rosetta was the name of the village where this stone was found; the story of how it eventually led to the world being able to read Egyptian hieroglyphics is one of gripping interest. (See Ceram in the bibliography.) The stone went to the British Museum, but copies had been made by the French, and it was finally cracked by a youthful genius, Champollion, who in his early twenties knew most languages of the east, ancient and modern, and 'for practice' kept his diary in Coptic! (Forty years later a French scientist took this to be an ancient text and wrote a learned paper about it!) Do read Ceram. If I was only allowed a library of twenty books it would be one of them.

A privately-printed book by two brothers, Naylor, tells of their walk from John o' Groats to Land's End in 1871. It is a big 600 page tome with plenty of photos. They must have been fit lads then for they set off from the Cross Keys here, had breakfast at Innerleithen, visited Abbotsford, looked at Melrose, and then walked on to Lilliesleaf, all in the one day! They had a good tea on reaching Melrose, visited the abbey and then returned to the inn and ordered another tea.

ON TO NEIDPATH CASTLE

Neidpath Castle lies less than a mile up the Tweed from Peebles and is well worth a visit. If keen to see the interior this would have to be before the 'last visitors' time of 16.30. One route onwards for tomorrow (the more scenic) will pass the castle, so even if too late today one can still see its superb setting and character then, or wander up this evening after supper.

Drop down to the riverside swimming pool from Tweed Bridge (west end of High Street) and follow up beside the attractive river. Ducks congregate at a weir, and do look back to admire Tweed Bridge, with Lee Pen in the distance. Before the last war the huge Tweedsmuir Mill covered this site and across the river once lay the sprawl of the Caledonian Railway Station and its sidings. A footbridge crosses a stream, there is a short diversion up a few stairs and down again, then the spacious Hay Lodge Park grounds lead on past a tubular footbridge over the Tweed. Up on the skyline, to the right, the top of a tower can be seen – all that is left of St Andrew's church.

The path across the river was once railway track. Peebles not only had its own line to Edinburgh but lay on the much-fought over route down the Tweed. All the railways in the Borders have gone, but Peebles has gained some bonny walk-ways.

At the end of the park take the riverside path which wends on to the castle, which appears ahead. There are some fine specimen trees and, across

NEIDPATH CASTLE UP-RIVER FROM PEEBLES – AND OUR FAREWELL TO THE RIVER TWEED

the Tweed, a rich forest of mature trees. Half way across the meadow, below the castle, we turn right, up a brutally steep path, to a gate which leads to the castle entrance/car park. Take a last look at the River Tweed which has companioned our way for several days. 'Haste ye back' to the Queen of Rivers.

The continuation for the Meldons and West Linton is described under tomorrow's section.

The castle is an L-shaped tower dating to the thirteenth century and, despite many changes and restorations over the centuries, remains very much the castle of one's imagination – from thick walls to dungeon pit. Fraser of Lovat was the best known owner early on, but his head was to join Wallace's on London Bridge. Through his daughter the castle passed to the Hays of Yester, Earls of Tweeddale. Tweeddale failed to hold the castle against Cromwell's forces. The Dukes of Queensberry eventually purchased Neidpath but the notorious (Queensbery Rules) Fourth Duke despoiled the estate to spite his heir.

Wordsworth was so incensed at the felling of 'a brotherhood of venerable trees' which left the landscape 'beggared and outraged' that he wrote a sonnet deploring the deed. It opened with the salvo 'Degenerate Douglas! ... unworthy Lord!' Yet, already nature was healing and today's richness being created.

> *...wrongs, which Nature scarcely seems to heed;*
> *For sheltered places, bosoms, nooks and bays,*
> *And the pure mountain air, and the gentle Tweed,*
> *And the green silent pastures, yet remain.*

The castle is now owned by the Earl of Wemyss and March, and stands among mature woodlands: a mix of oak, alder, birch, larch and spruce, much loved by red squirrels and woodland birds like tree creeper, goldcrest, woodpecker, owl and sparrowhawk. Open April–October, 08757-201.

PRACTICAL INFORMATION: PEEBLES

Tourist Information Centre, Chambers Institute, 0721-20138,
Telephone code for Peebles numbers is 0721-

ACCOMMODATION: Peebles is the St Andrews of the Tweed with whole clusters of B & Bs and many hotels. July and August can be busy so booking ahead is still advisable. The Beltane Festival (third week in June) can also fill the available accommodation.

Central: Priorsford, Tweed Green, -21910, Whitestone House, Innerleithen

Road, -20337, Rowanbrae, Northgate, -21630, 31 High Street, -22774, 105 Northgate, -21909, Cross Keys and Kings Orchard, Northgate, -20748. (An old, haunted coaching inn, frequented by Scott and his friends.) County Hotel, High Street, -20595, Crown Hotel, High Street, -20239, Green Tree Hotel, Eastgate, -20582.

Edinburgh Road (A703) and off it: North Lodge, Venlaw, -20211, 36 Edinburgh Road, -20300, 46 Edinburgh Road, -20226, Drummore, Venlaw High Road, -20336, Venlaw Castle Hotel, -20384. (Fine setting overlooking Peebles and not overpriced. Coming off the hill take track from Shieldgreen skirting Whitfold Hill and down by tree belt.)

West and north-west of the town: 102 Neidpath Road, -20527, Lindores, Old Town, -20441, 1 Rosetta Road, -21232, 21 Kirkland Street, -20525.

South of the Tweed: 21 Edderston Road, -29651, 12 Dukehaugh, -20118, 39 Dukehaugh, -21258, 9 Witchwood Crescent, -21206, 10 Gallowhill, -20372.

Near Peebles: Countryside Hotel, Glentress, -20100 (4 kilometres east on A72), Brookside, E Shiels, -21178, 3 kilometres east on A72, Winkston Farmhouse, -21264, (3 kilometres on A703, Edinburgh road, Chapelhill Farm, -20188 (245422: a former Tower of 1600), Cringletie House Hotel, -07213-233 (5 kilometres north, off A703), Eddleston, 4 Elibank Road, 07213-281 (7 kilometres out on the A703, Edinburgh road).

More expensive hotels include: Tontine Hotel, High Street, -20892, Kingsmuir Hotel, Springfield Road, -20151 and Tweedbridge House, Chambers Terrace, -20590 (both south of the river).

Further upmarket again: Peebles Hydro, -20602, Park Hotel, -20451, and Black Barony Hotel, Eddleston, 07213-395.

CAMP SITES: There are two, both well-appointed. Shops at both sites. Crossburn Caravan and Camping Park, Edinburgh Road, 0721-20501, Does take tents despite the map only showing a caravan symbol. At the Venlaw drive entrance it could be reached by the alternative route from Shieldgreen (see Venlaw Castle Hotel note). Rosetta Camping and Caravan Park, Rosetta Road, 0721-20771, set in twenty-four acres of magnificent grounds at Rosetta House.

TAXIS: Peebles, 0721-20329, -22594, -20832, Eddleston: 07213-646, Innerleithen, 0896-830486, -831028

MEALS: Very wide range. Half-day is Wednesday.

PEEBLES

to

WEST LINTON

Bart 41 OSLR 73, 72
OSPF 448 (NT 24/34), 447 (NT 04/14), 433 (NT 05/15)

Hilly drove-road country leads us to the edge of Peebleshire, at the charming village of West Linton. Accommodation is a bit limited so book ahead – and then enjoy a leisurely walk.

CROSSING THE MELDONS

Walk out to Neidpath Castle (again), where we finally take leave of the River Tweed. Exit by the castle drive and turn right at the A72 (back towards Peebles!). After a couple of minutes, cross to go up a steep, rough road, just before the town sign for Peebles. This leads up to a golf course which is first skirted, and then crossed to reach Jedderfield farm. In the interests of courtesy, and survival, take care not to stray into firing range.

Don't go into the farm, but continue up beside it to a gate at the top corner of the golf course and, once through the gate, turn left on a track which follows the edge of the field. As this swings along the top of the field there are wide views over Peebles to yesterday's hills. The track turns into a wood, hemmed in by double walls (as on Pennymuir a sign of an ancient route or a drovers' way). There are gates and a crossroads, but keep straight on to come onto open, grassy moorland.

On leaving the trees walk along to the jutting corner of the wall on the right. Left from here the Roman Road of the map heads off round the hillside: it is

Neidpath Castle proved too hard even for the Romans, hence their diversion up here.) The track slowly rises, and the White Meldon, and fields, come into view through the saddle ahead. We are aiming for the apex of our field, in front. Above us, on the right, is the communications' mast, 357 metres (which is not on the OSPF map), then the path runs down to cross a tiny stream.

Once through the gate follow the wall up to another gate which gives access to the heathery dome beyond. Slant up rightwards to largely bypass South Hill Head, aiming for the col between it and a small spur of a top (Clock Knowe) lying to the north-east , above the col to the White Meldon. From this col we continue on in the same line, to the Lyne–Eddleston road, then, beyond, to Harehope – all very visible looking down from our modest height. The picnic site and toilet block can be seen beside the road (and footbridge/stiles lead to them) with the snaking forest road above, and then another contouring the tree-clad Crailzie Hill to the col we go over.

Just angle down, using the odd sheep trod or, better still, walk along this north-east spur, and down to the main col to climb White Meldon, a short diversion that will reward with a view of hills unequalled on this walk: Dollar Law and the Manor Hills, the Culter Fells, the Broughton Heights, the Moorfoots back to Lee Pen, a last look at Minchmoor – such quantities of hill, such qualities of hill and vale, epitome of Tweed, and our farewell to Tweed. John Buchan who claimed this area as his own, wrote '...if Paradise be a renewal of what was happy and innocent in our earthly days, mine will be some golden afternoon within sight and sound of Tweed'.

White Meldon is the site of a huge prehistoric settlement, though little remains on the ground, even in the hollow between trig point and cairn. It could have been in use as long before the Romans as years have rolled since. Agricola's advance may have been the cause of its abandonment, for walls were left unfinished as if everyone had left suddenly.

Black Meldon, to the west, also has a summit fort, and the whole area is dotted with sites, one of which we will see shortly. Note the old road up this valley which contours from Lyne, keeping above the present road along by the Meldon Burn. We join this briefly. Descend to the road/picnic area/toilet. An interpretive board will fill in some more on the Meldon sites.

Head up the fence edging the forest. About 100 yards in from the road, cross the fence to take the line of the old road into the forest. This soon leads to a forestry road where we turn left to follow the road to Harehope. The jut of hillside we round at this spot is Green Knowe; along its east flank an unenclosed prehistoric settlement was excavated in 1961.

Our forest track eventually meets the main drive into Harehope so turn left onto this. Another variant of the drovers' road left Peebles at Rosetta and passed by Standalane Farm to skirt Hamilton Hill and on north-west, then north, past the rectangle of trees (Scots pines) before turning west, over the drive to Upper Kidston, over the fields beyond and down by the Meldon Burn to the road at Harehope gate – and so up to the farm. Some of the drove still runs between typical parallel fence/wall lines.

From Harehope Gate the drovers also used the old road to Edinburgh as far as Stewarton (really Nether Stewarton), then, just beyond, turned west by Upper Stewarton to cross to Greenside/Cowhope, and so through to the Flemington Burn where our route is rejoined. The drovers of course were heading in the opposite direction. One has to try and imagine the landscape before forestry came or even modern fields and farming. Beasts wouldn't follow down the valley (too boggy usually), but would graze and travel along the slopes on drier ground, hence the route by Harehope.

On reaching Harehope the road swings right to a white house, but we continue straight on to skirt right of the farm buildings, through a gate, and on up through a scatter of trees (mostly ash and beech) on a line between parallel fences. This leads to a sloping field. Go through a gate and turn right, along the foot of the field, through another gate, then turn left along the fence. When level with the

LOOKING UP TO THE WHITE MELDON, AFTER LEAVING PEEBLES

top of the field bear right through the trees for twenty yards to reach a big break. Turn up this ('cruel on the calf muscles' steep) to reach a forestry track.

The track makes a big loop so don't follow it. Head straight on and, suddenly, you are on the prehistoric ring fort site of Harestone Hill. This is a superb site both for its panoramic view and for itself, a clear circle of ditch and ramparts, 190 by 180 feet, once full of residential huts. Walk right across it and join the forestry road beyond, turning right to follow it as it swings up to the skyline pass.

When the road ends there is a small gate which leads out onto the col beyond and a grand feeling of 'the other side of the mountain'. We descend the hollow beyond, Wide Hope (the last *hope* name of the walk), keeping either down outside the forest edge or, easier, following what looks like the old drove line more to the west down the *shank*. The way ahead is clearly seen too, with the track angling up to round Drum Maw. Kestrels were hunting when I passed this way. There is a gate about 100 yards down the Flemington Burn from the forest edge and a track angles up to join the larger track contouring above. Turn left along this track (which runs up to remote Fingland) and savour the mini-meanderings of the Flemington Burn, which, if more douce, still echoes J. B. Selkirk's words on Border Burns:

> *Ah, Tam! gie me a Border burn*
> *That canna rin without a turn,*
> *And wi' its bonnie babble fills*
> *The glens amang oor native hills.*

If descending the Flemington Burn (as accommodation may dictate) those interested in prehistory will find the fort site on top of Whiteside Hill (168461) worth a visit. There are rings within rings from various occupations, hut platforms and other features.

Our track soon comes to a multiple junction. Bear right at the first split and go straight on, ignoring the path that comes in from the left and cross to go off, right, up the hill. The Landranger map is quite inaccurate, so follow this verbal directing. As the track then clearly heads up the Fingland Burn valley there shouldn't be any real difficulty. The scenery is reminiscent of the Cheviot ranges and very pleasant as we appear to be deeply lost among rolling ranges of hills. The marks of prehistoric and later settlements can be seen on the slopes of Drum Maw. We come to a gate then the track dips to the burn (the last drinking water till West Linton), before rising steadily up the flank of Drum Maw. See if you can pick out this conical hill from the Cauldstane Slap ascent tomorrow.

A gate leads into a strip of forestry (not shown on the Landranger map) and there is a short, very wet bit, which even ponies skirt. When the col is reached there is a sudden revelation of the sweeping view to the Pentlands giving a good preview of tomorrow's act. West Linton can be seen nestling at the foot of the hills. We join a better track coming in from the right (quarry), go through a gate at the end of the strip, then the track curves round and down (another track comes in from the right) and sturdy trees dot the hillside: oak, Scots pine, ash and some contorted thorns like giant bonsai. The path traverses a while, then, through another gate, turns sharply left, straight down the hill, a line we keep to, descending to the A701. There are lots of gates so these are not mentioned individually. The track is lined on the right by oaks and on the left by conifers, and when the conifers end there are bold beeches to mark our line. Don't swing off right into the farm.

The grassy track keeps on down to join a tarred side road at the hamlet of Damside and quickly twists down to the main road. Turn left along the A701 (pavement) to Romanno Bridge. The Inn (which does accommodation) may be a welcome pause. Before going on walk to the edge of the hamlet, on the B7059 Peebles road, look at the lower slopes of the hill ahead, overlooking this road. You'll see a field that is terraced from top to bottom – one of the most striking and

THE ROAD ON BY DRUM MAW UP THE FINGLAND GLEN

enigmatic of prehistoric works in Scotland, for they are plainly not natural (like the Parallel Roads of Glen Roy) yet there are no artifacts to help dating or who constructed them. There are several long, illustrated articles in the *Proceedings* (see bibliography).

Leave Romanno Bridge by the original A701 line beside the telephone box. This takes you back to the A701 over the beautiful old bridge that gives the place its name. Romanno was the name of a local family, extinct in the sixteenth century, but they may have had some Roman connection. The mysterious cultivations were once thought to be Roman, and every other old bridge is erroneously called Roman. Turn left along the A701, passing a school, right, then turning off right on a quiet country road marked 'Bogsbank 2'. There are plenty of Scots pine woodland strips, popular with masses of rooks, and some new roadside planting of deciduous trees. The road rises steadily passing Hamilton Hall, a farmhouse offering B & B. A level straight, on the crest, offers good views back to the hills we have crossed and on to the Pentlands where some of the ragged tops ahead ring to names like Deerhope Rig, Patie's Hill, Spittal Hill, Cock Rig, Braid Law, West Kip and Scald Law. The farms we pass have comfortably soft names: White Moss, Bogs Bank, Tarf Haugh. We cross the small West Water, as once did a railway line to Dolphinton (change) and Carstairs, but there is little sign of it now though West Linton still has a Station Road – the B7059. The station was called Broomlee and still exists as a private house.

If the railway has gone, so has much evidence of the coal mining which for centuries took place between the A701 and A702. (There is some open-cast working outside Carlops at present.) This railway's next station north was called Coalyburn. Only in 1799 were colliers freed from a serf-like attachment to the soil, being sold like cattle as owners changed, their children from the age of six (girls as well as boys), forced to work in utterly appalling conditions, on fourteen hour shifts, for less than the equivalent of ten pence a day. It was only in 1842 an Act was passed to ban the employment of women and children. We pass a discreet sewage works, an overspill cemetery and enter West Linton by a creeping bungaloid extension.

WEST LINTON

At the road junction there is an iron lamp standard and a round horse-trough (filled with concrete rather than water), erected by the local Band of Mercy, and commemorating Queen Victoria's jubilee in 1897. Facing it is the old toll house. You can still see the tiny window where dues were paid. It is set at a height so mounted travellers (as well as the drovers and those on foot) could pay with minimal inconvenience.

There is almost an English village atmosphere with the 'green', children's play area and white, tidy, tall-spired St Andrew's church rising behind the war memorial. Don't fail to have a look at the churchyard. Tucked in a corner are *bee-boles* (cupboards in a wall for holding the minister's *skeps*), and there are plenty of interesting early gravestones; one, of a full figure in cloak, buttoned coat and buckled shoes, is superb.

The church had its troubles in the long fight to win free of patronage which was so often abused in those days. Half the congregation walked out rather than have a minister forced on them. In Covenanting times the minister was suspended for his principles, as was his son who succeeded him. The church dates to 1782 but was enlarged in 1871 when the slender spire was added. You can see fine wood carvings inside – if it is open.

A gruesome story is told of a Linton student at the Edinburgh medical school finding a recently deceased local man lying on the dissecting table. Body-snatching was such a menace that armed guards often stood watches at night. At

*THE IMPRESSIVE PREHISTORIC TERRACES ABOVE THE LYNE VALLEY
JUST OUTSIDE ROMANNO BRIDGE*

least one raiding party was disturbed at Linton while, on another occasion the 'guards' crept out of the watch house and fired towards a noise. In the morning they found they had shot a stray horse!

The town has had its eccentrics. James Oswald (died 1726) so liked the marble table on which he dined that he decided it would make a pleasing gravestone – so he had the stone inscribed in advance and carried on using it. He was accidentally shot while duck hunting on Slipperfield Loch not long after. The 'table' was set up in St Andrew's cemetery, the inscription suggesting travellers might like to stop and picnic there!

Kenneth Paul was born in 1893 in an Angus manse, and became a teacher at West Linton in the Thirties. A keen youth hosteller, cyclist, walker and fanatical country dancer he eventually became a bit of an eccentric recluse, the house filling with junk. When he died in 1977 his will left the residue of his estate to St Andrew's church, to be used for social purposes. And the capital, despite grants and refurbishing the hall, is now a six-figure sum! An earlier pupil of West Linton (commemorated by a plaque at the school hall) was George Meikle Kemp, the architect of the monument to Sir Walter Scott which so dominates Edinburgh's Princes Street.

The Main Street jiggles up towards the Pentland-flanking A702 Edinburgh–Biggar road, with many houses set, Dutch-style, with their gables to the street so there are many little alleys and squares between them. The whole village has a 'preservation order'. In the centre is an 1861 clock tower which I suppose marks the work of an earlier eccentric, James Gifford, a local laird and stonemason. He filled his house with family portraits carved in stone, delightful in themselves and in their portrayal of seventeenth-century costume. He gave the village a well, which had the central figure of his wife, with his four children at the corners. (He then had a fifth child and the only place he could find to place its image and maintain the symmetry was on the mother figure's head!) Eventually this 1666 well decayed, and only the figure of the wife survives, now incorporated in the Clock Tower built over the site. A superb plaque of his carving stands on the wall of a house in Raemartin Square, which itself is on the site of the original Gifford house. An unusual sundial is sited on the corner of the roof of this building.

There is an Information and Exhibition Centre in the centre of the village, but it has limited opening hours (weekends in summer, 0968-60346). Another trim-looking church near it has been converted into a private house. (It was the old Secession church.)

The Old Bakehouse Restaurant is a welcome port of call. The ancient ovens, paddles, coppers, etc are still there and the atmosphere is completed by the waitresses being in period costume. I like West Linton very much; it wears its age gracefully and has not damned itself by the cheap trumpery of olde worldism. Though in Peebles-shire, West Linton seems to belong to the Pentlands, and is often given fairly casual reference in books on the Borders or Tweeddale. Dolphinton, the next village along the A702, is in Lanarkshire.

West Linton is a relatively modern name. It was once the more resonant Linton Roderick from the sixth-century Rydderich Hael, the Strathclyde king who supported Kentigern (St Mungo, who is buried in Glasgow Cathedral), and who established Christianity in the Borders. In 1160 the church of Lyntunruderic was conveyed to the church of Kelso so, until the Reformation, the monks must have journeyed over much of our route.

West Linton's annual celebration – the Whipman Play – is held early in June. Whipman was an old name for a carter and the festival dates back to the founding of the Whipmen's Benevolent Association in 1803. This body died with the introduction of motor vehicles, but the festival, after each war had seemingly ended its life, has somehow been revived and thrives. Linton, since 1631, had huge fairs, much helped by the droving trade which could see 30,000 sheep sold (including the Linton breed) and then driven over the Cauldstane Slap. 'Big as a Linton market' was a common phrase.

A SPLENDID OLD GRAVESTONE IN WEST LINTON

PRACTICAL INFORMATION: WEST LINTON

Telephone code for West Linton numbers is 0986-,

ACCOMMODATION: More limited than we've had up till now so book ahead. Check positions on the map too, several are well out of the village.

West Linton: The Linton Hotel, Main Street, -60228, Rycroft, Station Road, -60356, Raemartin Hotel, Main Street, -60464, Gordon Arms, (at A702 junction) -60208.

Beyond West Linton: Conveniently on tomorrow's route and worth the extra is the beautiful country house and garden of Medwyn House, -60542 (143523, one kilometre off the A702 on the Baddinsgill Reservoir road. Not overpriced; recommended). Next day walk on up the road for half a mile then turn right for Lynedale etc, SROW sign Carlops, which takes one to Stoneypath and the described route.

Carlops: Four kilometres north along the A702 is the Allan Ramsay Hotel, Carlops, -60258 which is a possibility but on no account walk up the A702. Follow tomorrow's route up to the Roman Road and in by Linton Muir and Hartside, good walking in the landscape of *The Gentle Shepherd*.

Before West Linton: A cluster of accommodation opportunities lie along, or just off, the A701. If West Linton cannot help one of these is the best alternative. Rowallan, Mountain Cross, -60329. (On A701, south-west from where we reach it off the hills and perhaps best gained by heading downstream to Flemington rather than over Drum Maw to Damside). Hamilton Hall, -60347 (Traditional farmhouse, 152482, named on the map). Romanno Inn, Rommano Bridge, -60781.

Further Afield: There is no taxi locally, the nearest being at Penicuik, nine miles to the north-east, 0968-72608. Accommodation in that area: Penicuik 0986-75885, -72035, -74154, -72557, -72683, -72035, -73030. Easter Howgate, 031-445-2265, Leadburn, 0986-72952, Nine Mile Burn, 0968-60930, Silverburn, 0968-78420. Penicuik Tourist Information Office, Penicuik Library: Mon, Tues, Thurs, 9.30–20.15, Fri 9.30–17.00, Wed, Sat 9.30–13.00. There is also the option of simply catching a bus in to Edinburgh for the night, as one can also do from Peebles to split the walk into two parts if required by limited holidays available.

CAMPING: No site.

TAXIS: See above.

MEALS: Limited but good.

WEST LINTON
to
CALDERS/
BROXBURN,
EDINBURGH

Bart 45 OSLR 65
OSPF 433 (NT 05/15), 419 (NT 06/16), 406 (NT 07/17)

Tarred roads will top and tail today, but the major feature is the crossing of the Pentlands by the historic pass of the Cauldstane Slap. From it we take a last look at the Border country , and a first look at the Highlands, seen over the Lowlands, which will keep us happily occupied for the rest of the walk.

Originally I'd planned to have an overnight stop somewhere like East Calder, but there is very limited accommodation in the area (an industrial sprawl, just not geared for visitors and tourists). There are no camp sites and few hotels or B & Bs. Rather than face frustrations and perhaps disappointment my simple solution was to walk on to Broxburn, and then take a bus into Edinburgh for the night, Edinburgh having two SYHA hostels, private hostels and all manner of accommodation. There could be time to see something of Britain's finest city, go to the theatre and dine out. This is a fun trip remember! This then leaves a pleasant canal walk to Linlithgow on the next day, with time enough to explore that historic town. However, there turned out to be just sufficient accommodation, even if it is rather scattered. The walk description is carried forward to Broxburn, but you may well stop before then.

THE PENTLANDS BY CAULDSTANE SLAP

Take the unsurfaced lane (The Loan) up beside the garage on the A702 (opposite the Gordon Arms); a leafy brae with plenty of posh houses. As the angle eases and we swing right, note the attractive house of *Sron Garbh* on the left. A painted plaque above the door gives the date 1935. As we come out from the trees, our avenue merges with the minor tarred road up from Lynedale. Lynedale and Medwinbank were hamlets along the old turnpike road with mills using the Lyne Water. Besides the clothmaking there was a wheelwright and furniture-maker. A millwright wrote the popular drovers' fiddle tune *The High Road to Linton*. Charles X, exiled from his French throne, stayed here while shooting over Slipperfield Moor.

The famous Brighouse Inn, dating back to the fifteenth century, is now the Medwyn House Hotel, having gone from Coaching Inn to Victorian mansion house. If you want a treat have a night there. The road running along to Carlops is part of the Clydesdale–Forth Roman road. We turn off it at the road to Stonypath ('Harperrigg 7' the Scottish Rights of Way Society sign informs us). Opposite this road some mine workings can just be made out. Mary Queen of Scots is said to have paid her troops in silver obtained here. The 'siller-holes' were last worked in 1753.

Walk up and pass through several gates on the right of the Stonypath farm buildings. The track rises above the Lyne Water to Tocher Knowe (sheep fank), and rounds Faw Mount to the lush, high, world of Baddinsgill. (Here is a *gill* word much further north of the border than you'll find *burn* south of it.) When we reach the field, before the Baddinsgill House woodlands, we turn left along by the wall, keeping between it and the wending stream of the infant Lyne, edged with aromatic water-mint, to cross a substantial footbridge and climb the bank to a tarred road just before Dipper Wood. (SRWS: 'Harperrig 5 ½ by Cauldstane Slap' etc.) The name Baldewynsgill appears in a map of 1411, but this route is as old as time.

Turn right and follow the road to its termination at the reservoir. The road stops being a public road for vehicles at a sheepfank, dips and rises (still plenty of thick trees) past the farm and ends above the dam of the Baddinsgill Reservoir, built in 1924 to supply water to Bathgate. The right-of-way continues through a gate and, suddenly, we are onto open moorland country where we will certainly enjoy the 'tumultuous solitude' of Christopher North (John Wilson) who lived at Roslin and walked these hills - often on night expeditions. The track is clear to the shoulder beyond the Ravendean Burn, then becomes a path (yellow markers) up to the pass, the Cauldstane Slap (*c.*380 metres). *Slap* just means *pass* and we are, again, given a sudden portal view, but over a very different world: the Lowlands and the scarred world of West Lothian, an undeserved Cinderella bit of countryside. The energetic can climb West Cairn Hill (562 metres) which has the clearer prehistoric cairn on top. It is only now that we are on the Tweed watershed for the Baddinsgill slopes drain via the Lyne to that king of rivers while, over the pass, the slopes drain to the Water of Leith and the Forth Estuary. The pass must date back to prehistoric times and few passes can be so well-defined. The influence even enters fiction. Stevenson, in his unfinished masterpiece, *Weir of Hermiston*, creates 'the four black brothers of Cauldstane-slap'. The rebel lords, after the abortive Raid of Ruthven, gathered in West Linton then rode over the Slap to Falkirk and Stirling to confront James VI. The restless James IV rode over the Slap 'before day' having 'boycht a horss' at Lithgow for five pounds. More anonymous were the drovers pushing for the Border and English markets with their cattle. Linton had its own important markets for the local Linton breed of sheep, 30,000 sometimes being sold in a year, and many heading over the Slap to Ochil or Highland destinations. A toll at Romanno did well out of the drovers, but then West Linton erected a toll to catch the traffic off the Slap and Romanno lost out, even though it went to court over the matter. The law, however, forbade the Linton Toll to double-charge carts, which were

BADDINSGILL RESERVOIR IN THE PENTLANDS

carrying oats to the mill and then bringing the meal back again. The earliest mention of the pass by name is in a charter of about 1370.

There is a stile over the fence across the col and a SRWS sign. The path leads down roughly parallel to the Baad Park Burn which is joined by the Cushie Syke (*stream of the wood pigeon*). Looking back the fort on the East Cairn shows well. At the far end of the reservoir are the ruins of East Cairns Castle, once home of Crichton, High Admiral of Scotland, who also acted as public-spirited policeman to the route over the Slap. John Buchan in his long poem *From the Pentlands* could have been describing this corner:

> *A land of peace where lost romance*
> *And ghostly shine of helm and lance*
> *Still dwell by castled scarp and lea*
> *And the lost homes of chivalry...*
> *That ancient land of heath and sky,*
> *Where the old rhymes and stories fall*
> *In kindly, soothing pastoral.*

Buchan would appreciate the fact that Harperrig Reservoir is stocked with brown trout. The stream flowing from the reservoir is the infant Water of Leith. Looking ahead, traffic will indicate the A70 line which we reach at the edge of the trees by the second pylon visible from the left. Nearing Harperrig there is a metal marker with EWCo 1859 on it (Edinburgh Water Company).

Harperrig, and the slopes above, provided a stance on the great drove road south. The farm always tried to cut its hay before the tens of thousands of cattle arrived, but if the droving season was a bane it also was a merry time with the farm entertaining the owners (the drovers slept with their beasts). Looking at the map at the back of Haldane's *Drove Roads of Scotland* (the definitive survey on droving) the Cauldstane Slap is a unique stretch with no alternatives. From Falkirk there was a choice of south or north of the Bathgate Hills, (we'll be following the latter), and south of the Pentlands the route soon has variants, but over the Slap the whole shebang had to travel.

Pass right of the first Harperrig field, keeping along by the fence to a gate/stile. There are some right-of-way signs or arrows but these may change. Anyway, an apex of fields juts towards the farm but we continue straight on across – watch the thistles – to walk down by the fence passing a big marker post, and so reach another gate/stile beyond which we find the footbridge of the Gala Ford. The green sward is a good brew stop.

Once across the footbridge turn left, then, through the gate, turn right to follow a (ruined) wall line right up to the A70. If in doubt the second pylon is always there as a marker. The view from the wind-battered trees as we reach the A70 is fine; after all, it is Little Vantage. Snipe and curlew relish these rushy fields and wheatears, wagtails and starlings nest in the walls. You can usually find a pipit's nest.

Gather your wits for the short stretch of A70. There is always the odd motoring maniac to endanger the pedestrian on this crest of road, a rather strange 'shelf' of land stuck onto the Pentlands and once known as the Lang Whang. At the far end of the rolling Pentland tops is the crouched lion shape of Arthur's Seat – in the middle of Edinburgh.

INTO THE LOWLANDS

We have just over half a mile of this Pentland-view walking before turning off left. Little Vantage is now a ruin, the site of a change house in pre-motoring days. On the left of the A70 we see a big walled garden (empty) behind the attractive late seventeenth-century farmhouse called Ainville. There is no signpost for our minor road (110637). Vehicles use the next road for East Calder, so this is never busy. A track leaves the minor road for a farm named Leyden. Maybe this is a connection with John Leyden rather than a foreign town. I'd like it to be.

The road loses height steadily. Rowan, ash and beech line the verge.

ENJOYING A PADDLE AT THE GALA FORD AFTER CROSSING THE CAULDSTANE SLAP

The last group before pylons cross have a marked wind-induced lean to starboard. Looking down to the plain we can see several pink-tinted *kloofs* which are old shale-bings, of which more shortly, when we reach them. The towers and lego-work of the Forth road and railway bridges can be spotted too. The road runs down by the farms of Latch, Cockmylane and Ormiston, then swings abruptly, right, alongside and then under the Edinburgh to Glasgow via Shotts railway. This was the old Caley route, a rival to the Falkirk route. (In the price war a century ago you could go Edinburgh–Glasgow for sixpence – 2 ½ pence!.)

Turn left at a T-junction in the hamlet which leads to the busy A71. The road across this for East Calder has been offset for safety. Cross carefully. Just one field on, where the pylon line crosses, turn off right, down the right-of-way, signposted 'East Calder'. This lane leads down to the B7015 at the east end of East Calder. St Paul's Primary School is passed shortly before reaching the B7015. A few minutes walk (left) takes one in to East Calder, a neat, well-appointed village with several pubs, chip shop, stores, etc. (The old Parish Church, abandoned in 1750, has some crudely-sculpted monuments in the graveyard.) The route itself turns right, and, a few minutes walk in that direction, is the popular Whitecroft Farm B & B, on left, just beyond a petrol station, and an excellent Chinese restaurant,

A TURNIP-HEAD FACE ON TOP OF A STONE IN EAST CALDER'S OLD GRAVEYARD

The Fortuner. As one passes the ivy-clad, arched entrance to the Almondell and Calder Wood Country Park, the route's continuation, Whitecroft Farm is a very convenient stopping spot. Phone at least one night before to ensure a place: Whitecroft Farm, East Calder, Midlothian, 0506-881810. The only other B & B is across the Linhouse Water in Mid Calder: 14 Caroline Gardens, Muirieston Park, Mid Calder, West Lothian, 0506-414047.

ALMONDELL COUNTRY PARK

The gateway is just west of the signposted car park. About sixty yards down the drive there is a notice board with a map of the park. The drive is lined with laburnum, various cherries, dark plums, larch, etc, so is colourful at all seasons. Walk down the long straight drive but watch out for the turn-off. It is easy to walk past it.

Just before the drive disappears, round and down a bend to the right, there is an opening, on the left, marked by a stone that looks a bit like a milestone. Turn off onto this path that wends through the trees to reach a T-junction (another marker stone) on the edge of the deep, wide dell of the Almond.

Not far upstream stands a huge nine-arched viaduct which is glimpsed through the trees. We cross this, so wander upstream on the path (which puts in an abrupt down and up) to reach the viaduct. Built about 1886 to serve the oil industry at Pumpherston, it has been given new life as part of the Almondell pathway system.

The Calders and Pumpherston have now been overshadowed by Livingston New Town lying to the west. In 1962 Livingston's population was 2,000, now it is 37,000 with over 150 industries, and the huge Cameron Ironworks, the area's largest employer, making products for the offshore oil industry. Grangemouth, the huge oil processing plant, we will see after Linlithgow. Considering the sprawl of industry our walk will retain a deep rural feel, right to the end. Livingston has one or two hotels but they are both expensive and not very convenient, even using a taxi. Livingston is a nightmare for pedestrians anyway.

Looking down left from the lofty height of the viaduct you'll see a path and a stream running along the far bank of the river. The stream is obviously artificial and is the main feeder for keeping the Union Canal's water level steady, not that it works in prolonged dry spells. The Cobbinshaw Reservoir up in the Pentlands (about five miles south-west of Harperrrig) was built to provide the extra water, which flows down the Bog Burn and becomes the Muirieston Water then joins the Linhouse Water in

Mid Calder before, finally, running into the Almond. Five minutes walk up from the viaduct there is the weir where the channel is led off. The River Almond, when it passes under the Union Canal, is seventy feet lower, hence the need to tap the river a couple of miles upstream. Just sixty yards downstream from the viaduct you can see another bridge, which is an unusual one as it is both a footbridge and the aqueduct for the feeder channel.

Once across the viaduct turn down the steep steps on the left and follow the path slanting down. Don't cut back under the viaduct. A small bridge, with the remains of a sluice, leads to the main valley path. The feeder channel is full of monkey flower, bittersweet, greater willowherb (an aquatic cousin of the rose-bay species which is also plentiful) and blue water mint.

We turn left, downstream, but it is only a short addition to walk up to inspect the weir that is really our first contact with the engineering interest of the Union Canal. There is another footbridge which gives a good viewpoint. Anyone who has stayed in Mid Calder overnight will come down this path.

To do so head for the junction at the bridge sixty yards down from the Torphichen Arms. Turn left onto the B8046 ('Pumpherston 1', 'Uphall 2¾') and after about 300 yards turn right into a car park (a police notice tells you to lock your car), from which a path leads off into the Almondell and Calder Wood Park.

The path crosses a road-wide concrete bridge and climbs steeply up the far bank then slowly descends again, passing the serried ranks of adolescent trees in a nursery, to reach the River Almond at a big weir, which is followed by a big sewage works and, after following the riverbank for five minutes, another weir – which is the one that feeds the feeder for the Union Canal. Cross the bridge to walk down the left bank to the high viaduct. This is worth going up onto, and a path breaks off, left, over a small bridge and climbs up steep steps to reach it. The interesting points are covered above, and from the viaduct we are all back on course, so to speak.

There is a roofed entrance, like an exaggerated church porch, below the viaduct (presumably in defence against idiots dropping anything overboard) and we continue down to the feeder aqueduct.

The feeder crossing the river is interesting, and produces an ingenious combination that allows pedestrians – almost – to walk on water. This unusual bridge dates to 1820, the work of Hugh Baird, the engineer of the Union Canal. To keep the canal topped up as much as two million gallons of water a day may be needed.

After inspecting the aqueduct cum footbridge walk down on the left bank path (singposted for the Visitor Centre). There is a meadow picnic site seen across the River Almond and then we come on the ruined stone bridge designed by the portrait-painter Alexander Naismith (or Nasmythe or Naysmith) and built about 1800. Surely it is worth restoration? Keep to the main drive. A parking place for disabled drivers marks the original site of Almondell House and, just beyond, is the Visitor Centre. It is open during office hours on Monday–Thursday and Sunday, but shut Friday and Saturday. Soft drinks, tea, snacks and chocolate are on sale if you need refreshments. There are a number of fine specimen trees – copper beech, cypress, sequoia, lime etc. Do go into the Centre, a lively, friendly place with interesting historical and wildlife displays, an aquarium and an audio-visual presentation.

The Visitor Centre building is the old stable block for the one-time mansion of Almondell, and once more we run into a connection with the 11th Earl of Buchan who so left his mark at Dryburgh. The Erskines were quite an interesting family. The 11th Earl was the last to live at the Kirkhill House, and much of its contents were taken to Almondell which had been built by his brother Henry, whose son inherited the title in 1829. Henry Erskine was a famous lawyer (he became Lord Advocate) and started building Almondell in 1790 to his own eccentric design. It was a disastrous enterprise, but he loved the setting which we enjoy today with the additional benefit of the trees being in their splendid maturity.

The house was burnt in the 1950s and demolished in 1969. Another brother of the 11th Earl was Thomas Erskine who became Lord Chancellor as Baron Erskine. Henry and Thomas lie in the family church at Uphall (St Nicholas), David, 11th Earl is at Dryburgh, of course.

On the road beyond the North Lodge of the park (not on our route) is an unobtrusive stone with an enigmatic dedication to William Wallace. Dated 1784 it doesn't take much guessing who erected it! The strangest structure the eccentric earl created was at his home of Kirkhill, on the outskirts of Broxburn. Its story is told in the leaflet available at the Visitor Centre.

Mathematician, astronomer, antiquarian and scholar, the Earl of Buchan constructed a scale model of the Solar System in and around the grounds of Kirkhill House in 1776. The model consisted of the Sun, Mercury, Venus, the Earth and its moon, Mars, Jupiter and its four moons and Saturn with its rings and five moons. Mars is now known to have two moons, Jupiter eleven moons and Saturn nine, and since the construction of the model, Neptune, Uranus and Pluto have been discovered; but even bearing this in mind, the model was extraordinarily accurate for that period. It was constructed to a scale of 12,238.28 miles to an inch, the Sun being represented by a stone sphere six feet in diameter, and the Earth by a bronze sphere 0.646 inches in diameter placed 645 feet away. The larger planets were made, like the Sun, of stone while the smaller planets were of bronze.

The model has disappeared, but a summary of the calculations which enabled the Earl to construct the model are preserved on the stone pillar which Buchan erected in the grounds of Kirkhill in 1777. The astronomical data inscribed on the pillar still largely holds true today, a fact which is all the more remarkable bearing in mind its date. Buchan also included on the pillar a prediction of the position of the planets on 20 May 2255 (why he chose this date is unknown).

The pillar was surmounted by a bell tower on top of which was a metal cross. After Buchan's death, the bell tower was removed and taken to his younger brother's estate at Almondell, where it was placed in front of the stables over a well (which is still there). The pillar remained at Kirkhill, but by the late 1970s it had collapsed. When the shell of Kirkhill House was sold for private restoration, the stones of the pillar were taken into safekeeping by West Lothian History and Amenity Society, and it was decided to rebuild the pillar, with bell tower and cross, in front of the Visitor Centre.

THE UNION CANAL

From the end of the Visitor Centre Buildings cross the grassy 'dog-free' area of the old walled garden to reach the graceful, modern, single-tower suspension bridge. A plaque on the far side is inscribed Mandela Bridge. Opened 1986 in tribute to those in South Africa who struggle for freedom and dignity. 'The Cathedral of Peace is built of many small stones.' Another plaque is a Civic Trust Award for the structural steel design of the bridge. It is dated 1971.

Beyond the bridge our path picks up the canal feeder channel which we follow to its end. A flight of wooden stairs climbs off right and a notice points our route ahead: 'Linns Mill Union Canal 1 ¾ miles'. (Lin is more correct.) The path is perfectly clear to follow, even if frequent stiles make it a bit of a steeplechase, and the feeder twice vanishes into conduits, these tunnels necessitated by the looping river pushing hard against our side of the steep valley, and leaving no room for a water channel and not over-much for our path.

After walking along a hawthorn hedge a stone bridge over the feeder is the entrance drive to Shiel Mill (ponies), then a quiet stretch ends with the feeder going underground. We angle along and up, passing under the line of pylons, and down again to rejoin the feeder which flows through pleasant beechwood here. The river loops away from our side, and on the prow opposite is Illieston Castle, a well-preserved tower house, built by John Ellis in 1665 but with earlier buildings going back much further. James II and James IV used it as a hunting lodge.

Another bridge crosses the feeder which then goes into another culvert. These tunnels were repaired in 1989/90 as part of the ongoing work of restoring the Union Canal to something of its early condition. (The culverts were leaking and the bank had slipped away in one place.)

The path leaves the trees at another bridge, and contours round the top, wooded edge of a curving field. The buttressed arches of the splendid aqueduct appear downstream, while back across the river, Illieston stands boldly against the skyline. There is another small bridge, and when the water again disappears into a tunnel we turn up a flight of steps to reach a minor road. Turn left down this, and left at a fork, a drive which passes below the arches of the aqueduct. Inhibiting notices declare that the road is a private one to Lin's Mill but, through the arches towards the white gates, one turns right up a flight of steps to gain the Union Canal, at one of its most impressive spots, the Almond Aqueduct, the third largest aqueduct in Britain.

There is no mill now but Lin's Grave is hidden away in the woods of the private grounds. It is inscribed 'Here lyeth the dust of William Lin richt heritor of Lins Miln who died in the year of the Lord 1645'. He was one of the many victims of the plague which ravished Scotland that year.

Make sure you go under the arches before turning up onto the canal towpath (there are steps on the near side as well): the towpath over the whole system, with very few breaks, lies on the right (north) side as we walk it. The other side is usually impassable to pedestrians.

Have a look round the corner, and at the basin where the feeder culvert brings in the water we've walked beside to keep the canal level topped-up. An old notice board has lost its wording, but a date 1821 on the wall gives the date of this building. The canal east of here has been well restored and is popular with cruises based on Ratho or Edinburgh. The Bridge Inn or the cruising restaurant *Pride of the Union* are well-liked dining spots. Among the cruise boats the Seagull Trust arranges trips for disabled people.

In its heyday Ratho had fourteen pubs. The Pop Inn, next to the canal, is reputed to have had a door at each end of the building so the bargeman in charge of the towing horse could enter by one door, enjoy a pint *en passant,* and exit by the other door without having fallen behind his charge. About 1845 Ratho House was turned into a distillery, the annual production of 42,000 gallons being largely consumed locally. Canal work was a drouthy business obviously. Ratho was actually a change house and fare stage for tolls. A son of the Bridge Inn owners was the last person to be publicly hanged in Edinburgh, in May 1864. One of Edinburgh's regular exports via the canal was manure (horses rather than horse power in those days) and this led to great fertility on the canalside farms. Maybe this lingers on as two local farms hold world records for wheat production. Coal (and building stone) was the big import to the city, and the major reason for the canal being built. The passenger side was never lucrative and was killed by the railways.

Those who suffer from vertigo had best cross the aqueduct with their eyes shut, for the setting is impressively high and exposed with the narrow cobbled pathway edged on the left by the iron trough of the canal and, on the right, an airy iron railing does little to hide the seventy foot drop to the river Almond. There is a superb view north, down the river, to Telford's Almond Valley Viaduct of the main Edinburgh–Glasgow Railway. This was built in 1842 and, with thirty-six arches, it rather outdoes our five There is a

HOW IT ONCE WAS – A SCENE IN THE HEYDAY OF THE UNION CANAL – AT THE ALMOND AQUADUCT (PHOTO: COURTESY LUCS)

control sluice from the canal, in the middle of the aqueduct (south side), which tends to dribble water. In winter this overflow has been known to freeze solid, creating a pillar of ice seventy feet high. At the west end of the aqueduct there is a milestone marked '10 ½' (to Edinburgh) and '21' (to Falkirk and the Forth and Clyde Canal). About 100 yards on there is an overflow channel, lined with granite setts, which crosses the towpath.

A bank prevents us from seeing any view, but the noise of the M8 will be noticed. The first bridge we come to is numbered 19 on the arch, and just before it a minor road once gave access to a landing stage. Beyond bridge 19 a hedge blocks the view for a while then, suddenly, it ends and we are looking out onto a landscape typical of West Lothian: an industrial estate backed by shale bings (our route goes on through between them), and fronted by sweeping rail and motorway routes and, as like as not, aircraft at low altitude as Edinburgh Airport lies just beyond the great railway viaduct. We are likely to be passing at peak flight times, either morning or evening, which will delight plane-spotters. This will be the most conspicuously industrialised moment of our walk and, as such, will have a certain curiosity value even if we see surprisingly little of it in passing. The canal, keeping to its contour line does a big loop round Broxburn, and is cut by the M8, but we cut across to rejoin it at the ginger-headed mountains. Just beyond Bridge 20 turn off onto the minor road which goes under the railway and over the M8.

A VICTORIAN PICTURE OF AN EIGHTY FOOT ICICLE FORMED FROM THE CANAL OVERFLOW AT THE ALMOND AQUEDUCT

The railway is the old Edinburgh–Uphall–Bathgate–Coatbridge–Glasgow line, which breaks off from the main Edinburgh–Glasgow line west of Ratho (Newbridge Junction), and was originally built in 1849, to Bathgate, being extended to Airdrie and Glasgow in 1879. It served the coal, iron and shale oil industries, and passenger trains were few. The last was in 1956! The creation of Livingston New Town failed to keep things going, and the line west to Airdrie was lifted in 1982. Bathgate station was gutted by an arsonist. Out of this dismal history came resurrection, and the line to Bathgate (an unusual modern station) is now a vital commuter route.

BROXBURN AND UPHALL

The bridge over the motorway is a good viewpoint. Beyond the big, many-arched railway viaduct lies Edinburgh Airport, so aircraft will no doubt be much in evidence. The first building, right, at a junction is the Astor Motel (see below), which is one accommodation choice with a certain irony for pedestrians on a walkers' way: a night in a *motel*.

Continue on to pass through the hamlet of Burnside, in the hollow between the Caw and Brox Burns, and so reach the A89. The road we have just come along is indicated 'Newhouse Road' – and the same name appears across the A89 – our continuation. There is no vehicular access to this short road, which leads through to the A899 where we turn left along into Broxburn and Uphall.

If not staying in Broxburn or Uphall (or visiting one of the many pubs or friendly coffee houses) then the A899 is left after about fifty yards turning off right, just over a bridge, onto a footpath. The footpath entrances are opposite Hall's factory, leading to a sturdy footbridge over a tiny burn, and, after only ten yards, a crossing of paths. Take the one straight on (the only path not tarred) which runs along, very straight, with a hedge to the right. (The occasional sickly-sweet smell comes from Millar's sweetie factory on the other side of the hedge.) Not long after a grass area appears, left, we come on a road; simply cross this and carry on along the grassy footpath towards the red bings, with the hedge now on our left side. This leads (crossing one more tarred road) to the Union Canal, just before Bridge 29 and is described under tomorrow's walk.

The A899 leads straight into Broxburn (Main Street). Note the church, on the right, as the way out tomorrow starts from there. Broxburn has a wide range of shops, coffee houses, pubs, etc, and is a friendly place despite a rather unpretentious appearance. It straggles along north of the Brox Burn, a town which grew with the shale oil industry after 1858. In

1861 the population was 660, in 1891 it was 5,898. With that industry gone there is a scruffy air of survival only. They were either *affy wild* or *unco guid* in Victorian times. I lost count of the churches along the long High Street to Uphall. The West Church is 'weird and wonderful Gothic', and the Roman Catholic church the real showpiece. St Nicholas Parish Church, on the B8046 out of Uphall, is the only old church. Uphall was once Strathbrock (*valley of badgers*) and Broxburn is from the same old word brock for badger (*badger stream*). Uphall is a name which seems to cause pronunciation problems, goodness knows why. It is just as written, Up-hall, but people will produce Uffle and such like.

The Earl of Buchan built his solar-system model at the family home of Kirkhill. The family were connected with the area until after the Second World War. The Broxburn Roman Catholic church was built in 1880 for the Dowager Countess of Buchan. She presented it with the font which has had a varied history. Dating to pre-Reformation times it was ejected from the new kirk and ended being used as a cattle water trough on a local farm. When it was recognised for what it was the farmer gave it to the countess.

As already mentioned, my first idea on hitting Broxburn was to immediately take a bus into Edinburgh for the night – or even two nights – for it would be interesting to spend a day seeing some of the Roman and other antiquities connected with Dere Street, the Borders and the Antonine Wall, in the Royal Scottish Museum. This is still a reasonable option. Most of the local accommodation is fairly basic and sometimes noisy. I'll list the local accommodation and you can make the decision. The only standard B & Bs (very good) were those back in East and Mid Calder. (Booking ahead advised.)

PRACTICAL INFORMATION; CALDERS/BROXBURN

ACCOMMODATION: The Buchan Arms Hotel, 2-4 Main Street, Broxburn, is the only local accommodation. Westwards, Broxburn runs on into Uphall where the Oakridge Hotel, Main Street, Uphall, is likewise the only accommodation. It is a bit of a drag from one to the other but you could use bus or taxi (taxi rank just along from the Buchan Arms). The Union Canal circuits west about Broxburn so, coming back, you could turn off onto it rather than walk along the Main Street again.

At the west end of Uphall is Houston House, a beautiful castle-mansion, once owned by Mary Queen of Scots' advocate, Sir John Shairp. The Shairp family lived there for 350 years: cavaliers and squires, lawyers, MPs, academics (Principal Shairp of *The Bush Aboon Traquair*, was a great walker and a minor poet) and all respected the building's character so it is a classic example of a seventeenth-century tower house. It became a hotel in 1969. There are six single and twenty-four double rooms but the prices will put it beyond most walkers: 1990 quotes were £73 single, £83–£110 double. *Table d'hôte* dinner works out at £25 but the cuisine is renowned and a good alternative to an Uphall chip supper!

The Tally Ho, 7 Main Street, Winchburgh, does accommodation and is another possibility, as is the Astor Motel, Newhouse Road, East Burnside, Broxburn which sits at the junction (097714) which we passed just after leaving the canal. If determined not to go off to Edinburgh, Kirkliston, two miles east of Niddry Castle has a hotel at its central crossroads, Newliston Arms Hotel, Main Street, Kirkliston. Go under the M9 at 111746 to reach the B9080. There is no way over the M8 between junctions 1 and 2. Kirkliston Church has a showpiece Romanesque doorway and an airy setting on the hill. Using a taxi and returning next day is practical - today has put in many miles and we deserve a restful evening. There is also Newton Guest House, two miles North of Winchburgh 031-331-3298 and a B & B at Dechmont, one mile west of Uphall.

ACCOMMODATION SUMMARY (IN ORDER OF CONVENIENCE): East Calder: Whitecroft Farm, 0506-881810. Mid Calder: 14 Caroline Gardens, 0506-414047. Broxburn: Buchan Arms, 0506-856447. Uphall: Oakridge Hotel, 0506-856465, Houston House, 0506-853831. East Burnside: Astor Motel, 0506-850933. Winchburgh: Tally Ho, 0506-890221. Kirkliston: Newliston Arms, 031-333-3124. Newton: Newton Guest House, 031-331-3298. Dechmont: 70 Main Street, 0506-811291

CAMPING: not practical

TAXIS: Broxburn: 0506-857467, -854867, -853838. Winchburgh: 0506-890600, -890590. Mid Calder: 0506-880022.

BUS SERVICES: Eastern Scottish (031-556-8464) operate services 16, 17, 18, Edinburgh/Broxburn every twenty to thirty minutes. City terminus is St Andrew's Bus Station in city centre. Waverley Station (trains) and Tourist Information Centre at Waverley are just five minutes walk away, across Princes Street.

MEALS: Limited but ranging from chip shop and bar meals to *haute cuisine* at Houston House.

OPTIONAL EXTRA DAY IN EDINBURGH

A capital city obviously has a huge range of places and activities to attract the visitor. The Tourist Information Centre has plenty of maps, literature and information – so use it for whatever one's personal ideas for a day in Edinburgh. The one place I would advocate, as bearing on our walk, is the Roman Room in the Royal Scottish Museum, Queen Street, 031-556-8921. The Roman world is so superbly displayed and described that even the originally unenthusiastic come away converted. Don't miss it. We only see the surface scratches of Roman life as we wend Dere Street or Antonine Wall, here we are taken to the heart of it. Allow plenty of time for the museum.

ACCOMMODATION: The main Tourist Information Office is five minutes walk from the bus terminus. Exit onto St Andrew's Square and turn left to walk onto Princes Street. The Tourist Office is almost opposite, on top of the Waverley Market. They can book accommodation. Or send for a list in advance: Tourist Information Centre, Waverley Market, Princes Street, Edinburgh EH2 2QP. 031-557-2727.

There are two Grade 1 youth hostels in Edinburgh. Eglinton, 18 Eglinton Crescent, 031-337-1120 and Bruntsfield, 7 Bruntsfield Crescent, 031-447-2994.

There are also one or two private hostels (ask, as above). During the International Festival (last two weeks of August) all accommodation is heavily booked-up.

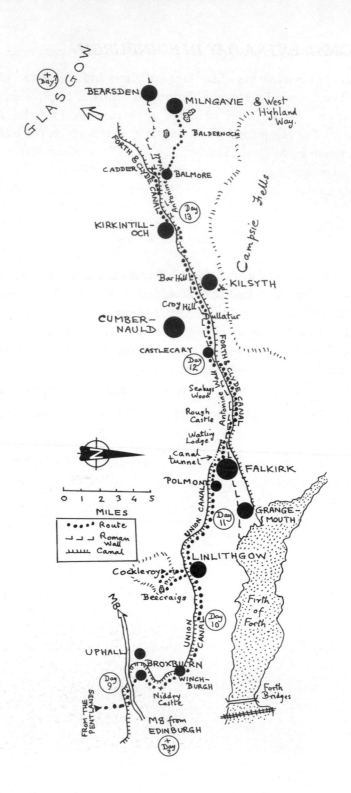

GLASGOW

BEARSDEN   MILNGAVIE & West
           Highland Way.
           + Baldernoch
FORTH & CLYDE CANAL
CADDER   BALMORE
         Day 13
KIRKINTILL-
OCH   Campsie Fells
         Bar Hill   KILSYTH
         Croy Hill
CUMBER-   Dullatur
NAULD
CASTLECARY
         Day 12
                  Seabegs
                  Wood
                  Rough
                  Castle
                  Watling
                  Lodge
         Canal
         tunnel →   FALKIRK
         POLMONT
                          GRANGE-
                  Day 11 MOUTH

N

0 1 2 3 4 5
MILES

•••• Route
┘ ┘ ┘ Roman Wall
ᴜᴜᴜᴜ Canal

Cockleroy   LINLITHGOW
Beecraigs
                          Firth
                          of
         Day 10   Forth

M8

UPHALL
         BROXBURN
         WINCH-
Day 9   BURGH   Forth
         Niddry   Bridges
         Castle

From the
Pentlands
         M8 from
         EDINBURGH
         + Day ?

144

BROXBURN

to

LINLITHGOW

Bart 45 OSLR 65
OSPF 406 (NT 07/17), 405 (NS 87/97)

The first full day of canal towpath walking, a fairly short day to allow time for exploring historic Linlithgow, and possibly visiting Cockleroy and Beecraigs. The Union Canal makes for easy walking as it follows a single contour line, and so has no locks or hills, a very unusual feature.

A UNION CANAL DAY

In the old days the lack of locks allowed travellers a speedy crossing between the cities of Edinburgh and Glasgow. The once-thriving service took as little as thirteen hours, and cost the equivalent of 7 ½ pence. At one time there were plans to run the canal through Princes Street Gardens in Edinburgh and down to Leith Docks, but fierce opposition blocked this extension.

The Union Canal opened in 1822, but with an inter-city railway coming in the 1840s it then began a century of decline. Now, for recreational purposes, the Union and the Forth and Clyde canals are slowly being brought back to life. Covered in a scum of weed, decades of litter, and overgrown, they are still a precious asset, and I hope all of us who walk their lengths will become champions in their defence and restoration.

Look out for details of construction. Bridges are numbered from Edinburgh and there are sixty-one of them, plus several new ones and of course, all those where the canal does the bridging, which is often much more exciting.

Tow ropes have often worn grooves into stonework, there are half-mile posts, wharves, winding-holes for turning boats and odd features on the bridges (which are, on the whole, much of a muchness). The smart new canal was nicknamed The Mathematical River, partly because it followed the one contour (240 feet, and also because it maintained a regular width (35 feet) and depth (5 feet). While on figures, in 1834 no fewer than 121,407 passengers travelled the canal. Meals, music, even gaming tables were provided to pass the time and there was a night sleeper service which was popular with both business men and honeymoon couples. The canal cost £400,000. Linlithgow Palace was garrisoned as the people were doubtful about the wild Irish navvies on their doorstep. Two have a deserved notoriety, their names Burke and Hare.

Leaving Broxburn walk back along the A899 (Main Street) to the Parish Church. Immediately before the kirk, turn left along Church Street. Ahead are the floodlights of Broxburn Athletic FC, with scabrous red wastes beyond. There is a big sports centre and children's play area to the left as we walk along. This whole area has had imaginative civic landscaping with a pleasant planting of trees and shrubs: rose, weigela, red thorns, golden-leaved elders, purple berberis. At the end of the houses we bear leftish, up the gated road, with football pitches (Buchan Park) on our right, and willows and aspens on our left. There is another gate, a bike track and a manège (equestrian riding arena), then the road ends by a launching slip on the Union Canal. Turn right and Bridge 28 is soon reached.

The canal is very silted up and cluttered with overmuch litter (black mark Broxburn!), nor are the red ash bings very attractive in their raw, disturbed state. All the more surprising then to find tits working through the alder and willow planting, moorhens fussing in the canal and foxgloves colonising the slopes beyond. A high percentage of the foxgloves are white, maybe due to the poverty of the soil or its chemical composition. Further along the canal are banks of scented stock. (In September the slopes of the bing chitter with the sound of explosive broom pods.) A canal is often an artery of life in an otherwise dead landscape. The brick-red colour of the bings is hardly surprising for much of this spoil has been turned into bricks, or used for land reclamation at Grangemouth or for motorway construction, etc. The word *bing* has its derivation in the Gaelic *ben*, meaning a hill.

Shale oil manufacturing was a typical Victorian enterprise. James 'Paraffin Young' first came to West Lothian in search of 'cannel coal' (candle coal – used for lighting as it burnt with such a bright flame), and this led on to developing a process to extract paraffin oil and wax from the oil-bearing shales. So the oil industry began here. At its peak there were 120 works (employing 13,000 workers), but by 1873 the number had dropped to thirty as the oil wells of the USA began to produce their black gold. Young died in 1883. The last works closed in 1962. Dr James Young was a chemical engineer from Glasgow. A fellow student who became a lifelong friend was David Livingstone, and much of the sponsorship for the latter's travels came from Young. Victoria had Falls named after her but there is a branch of the Lualaba named Young River. With our quiet setting (aircraft permitting), it is hard to imagine the atmosphere 150 years ago when dozens of chimneys poured smoke into the air. Grangemouth is quite modest in comparison to pictures of the old oil industry.

Bridge 29, abandoned and in poor state, is twinned with an equally abandoned railway bridge covered in inarticulate graffiti. (The closure of the shale works led to their decay.) As we walk on, a line of power poles runs overhead for a while; when these angle off there is a length of straight towpath for *c.*250 yards and just before the bend resumes, there is a break on the right (096737) which we take. (Niddry Castle is seen directly ahead on the straight bit.) A track comes to the canal at this point. Go through and left along this track to reach the minor road beside the bridge over the main Edinburgh–Glasgow railway line. Look over the bridge. The railway cutting is far, far deeper than the canal's! Further along it goes *under* Winchburgh.

NIDDRY CASTLE AND SUCCESSIVELY, RAILWAY LINE, UNION CANAL AND SHALE BING AT BROXBURN

Just over the bridge turn left along what is the drive of Niddry Castle, a rather stark tower standing below the man-made red-mountain. The castle was long undergoing restoration and, at the price of a donation, one could visit (Sundays 10.00–16.40, May–September, 0506-890753) to see the work in progress. There is an award-winning archaeological dig as well. (The castle has been put on the market, so its status may have changed. The right-of-way still leads past it however.)

Niddry Castle was built by the Seton family in 1490. Lord Seton was one of the gang who helped Mary Queen of Scots escape from Loch Leven Castle, and she was brought to Niddry, briefly, before the battle of Langside led to her final flight and imprisonment in England. Mary was three times as long a prisoner of Elizabeth as she was a free queen in Scotland. The castle was sold in 1676 and abandoned early the next century.

Trains are apt to go thundering past on the Edinburgh–Glasgow line which runs parallel to the canal most of the way to Falkirk. The train journey between capital and largest city takes well under an hour and speeds of 100 miles per hour are reached. The whole line is superbly engineered, having been built as a fast line in 1842. There are grand views of the Forth Valley and the Ochils and, if returning by this route at the end, there will be plenty of personal associations.

Skirt the castle on the right (east) to drop down onto the golf course,

WINCHBURGH: ROW OF OLD WORKERS' COTTAGES, NOW CAREFULLY PRESERVED

and cross it to walk up to Winchburgh on a path outside the golf course and below the shale 'mountain' (which is being quaried, slowly, and as yet only on the far side). It is worth wandering up this artificial hill for the view, and to see how nature is slowing greening-over the barren waste. They are beginning to be positive, rather than negative features in the landscape. I trust some will be allowed to survive, both as wildlife sanctuaries and monuments to an important industry.

If not interested in climbing the bing (not a Munro or even a Corbett) then continue on from the golf course (car park and Portacabin club house), aiming for the obvious white (masonic) hall building where the village begins. Castle Street goes up through the old mining 'rows', built in the 1890s and the foremost example of a mining community in Scotland, to the Main Road (the 1903 school is now a Day Centre). Plans are afoot to create a museum/trail connected with the oil industry. Turn left and walk along past the shops. The Star and Garter has a carved bird and the date 1903 on it. *The Buildings of Scotland* notes 'In the middle, a pompous Police Station, 1904'. It is now a pharmacy. There's a dragon on the cast iron gulley box. As a result of the Irish influx when the canal was built there is still a strong Catholic element in Winchburgh and the May Queen ceremony (last Sunday in May) has a distinctly continental atmosphere. The church is St Philomena's.

The Tally Ho (which does accommodation besides welcome refreshments) stands at a junction, and continuing, in the Linlithgow direction for 120 yards, brings us to the Union Canal again. The Tally Ho has many photographs of Winchburgh in the days when the oil and brickworks were in full swing. Bricks were much needed for buildings connected with the oil industry so it is ironic that industry's waste is now a source of raw material for brickmaking.

A footbridge has been added alongside the B9080 span and, like other Winchburgh bridges, seems to be used by locals for throwing their litter into the canal. Steps, on the other (north) side of the road, lead us back down to the towpath, a green tunnel of jungly growth and shading trees.

> *… woods whereto my soul,*
> *Out of the noontide beam,*
> *Flees for a refuge green and cool*
> *And tranquil as a dream.*
>
> (de la Mare)

*ONE OF THE STAGING POSTS ON THE
UNION CANAL, NORTH OF WINCHBURGH*

The next three miles of canal still have a jungly hold of trees, great on hot summer days, if a bit claustrophobic. About the only features are the bridges one goes under. I think I counted ten or eleven before there was the novelty of the canal bridging the road to enter Linlithgow. (A road goes under the canal at Philpstoun as well.) Steps or a scramble can lead one 'up for air' at most of the bridges.

CRAIGTON BRIDGE (NUMBER 35) ONE OF THE FINER BRIDGES ON THE UNION CANAL

There is a long wharf on the far side not long after rejoining the canal then, beyond Bridge 33 the second/third staging post marker. (Traffic was charged for by stages just as buses are now.) The canal bears quite a similarity to Kipling's 'great, green, greasy Limpopo River'. Bridge 34 has been rebuilt with modern concrete, but retains the number stone. A pre-Reformation parish here has all but disappeared. Priestinch, by the railway, is a hint of its existence and, by crossing the bridge to follow a woodland path (The Lady Walk) along the south bank, one can glimpse the gables of the ancient Auldcathie Church, marooned out in a refuse disposal landscape!

Keep to the south side path (unless very wet weather), parallel to the canal, to reach Craigton Bridge (No 35) which is better than most with some good stonework and decoration. It needs some care and attention though. Maybe we need enthusiasts to adopt canal bridges to look after their welfare. Bridge 36 is of redder sandstone, has no parapet at all and is overgrown and abandoned, as is the bigger Bridge 37. The stretch between them has clear 'kicking stones' - jutting stones running along between towpath and canal which allowed the horses to obtain purchase as they heaved at an angle, as they had to when towing heavily-laden barges.

Bridge 38 at Fawnspark has a car park beside it. The farm across the canal basin breeds Clydesdale horses, and if lucky you will see some of the delightful foals. This is a popular place for fishermen. The canal has pike, perch, roach and eels in plenty, also bream, tench and carp. A busy wee road crosses Bridge 38 so it has been strengthened with ties.

Beyond Fawnspark the canal becomes a bit like a railway cutting, being hemmed in by the last of the shale bings we'll encounter (bikes, with or without engines, find them a challenge). Concrete abutments on both sides point to a crossing at one time. Bridge 39 is reached as we emerge from the bings, crossed by a farm track and overhead power lines and best reached from the overflow weir just beyond. The road from Philpstoun southwards passes under the canal. A mere hamlet now it was a place entirely dependent on the oil industry. The name dates back to Philip d'Eu, a twelfth-century Norman who was granted land here. Swan feathers on the bank indicate a favourite preening spot. We noticed a scent of aniseed here – which comes from the feathery leaves of sweet Cicely (*Myrrhis odorata*), which grows all along the canal. So do brambles – a bonus for a September tramp. There's another underpass just beyond Philpstoun with great bites of semicircular masonary, now only linking fields.

We've had a slow transformation and the canal, from being deep in its private jungle, now runs along high, open country with fantastic views over the rolling Lowlands to the swelling Ochils on the skyline. The tower on the hill to the north is above The Binns, home of Tam Dalyell, the lively local M.P. An ancestor of the same name was a dreaded persecutor of the Covenanters. He was captured at the battle of Worcester, later reorganised the Russian army for the Tsar, won the battle of Rullion Green (1666) and raised the Scots Greys in 1681. They wore a grey cloth imported from the Netherlands, which the general ordered to try and make his men less conspicuous in the field (a use of camouflage that was not in general practice for another 200 years!). His portrait shows stern features and a huge white beard.

Overlooking the Forth Estuary beyond The Binns is ancient Blackness Castle and the palatial Hopetoun House, all worth visits on a more mobile trip. South of Bridge 40 is Champfleurie House, a French name.

Bridge 41, Kingscavil Bridge, was the site of one of the change houses along the canal. The name means the 'King's plot of land' but the house and estate early on belonged to the Hamiltons. Young, newly-wed, cheery Patrick Hamilton was to be burnt at the stake as the first martyr of the Reformation. Prince Charles slept in the old house in 1745 while his army lay at Threemiletown (Scots miles, longer than English). As we near Linlithgow we are passing below Pilgrim Hill, and the name St Magdalene was once that of a fair and hospice on the town's outskirts. The town has

THE UNION CANAL: THE MANSE BASIN, LINLITHGOW, BUSY WITH WEEKEND BOATS AND MUSEUM

spilled out in a huge, impersonal suburb, Springfield, which catches the eye (a sock in the eye?) as one nears the town. After Bridge 42 however we have the Palace and St Michael's in view.

LINLITHGOW, TOWN OF BLACK BITCHES

The canal passes over the B9080 as the town is reached. Below is what looks like a distillery with its pagoda-like towers, features which have been carefully preserved in turning the one time St Magdalene distillery into luxury modern houses. The 1960s saw much of historic interest swept away by the unimaginative local council, so this is a contrast. Liking or loathing is the reaction to the 1964 aluminium crown of thorns on top of St Michael's Kirk over beside the Palace. We come to the bowed parapet of another lane going under the canal. Immediately below is the station, then the flat roofs of the ugly Regent complex, one of the several so-with-it intrusions of twenty to thirty years ago which spoilt the character of the town. Beyond the grassy area is the Low Port primary school (once the Academy) with its turrets and glimpses of the loch. The Regent complex stands on the site of the old Nobel Works built in 1701, the Explosives Factory as it became in the world wars. ICI purchased the works and then closed them down in the sixties. The grassy area below the castle is called the Peel, there being such a defence long before stone castles were built. Originally the canal had hoped to make use of the loch but the need to keep to its contour prevented that. The Pugin Roman Catholic church and Laetare International Youth Centre lie east of the school.

THE SIXTEENTH-CENTURY DOOCOT, LINLITHGOW

Bridge 43 is our real entry to Linlithgow and its Manse Basin. Note how the corner of the bridge has been deeply worn into grooves by tow ropes. The canal comes to life here as there is a museum and a collection of craft. The museum is open on weekend afternoons and is the creation of LUCS, the Linlithgow Union Canal Society, an enthusiastic body of volunteers who have done much to revitalise this section of the canal, tidying the area, upgrading the towpath, rescuing everything old and interesting, running trips in the *Victoria* (a replica steam packet), and other old boats, hiring rowing boats and so on. The museum is a fascinating record of the canal's past and there is a short audio-visual presentation. If you are here midweek then you'll just have to return at a weekend!

From the basin we look over Strawberry Bank to a garden with a sixteenth-century beehive-type doocot holding 370 holes. It has stone courses sticking out to prevent rats climbing up, and a tiny door. Pigeons were popular in medieval times as they provided fresh meat in winter. Only nobles were allowed such, the common people just had old salted beef. There were no root crops then for winter feeding so each autumn animals were slaughtered – or driven south to English markets by some of the tracks we've been using.

Turn east from the garden to cut down a road, barred to traffic, which leads to the High Street after passing under the railway. The station is probably the best-preserved (and thoroughly modernised) on the Edinburgh–Glasgow/Stirling lines. There is a lively painting in the hall. Linlithgow had an ancient right to levy tolls which it had done on roads and then on the canal. The railway however refused to pay and despite various courts upholding the town, the House of Lords finally favoured no tolls for railways. The road comes out onto the High Street near the High Port, beside the Star and Garter, best viewed from across the road, but then return to the south side to walk along the High Street.

There is a charming portrait of Linlithgow in the titular essay, *Dreamthorp*, in a book written about 150 years ago which I'd enjoy quoting. The author, Alexander Smith, is still remembered for this coined title and for a second book *A Summer in Skye*. He was only thirty-seven when he died, in 1867.

> The several towns and villages in which, in my time, I have pitched a tent did not please, for one obscure reason or another but when, on a summer evening about the hour of eight, I first beheld Dreamthorp, with its westward-looking windows painted by sunset, its children playing in the single

straggling street, the mothers knitting at the open doors, the fathers standing about in long white blouses, chatting or smoking; the great tower of the ruined castle rising high into the rosy air, with a whole troop of swallows skimming about its rents and fissures; when I first beheld all this, I felt instinctively that my knapsack might be taken off my shoulders, that my tired feet might wander no more, that at last, on the planet, I had found a home. From that evening I have dwelt here, and the only journey I am like now to make, is the very inconsiderable one, so far at least as distance is concerned, from the house in which I live to the graveyard beside the ruined castle.

Robert Burns was less flattering, Linlithgow he said 'carries the appearance of rude, decayed, idle grandeur'. William and Dorothy Wordsworth stopped off for breakfast on the way to Edinburgh and the Borders at the end of their *Highland Tour*.

For centuries Linlithgow was an important leather-making centre and, like Selkirk, could be somewhat smelly. All the traditional industries have gone, though they are commemorated in the various guilds with their deacons. Linlithgow still elects a Provost and the people of the town, regardless of sex, are Black Bitches. A black bitch appears on the town's coat of arms. There are actually two coats of arms, the second portraying St Michael having a go at the dragon.

David I built a house here in the twelfth century, but like most Border or Central towns it suffered from the visits of several English armies. They burnt the town in 1424. But with the Stewarts came prosperity. James I began the building of the palace and most of his successors added to it. Mary Queen of Scots was born in the palace in 1542. When James VI became James I and flitted to London this became a neglected second home. Cromwell used it as barracks for nearly a decade. It hosted Bonnie Prince Charlie, but it was finally gutted after being occupied by Butcher Cumberland's troops. 1989 saw the burgh's 600th anniversary of receiving its charter from Robert II, at the time when, in England, the Black Prince's son was king and Chaucer was penning his tales. Linlithgow is twinned to Guyancourt, a town near Versailles. The population is now about 12,000, many working in the oil town of Grangemouth or Edinburgh or Glasgow.

But to return to our route at the east end of the High Street. The Star and Garter is an old coaching inn, a solid, square Georgian building. Walking along from it we come on St Michael's Well which has a stone dated 1720 and the words 'St Michael is kinde to straingers'. The figure above came from the earlier Cross Well.

Across the High Street are several sixteenth/seventeenth-century houses, the Hamilton Lands, restored by the National Trust for Scotland in 1958. Two have gables facing the street with steep red pantiles. Crow step gables were designed to allow beams to be placed across a roof which was too steep for ordinary construction. The whole of the East High Street is a mixture of styles and dates with the shocking 'stoppers' to east and west, a visual vandalism hard to conceive these days.

The Victoria Hall, when built in 1889, had hefty Gothic towers but these have gone as has the usefulness of the building. After the last war the hall was used as a cinema, then a bingo hall and now, its nadir surely, it is an amusement arcade.

Just before the Cross, above the sign of The Four Marys, is a tablet commemorating a Dr Waldie who introduced chloroform to Simpson and the medical profession. Continuing briefly along that side there are municipal/regional buildings with a fine example of a Provost's lamp. On the wall of the Sheriff Court is a tablet commemorating the assassination of the Regent Moray in 1570. Designed by Noel Paton it manages to spell Moray wrongly and has the wrong date!

This murder was one of the first-ever such deed using a firearm and was very carefully prepared, a sort of successful sixteenth-century 'day of the jackal'. Hamilton of Bothwellhaugh, after firing the shot, made his escape to the continent and, cashing in on the deed, became a professional hit-man. The Archbishop, whose house he'd used, was hung.

The town centres round the Cross Well. Cross and Gibbet have long gone, and the well has had a chequered history being rebuilt in 1659 after being damaged by Cromwell's troops. In 1807 it was completely rebuilt, copying the old design, the work being done by a one-handed stonemason.

The original Town House was also destroyed by Cromwell, but rebuilt by the king's master mason John Mylne in 1668. Fire damaged it in 1847 when its Italian-style arched portico was replaced by popular wrought-iron work. The present double stairway superseded this in 1907. The well-stocked and helpful Tourist Information Office is housed here and is worth visiting. If you have not done so already they can book local accommodation.

The Kirkgate leads up from the Cross to reach the Palace gateway. Panels above have the painted and gilded coats of arms of the Orders of the Garter, the Golden Fleece, St Michael (all conferred on James V) and the Thistle (which James V is thought to have founded). The porch at

Abbotsford was based on this entrance – Scott also cribbed bits of Melrose Abbey and Stirling Castle quite apart from accumulating original old features. Through the arch, on the right, is St Michael's Parish Church, a large cathedral-like building with a long history. Dedicated in 1242 most of it dates to a rebuilding after a 1424 fire. Its main fame is perhaps the window tracery, notably in the St Katharine's Aisle where James IV saw the ghost (a put-up by his worried wife?) who warned of impending doom if he marched an army south – to Flodden as it proved. The Reformation took its toll of the decorative statuary, Cromwell actually quartered his troopers and their horses there, and it accommodated Edinburgh students during the plague winter of 1645–46. There's a mortsafe lid still lying on the Livingston vault.

The Creation Window is dedicated to the leader of the Challenger Expedition which explored the world's oceans last century, and the huge window depicts a vast range of animals, birds and fish, including a lobster – red in colour!

Most heart-rending is the story behind the child Samuel window for it commemorates the little daughter of a previous minister who died when her hair caught fire as she dried it before a blazing fire in the Manse. A sister had

THE CROSS WELL, LINLITHGOW

previously died when she went through the ice while skating on the loch with her fiancé.

Linlithgow Palace's most famous tale is its capture for Robert the Bruce by a local farmer William Binnie who regularly used to deliver hay to the garrison. One day he hid men under the hay and stopped the cart in the entrance so the portcullis and gates couldn't operate. More men rushed in – and the palace was won.

Edward I had built a peel and the name survives in the parklands round the palace. These have seen many uses, but it is thought the water level was originally higher, leaving the palace almost on an island. Yellow water lilies have flowered in it for hundreds of years, and it is a bird sanctuary, an SSSI, and used for boating and sailing. Hundreds of swans sometimes gather in winter so the air rings with 'the bell-beat of their wings' (Yeats).

The complex story of the palace building I'll leave you to learn from one of the booklets available. You may find the human guide is a ten year old 'monk'. I'd love to see much more rebuilt and *used*. Buildings were never meant to be fossils.

The wider Western High Street has attractive features and, once the rebuilding of the hideous sixties 'boxes' on the north side is completed, should look very attractive. That such flat-roofed, un-Scottish erections were permitted was sad (they were even given a Saltire Award!), and bad enough they are now having to be restored after only thirty years. They replaced houses centuries old. This is often the story though: the Roman Wall was

THE FOUR CRESTS ABOVE THE ENTRANCE TO LINLITHGOW PALACE

only seen to be valuable fifty years too late to save much of its structure, the canal was only seen as a valuable resource after the M8 and other crass developments had smashed sections of it.

Walk along to the restored sixteenth-century West Port House and back if you like. The New Well still stands though as many as ten wells once gave rise to that jingle 'Lithgow for wells'.

BEECRAIGS AND COCKLEROY

If Linlithgow has been reached early enough a side trip to Cockleroy is well worthwhile. This is a hill to the south, in the Bathgate Hills as they tend to be called, and though only 278 metres (912 feet), like the Eildons or Peniel Heugh, the view is out of all proportion to the altitude. Allow three to four hours for the round trip.

Start at the Manse Basin (Bridge 43) and walk up Manse Road. Once clear of the suburbs a road branches right for Bathate, but we keep on for Riccarton. Cockleroy is visible to the south-west, a whaleback of green. Oddly our road wiggles down for a bit. There's a farm drive going off right at the bottom, and about 250 yards on there is a signpost at a stile to the right, 'Public path to Beecraigs'. We take this, aiming for the apex of the field, just

LINLITHGOW PALACE AND ST MICHAEL'S CHURCH FROM THE EAST

left of the trees running along above the farm of Hillty. Nearing the farm you'll see it is an interesting old building (the seventeenth-century home of a Seton who served Gustav III in Sweden). Just inside the wood at the top corner there are some steps.

Head on up the edge of the field, briefly, to a gate, turn left through it and then right immediately to continue up a sort of 'green lane'. After about fifty yards there is a rough cross-tracks. Bear left and just follow the path (odd steps) up the crest of a spur. The whole landscape here, though well-disguised by the thorn trees, is artificial in that it has been shaped by limestone workings. The cutting on the right for instance suddenly disappears (allowing access to fields, but we keep on up leftish) only to reappear as a bigger, deeper gash in the bottom of which are some large quarried caverns, very easy to miss unless consciously looking for them. The curious can scramble down for a closer look.

The path comes out onto a minor road at a junction where our continuation is signposted 'Beecraigs Loch'. The fields to the east and down round the Loch are used for grazing red deer, which may be visible. The caravan/camping site lies right, among the trees, then, first left, is the Country Park Centre where you can pick up a leaflet to the park and look at the various displays.

From the far corner of the car park there is a walkway down to the

RED DEER AT THE BEECRAIGS COUNTY PARK

loch which is designed to allow clear observation of the deer. They are not tame animals or pets in any way, but are farmed commercially just like cattle or sheep, or like the trout at the fish farm beside the loch where we come out on this route. From the fish farm walk on round the south side of the loch, to reach the Loch car park at the loch's western side, which is at the foot of the road we were walking down before the Park Centre turn off. If missing this interesting diversion there is a path just inside the wood on the right which offers softer walking than the tarmac.

South of the Loch is a field archery course, the toxophilite equivalent to a golf course except arrows are loosed instead of balls lost. There are fishing, sailing and canoeing courses based on the Loch with its tree-covered Dagger Island, orienteering chances everywhere, pony trails and even a climbing wall, details of which can be had from the Park Centre, 0506-844516.

From the top of the Loch car park take an unmarked footpath up a break in the trees. At a T-junction turn left along to join a forest road. There is a small bridge over a tiny burn immediately before. Turn right and, ignoring any branching tracks to right or left, keep on up alongside the burn which is eventually crossed by a wee stone bridge to reach the Balvornie car park.

Cross the minor road to pick up the way marked 'Cockleroy Walk' (pale blue arrows). It heads off into the trees from beside the toilet block beyond the pond, pleasant and gentle walking. Keep an eye open though, for the marked route suddenly breaks off at right angles to head right, and then left up to another tarred road with the Cockleroy car park on the other side. Cross to the path heading on into the forest from the map board; it becomes a dark tunnel so there is a sharp contrast to suddenly come out to the breezy open hillside beyond (gate/stile). A five minute steep ascent lands one on the summit of Cockleroy with its view indicator, trig point and 360° panorama which some will rate the best view of the whole trip.

Eye-catching, for us especially, is the unmistakable wide saddle of the Cauldstane Slap. The rock fin of Binny Craig, the crouching lion shape of Arthur's Seat, the hunky stump of the Bass Rock all lie to the east. Working anti-clockwise, the Forth Bridges are well seen, the Lomonds are bold, behind Linlithgow are the Cleish Hills, then the long horizon of the Ochils. The big, high chimney is that of the Longannet Power Station. Grangemouth is a jungle of chimneys and cooling towers and, beyond, is the Kincardine Bridge. (The dusk view when all these areas are lit up is quite spectacular.) Running away to the west are the Campsie Fells (our walk finishes where the left edge dips down) while real Highland hills poke their heads over: Ben Vorlich, Ben Ledi, Ben More (Crianlarich), Ben Venue, Ben Lomond. Balancing the Bass Rock in the Forth, a clear day may reward with a view of the ragged peaks on the Isle of Arran in the Clyde Estuary.

Nearer, below us to the south-west, is the obvious Lochcote Reservoir. Not so obvious, but between it and craggy Bowden Hill to the north, lies a flat area which was a loch till drained last century. A *crannog* (lake dwelling) was discovered then. Just to be different Beecraigs Loch is man-made, the work of Prisoners of War during World War I. Both Cockleroy and Bowden Hill summits are the sites of prehistoric forts, though there is nothing much to see. Quite magnificent however is the excavated and preserved multi-period prehistoric henge, circles and tomb on Cairnpapple Hill, due south, next to the obvious relay mast – one of the Top Ten prehistoric sites in Scotland so *nota bene* for a future visit. The knobbly nature of these hills is akin to what we saw north of the Cheviots, and points to the same volcanic origins.

The grassy depression on Cockleroy is called Wallace's Cradle. The patriot used the hill as an observation post and safe spot in the dangerous Lowlands where all his days were spent. He held a parliament at Torphichen, another historic site to visit one day.

Cockleroy is not a French hybrid word but murdered Gaelic, *cochull-ruadh*, the red cowl. This waist-of-Scotland not surprisingly is a real mix of

PART OF THE WIDE PANORAMA ON TOP OF COCKLEROY. LINLITHGOW LOCH LIES BELOW AND THE HILLS OF FIFE BEYOND

Gaelic, Norman and old British names – and some guid Scots ones too like Burghmuir or Cauldhame. Beecraigs is also Gaelic in origin, from *beithe* (pronounced bey) meaning birch.

Cockleroy has a very personal association now as it was the last hill climbed by Storm, my canine partner on so many adventures – ever since his walk from John o' Groats to Land's End when we went through the Slap and the Borders to pick up the Pennine Way. He was with me for all the canal explorations, his very last day's walk being over and round the Avon viaduct area with the canal ranger. Deaf, going blind and a bit unstable on his legs, he went on a lead whenever we crossed a viaduct – for my peace of mind. He romped as ever, but thirty-six hours later had a heart attack. Walking the route through shortly after was a cruel reminder of a marvellous companion who was known to so many walkers.

Head off northwards on the bare crest of the hill (Longannet chimney ahead) until it steepens, when one can peel off down right by a small copse of trees and on in the same direction, aiming for the near top corner of a big, long rectangular field (the reservoir is at the far top corner). The field arrangement is not as per Pathfinder map, and one comes on a fence in the way, but there's only a slight diversion along it to a gate at the far end.

Follow down outside this big field initially until a wall crosses our bows. There's a water trough and a stile takes us over to walk down the edge of the big field which is abandoned further on to join the drive from Williamcraigs. The exit is not too obvious, but is just a little below the bottom level of the clump of trees on the other side of the field. The drive passes a walled entrance, beyond which, on the left, is the top of the golf course. Descend to the club house. The road then does some wiggling down to creep under the canal but we can head onto the south bank and follow a footpath eastwards for a short distance before crossing the next bridge (No 46) onto the more familiar north bank. This leads along above what looks like a factory but is a school (Linlithgow Academy). The tall spire is that of the old Free Church of St Ninian's, near the West Port.

The next bridge may or may not be a bridge. It was filled in, blocking navigation, when the canal was closed but in 1991 work started to rebuild it so the dramatic six miles west can be enjoyed by canal-users. Hopefully it will be a proper Bridge (45) again in the early life of this guide. Back gardens entertain us along to Bridge 47 (its number is hidden under a boxed-in-pipeline), and so back to the Manse Basin and Bridge 43.

If time is a bit short then a taxi could be taken to either the Beecraigs' Loch or Balvornie car parks so at least Cockleroy could be climbed.

PRACTICAL INFORMATION: LINLITHGOW

Tourist Information Centre, Burgh Halls, the Cross, 0506-844600. Open all year.
Telephone code for Linlithgow numbers is 0506-

ACCOMMODATION: Accommodation is adequate but July and August can be busy as can the time of the Riding The Marches, held each year 'on the first Tuesday after the second Thursday in June'. There is a wide range of cafe and pub facilities, several 'carry oots' but a sorry lack of restaurants open in the evening.

Hotels: West Port, -847456, Star and Garter, -845485.

B & Bs: 23 Friarsbrae, -842667 (south of Bridge 44), Teviotdale, Union Road, -847188 (between the railway and High Street). 130 Barons Hill Avenue, -843746 (east off Blackness Road). 137 Barons Hill Avenue, -843903, 13 Carse Knowe, -845328 (further east, off Springfield Road), 43 Clarendon Crescent, -842574 (off Manse Road). Jock's Hill House, -845698 (west of the loch), 11 Jock's Hill Crescent, -842866 (west of the loch), St Anne's, St Ninian's Road, -842509 (west of the loch), 51 Braehead Terrace, -844915 (south-west beyond the Academy).

Outside town: Williamcraigs, -845470 (high above the golf course), (985754) Woodcockdale Farm, -842088 (just off Bridge 48 northwards), (974759) Belsyde Farm, -845328 (further south (976754).

CAMPING: Loch House Farm, -842144 (off A706 out towards Bo'ness, west of the loch just over the M9). Beecraigs Country Park, -844516 (April–September; high above the town).

TAXIS: -845313, -845476.

MEALS: Surprisingly limited in town. Most rural B & Bs will provide dinner if required, West end of town has a popular pizza/curry/chips carry-out establishment and there is an Indian restaurant at Linlithgow Bridge.

LINLITHGOW

to

FALKIRK

Bart 45 OSLR 65
OSPF 405 (NS 87/97)

This is a relatively easy day, entirely along the Union Canal to its end at Falkirk. Accommodation being limited the best option is to return to Linlithgow, which allows today to be walked lightly laden. If not already undertaken the walk up Cockleroy would be a pleasant evening extra.

A DAY ON THE UNION CANAL

Pick up the Union Canal and head west again. Bridge 45 (Preston Road), while still a conduit, had its road approaches marked by a warning triangle with a swan symbol, the first of its kind, and the result of a schoolboy's lobbying the authorities.

We soon shake clear of the town and the views remain extensive as we skirt the hills to the south, the 'Lowland Trossachs', of Cockleroy and Bowden Hill with Beecraigs Country Park and Torphichen hidden in their folds. Bridge 46 marks one route off Cockleroy (already described), and then there is the road passing under the canal, which leads to the hilly golf course to the south. A pipeline over the canal is more obvious at this point. Another underpass from the derelict Kettlestoun Mains leads to long-abandoned quarries. (Building stone for the New Town of Edinburgh was an important part of the canal's trade.) A collapsed section of canal (blocked off and filled with vegetation) is also due for renovation, so we may soon see the LUCS boats cruising out to the great Avon aqueduct.

Over to the right we see the impressive railway viaduct.

Some cobbling leads to the next bridge which has a wrong 45 carved on the east side and 47, correctly, on the west. This is a much-repaired small bridge, with bricks replacing parapet or railings, and is the drive to Williamcraigs (B & B). The A706 runs close to the canal for a bit.

On the other side a concrete structure may be noticed. This is an intake for a stream which angles down more or less parallel to the canal. When not needed the stream runs through below the canal as a scramble down the bank would show. Fifty yards on is Woodcockdale, one of the old change houses where relays of horses for towing would be changed over. The human carriers had priority over goods barges to the extent of having a rising, sharpened prow to cut through any tow ropes that got in the way. A horseman usually went ahead to clear the way less dramatically. The building has been well preserved. At present it is used by the 1st West Lothian Sea Scouts but there are plans to turn it into a riverside pub. Woodcockdale is a very English-sounding name but is first noted as such in 1491.

Bridge 48 is a much-patched one, as the A706 takes a hammering from heavy traffic. Under the bridge, on the south side, there is a 'stop-

WOODCOCKDALE – CHANGE HOUSE WHEN THE CANAL WAS FULLY OPERATING.
SEVERAL SWAN FAMILIES ENJOY THIS AREA

gate', rather like a solitary lock gate. This helps to regulate levels if there are fluctuations and can cut off sections of the canal to allow them to dry out for maintenance work – as will happen for the Kettlestoun restoration effort.

There's a winding basin and ruined landing stage not far beyond Bridge 48. A swan's nest sits at its edge. Somewhere along here is the boundary between two swan family territories. In 1990 there were six or seven cygnets raised by each pair. All the swans are ringed and studied. In winter they tend to gather on Linlithgow Loch – or live on the eastern seaboard anywhere between Montrose Basin and Northumberland.

The next stretch has a sad number of dead and dying elm trees, the result of the lethal Dutch elm disease. This is caused by a fungus which, once into a tree, stops the water rising and kills it eventually. The spores are transferred by clinging to the hairs of a specific beetle which then lays its eggs *under* the bark of elm trees, a sad cycle which has defeated all efforts at control – so we have these stark skeleton trees lining the banks.

The canal puts in a bend, and we find ourselves suddenly confronted by its most spectacular engineering feature, the great Telford-inspired Avon Aqueduct. Only Telford's 1805 Pont-y-Cysyllte aqueduct is larger.

THE GRANDEST AQUEDUCT IN SCOTLAND AS THE UNION CANAL IS CARRIED OVER THE AVON VALLEY

The 1823 *Companion* declares 'This noble edifice, which, for magnificence, is scarcely equalled in Europe, consists of twelve arches, is nearly 900 feet in length and 85 in height...The woody glens, the rugged heights, and the beautiful Alpine scenery around, must raise sensations of pleasure in every feeling heart'. The writer would have found the imposing twenty-three arched railway viaduct (also Telford's) downstream less to his delight. The coming of the railway was the death knell of the canal. Both are impressive. The railway viaduct is much more visible however. Distant views of the aqueduct are masked by the huge trees that choke the Avon banks. Upstream is the Muiravonside Country Park.

Avon waters drain from the Bathgate hills to the River Forth. Half a mile below here an old priory was largely washed away by one spate, so only a gable stands on the edge of the dell. In pre-glacial times the Avon flowed through what is now Linlithgow Loch to reach the sea at Blackness.

Beyond the railway viaduct is the site of the Battle of Linlithgow Bridge, 1526, when the Earl of Lennox was killed after being captured in an abortive attempt to rescue the young James V (born in Linlithgow) from the clutches of the Earl of Angus, the head of the notorious Douglases. The Avon was much used for driving mills and last century saw several paper mills established. Thomas Chambers, from Peebles, owned the Lochmill works and introduced spectacular machinery. The Chambers Hall was his gift to the town.

The aqueduct is still spectacular and, from below, very graceful. It was only possible thanks to Telford's ingenuity in using an iron trough to carry the water instead of the usual puddled (kneaded) clay, which was

MUIRAVONSIDE CHURCHYARD – A QUARRYMAN'S GRAVESTONE
SHOWING A QUARRYMAN HARD AT WORK

much heavier and just couldn't be carried on slender, practical arches. Once across on the north side, if you go down a little, you'll see a grated opening which allows inspection access to the interior of the viaduct. Inspectors can walk across *inside!*

If pioneering techniques went into these canals some of the ships to use them were historic. Henry Bell's famous *Comet*, the world's first practical seagoing steamship, was brought through the Forth and Clyde Canal for her first overhaul at Bo'ness, where Bell had served his apprenticeship. The spectators ran from the harbour as she arrived. They assumed, from the smoke, that the ship was on fire and might blow up at any moment.

Not far beyond the aqueduct there is a milestone marked '7 ½' (to Falkirk) and '24' (to Edinburgh). Note how the pointed side faces the canal so passing barges could read both facets at a glance. The pillar next to it is rarer, being another of the four 'stage' posts, the last if heading west. On the other side of the canal there was once a dry dock. The stern of the last remaining steel barge can be seen in the dock, but is so rusted at water level as to be beyond salvaging. The dock worked very simply by just stopping the end next to the canal, and then releasing the water inside which drained down into the Avon valley. The modern house that can be glimpsed sits on the site of an old canal cottage. Study has shown that the swans nesting by the dry dock have been there for at least ten years. They eat floating duckweed which tends to accumulate in sheltered spots like this. The canal is very rich in pond life as can be imagined. Immediately before the next bridge, there is another stretch with clear kicking stones.

A couple of minutes beyond Bridge 49 there is yet another area of major interest. Abutments on both banks point to a railway crossing, and then (on the far side) one can look in to a large square basin, the Causewayside or Slamannan basin. Coal was transferred here to barges, the lines jutting out over the basin, so, when the doors were opened, the coal fell straight into the holds. The railway will be mentioned later. There are plans afloat to restore something of past activity here (once the blockages to Linlithgow are cleared) with a charabanc ride linking canal and Bo'ness steam line, a delightful prospect. The Manuel (Emmanuel) Mine has now disappeared.

Not long after Bridge 50 there are signs of yet another old railway crossing, then Bridge 51, alas, is also a culvert and thus a barrier to canal traffic. There's a picnic site on the south bank. Cross this minor road, but, instead of returning to the towpath, walk up the side road signposted for

Muiravonside church: a rather stark building but there are many clear and interesting gravestones of the late eighteen-century. Continue up the lane between the church and its graveyard extensions to reach the Kirk Bridge (No 52) over the canal: a good viewpoint for Stirling Castle, the Ochils and Saline Hills (pronounced *sal-in*), and with the familiar shapes of Stuc a' Chroin and Ben Vorlich visible. The extensive Manuel Works (refractories, terracotta products, etc) lie beyond the graveyards and, in the middle of this sprawl, is the square tower of Almond Haining or Castle, once a seat of the Earls of Linlithgow and Callendar, but derelict for over 200 years. There have been several attempts to buy the castle in order to restore it, but the owners refuse to sell or do anything themselves, a sorry state of affairs.

The A801 road, linking M8 and M9 is a new creation and has a picnic area beside it in case you feel deprived of fumes and the frantic motor world. Turn leftish to cross the road. The canal is sadly culverted and, being new, does not figure in the original numberings. Opening the canal here again will be a big task.

Bethankie Bridge follows; this time the canal does the bridging, and the feature is easily overlooked as there is just a short curve of parapet. The old road goes under a six and a half feet arch, and another arch crosses a burn which then goes under the road.

We have a clear view down on the vast array of cooling towers, etc, that mark Grangemouth, but they soon drop out of sight as we walk this open stretch, the railway in a cutting beside us and new Polmont houses ahead. Despite the feeling of suburbia only a farm track crosses Bridge 53 and we hardly see Polmont thereafter as we enter a hemmed-in cutting leading to the large span of Bridge 54. An iron pedestrian bridge has been

THE OCHILS AND GRANGEMOUTH, WHICH WE ONLY NOTICE IF WE LEAVE THE CANAL

added on the west side. There is a derelict wharf, an overflow into a burn, and the usual urban litter. One is at a loss to know why people cannot put litter in their dustbins rather than carry it out and dump it in the nearest piece of wood or water. West Lothian had plenty of these squalid sites/sights, but the worst comes in the next few miles with the bridges vandalised, covered in graffiti and often with pipes and other additions.

A modern, concrete footbridge is followed by a sharp bend then we are looking down onto the railway again, with sidings and a yard, as here the lines to Stirling and Glasgow diverge, the former going by Falkirk Grahamston station, the latter by Falkirk High. Somewhere near here, in 1984, a commuter train on the Edinburgh–Glasgow run was derailed with the loss of thirteen lives – after hitting a cow which had strayed onto the track.

Bridge 55 is a messy area with a pipe crossing, the bridge walls a mass of graffiti, and all sorts of junk, from furniture to car parts, dumped into the water. Beyond, on the other side, is the high-wire enclosure of an HM Borstal Institution, which seems eminently suitable. Beyond the next bridge, 56, we lose the towpath as there is a road alongside an industrial estate. The canal is wider (like an elongated basin), there is a small overflow outlet, a winding basin, an exotic swan's nest, a swing bridge and a tinkers' village. Then the scenery reverts to deep rural again!

Bridges 57 (a pipe on brick pillars on front of it) and 58 lead from nowhere to nowhere, hardly even marked by farm use, but the rural is ended by the massed jumble of Hallglen Estate, as architecturally grim as the Borstal, with its off-white uniformity and cellular structure. Who needs barbed wire? Bridge 59 somehow hasn't made the OS maps, not that it is much of a bridge: the number is missing from the east arch, parapet stones lie in the water and it has its share of graffiti too.

There is quite a deep, wooded dell on the right and an overflow cobbled area exits through a wall with square holes in it. A second bit of walling is the parapet of the canal passing over the Glen Burn itself. This is actually a very beautiful sweep of the canal – only the three miles of Polmont are soiled and sad – and slowly, unobtrusively, the trees close in and we are walled in deeper and deeper. Two unusually big, and high, bridges follow in quick succession: Number 60 being the B8028, and Number 61, the Glen Bridge, no doubt the most photographed of all the Union Canal bridges because of the faces.

There are carved faces above the key stones, that on the east is radiant and smiling, that on the west glum and miserable. Accounts vary as

BRIDGE 61, THE SMILING AND THE GRUMPY FACES

to their meaning. Did one smile at the long miles built from the capital? Did the other grimace at the work just ahead in creating what was probably the first-ever transport tunnel in Scotland? Above the faces are ovals with the number 61 and the date 1821. Along the 100 yards leading up to the tunnel are the best examples of kicking stones on the canal.

There was really no need of a tunnel but the eighteenth-century industrialist William Forbes who had bought Callendar House (forfeited from the Jacobite Livingstones) objected to the proposed route, as it was too near to the palatial chateau he was making out of the old house. (The building and its parklands now belong to Falkirk District Council. There's a good stretch of Antonine Wall visible in the park.)

A 633 yard tunnel was quite a construction feat when you think it was cut by navvies working with horses at best – and none of today's power tools. The tunnel can be quite dark, but seldom so dark you can't carry on. There is a very sturdy rail for safety. (Which did not help my old dog Storm on one occasion for he walked overboard and had to be hauled out by the scruff of the neck.) Some water drips from the roof, and far enough along to be seen, there is a thick pillar and base boss – a sort of stalactite.

One comes out from the tunnel to a park-like area, with tidy grass verges and well-made paths, Falkirk's vast sprawl half-glimpsed and a view to distant Ochils. There is a basin before the Bantaskine or Walker's Bridge (No 62 – which is the last), and the towpath is even tarred. A nice moment comes when the screening on the right finishes and there is a close view of the Campsies. Ben Ledi lies to the right of their sprawl.

THE MANY FACETS OF FALKIRK

The slopes above Bridge 62 saw the last Jacobite success in 1746. There is nothing to see on the ground, some of which is built over. The monument is a crude concrete obelisk. Lord George Murray managed to surprise Hawley, who was camped at Falkirk, and drove his forces back to Edinburgh. The Jacobites then moved to Stirling. And Falkirk was no doubt glad to see them all away. That was in a windy, sleety January battle. Culloden came three months later. The Livingstones, Earls of Linlithgow, had Jacobite leanings and were forfeited after the Fifteen but the Falkirk 'Bairns' (as the town folk are still called) refused to pay rent to the York Building Company and the estate was leased back to the Countess of Kilmarnock, the Livingstone's heiress and her husband, who came 'out' for Prince Charles, was captured and beheaded. Ironically, Hawley was dining with the widow when the Jacobites attacked his forces. Callendar House saw most of the regular figures of note: Mary Queen of Scots, Cromwell, (it was Monck's Scottish HQ) and Charles Edward Stewart, en route for Derby. One of the unenthusiastic participants in the battle was the Gaelic poet Duncan Ban MacIntyre who is forever linked with Ben Dorain. An earlier Livingstone was principal guardian of Mary Queen of Scots and the nobles at Callendar House in Falkirk had to decide if she and Edward, son of Henry VIII, should be betrothed. They decided no, and Mary went off to France for safety. One of her Four Maries was Mary Livingstone.

The first bloody battle of Falkirk was back in the time of the Wars of Independence. The battle here was the sad end to Wallace's efforts to free Scotland from English interference. He had finally succeeded in driving out all the English garrisons, had been appointed 'Guardian of Scotland' and carried fire and sword into Northern England. Edward 1 was in Flanders (fighting the French king over lands he held from him) but was forced to return and invade Scotland in 1298. Wallace's smaller, less-trained force was caught at Falkirk and, despite bloody resistance, was simply massacred by the sheer weight of English numbers and the deadly longbow which weakened the 'schiltrons' of fierce spearsmen. Wallace fought on, tried in vain for continental support and, on his return, was betrayed. Edward had him barbarously hung, drawn and quartered as a 'traitor' which ensured he has been revered ever since. In the dirty political game of the time only Wallace the visionary but practical warrior, and James Douglas, never gave any alliance to Edward the Hammer. A remarkable man.

This central corridor of the country was much fought over, for Stirling was the lowest bridging point and so forced communications in that

THE SPLIT AT THE END OF THE UNION CANAL. OFF RIGHT LIES THE TERMINAL BASIN AND IN FRONT THE LINE OF THE FLIGHT OF LOCKS LEADING DOWN TO THE JUNCTION WITH THE FORTH AND CLYDE CANAL

direction, for good or ill. We seldom remember how greatly history is affected by geography, both in the big events and battles and in everyday social activity and trade. Falkirk as the 'epicentre of Scotland' could hardly escape. Now it is a town of 40,000 inhabitants and a busy place despite the decline of older industries. Coal mines and iron foundries made it a leader in the Industrial Revolution. The Carron Iron Works, established in 1760, later gave their name to 'carronade', a light gun used by many navies. (The works are now defunct.)

The approaching end of the canal can be judged by a white vehicle barrier across the towpath, just before a ramp in the bank where small boats can be launched and, angling off down right, a dirt road, which we will take briefly. The Union Canal has kept to its contour for all its thirty-one miles but here, of necessity, there were eleven locks to take it down to join the Forth and Clyde Canal at Port Downie Basin (a drop of 110 feet/33.5 metres). The locks no longer exist but if we walk down the dirt track to the first opening in the trees, on the left, we can see the remains of one of the locks. From there cut back up onto the canal towpath and walk on again. Shortly after, the canal just stops, a rather odd sensation, after our miles of walking along its banks. The *Govan Seagull* may be moored there, one of the Seagull Trust boats which takes parties of disabled people for cruises on

THE ORIGINAL 'UNION' OF THE CANALS – FORTH AND CLYDE ON THE RIGHT, AND THE NOW FILLED-IN PORT DOWNIE BASIN AND THE LOCKS OF THE UNION, LEFT (PHOTO: COURTESY STRATHKELVIN DISTRICT LIBRARIES)

the Union.

From this anti-climax spot turn down the road, which soon swings left under a tall brick railway viaduct (the lower end of the dirt road comes out just before the viaduct – the line of the linking locks). A broad, grass-lined road leads on but after a few minutes note Tamfourhill Road on the left as this is our continuation westwards. We soon complete the link with the Union Canal. This lies just beyond the Barr's factory and, perhaps most welcome, is the historic *Union Inn*, beside Lock 16, where the canal union once took place (Port Downie). The inn is a three storey, ashlar-fronted Georgian building which must have seen a hectic century during the joint canals' period of life (1822–1933). Sunday afternoon cruises are operated from here in the summer by the local canal society.

The Forth and Clyde Canal had a longer life span than the Union – from 1790 to 1962, a complex history completely ruled by commercial activities. Work started in 1768 under John Smeaton and the canal ran to thirty-nine miles, including a four mile city link. In the days of sail not having to go north around Scotland was a great boon. The Industrial Revolution gave increased traffic – until the new fangled railways proved cheaper, and the canal declined steadily, the last passenger services (*Gypsy Queen*) halting with the war. The canal was officially closed in 1963. Sadly new roads, etc, were built across it and now that leisure use is increasing there are frustrating 'gaps' in the navigation. However, the British Waterways Board are slowly bringing much of it back to life. And to us it offers a superb walkway, green and full of life, with views which will delight. Canal enthusiasts might like to spend some time at the end in Glasgow to see the magnificent Kelvin Aqueduct and the flight of five locks at Maryhill, major works which have been declared Ancient Monuments! They were built with monies raised from the forfeited Jacobite estates after the 'Forty-Five.

Perhaps the most enjoyable walk into the centre of Falkirk is to keep to the flight of locks dropping eastwards. There are thirteen in all down to Bainsford, north of the town, with the first five forming a regular flight down to the A803 through Camelon. Lock 14 has a coping stone at the tail of the lock inscribed 'Repaired by J Wyse 181?' (last figure is now illegible). The Rosebank Distillery lies across the A803. The canal is culverted but facing the road, on our left, is the rounded 'prow' of the brick-built distillery warehouse, now a restaurant. Round the far side of this restored building are the British Waterways offices where, if you have not obtained them yet, you can pick up some interesting literature on the canals. The canal rangers are based here and, in summer, they lead a series of excellent exploratory walks.

THE FAMOUS UNION INN AT LOCK 16 – WHERE THE UNION CANAL MET THE FORTH AND CLYDE CANAL

From the roundabout follow the A803 for a mile into town. The last mile or two of towpath give only a glimpse of the size and character of Falkirk. Falkirk and its surrounding towns are part of a huge sprawl of heavy industry, oil refineries, vast housing schemes and a jumble of chaotic urban development and clashing building styles. The river and town of Carron were the heart of the boom years of foundries, furnaces and factories.

It was an East Lothian entrepreneur who began this industrial revolution, but his local mine-owner would not reduce prices to make production viable. The famous Abyssinian traveller, Bruce of Kinnaird, had pits near Falkirk and *he* delivered the goods. So Carron, now swallowed up in Falkirk, became the heavy iron industry centre of Falkirk.

Roman camps, town walls and old buildings have all gone but many eighteenth-century buildings are now carefully preserved, there is a Town Trail for pedestrians (and a longer Town circuit for motorists), an excellent museum and the rebuilt town centre, of huge glass and concrete modernity, is well surrounded by parks and gardens.

Of interest to walkers were the annual Falkirk's Trysts, the largest cattle marts in the country. The scale was enormous: 60,000 cattle and 100,000 sheep are said to have been sold in one day. The drovers' routes, from the remotest Highlands, are one of our treasured legacies. The Highlands were peopled then of course, but this does show a level of population and production that could be obtained again were the powers that be genuinely interested in the Highland economy which stutters along on a selfish, feudal, system of land ownership inimical with past history and future hopes. Beasts could not be fed in winter so the great trysts saw the surplus sold off. Many were walked on to the industrial cities of England, or even to Smithfield Market. The tryst was held to the south-east and moved to Rough Castle and finally to Stenhousemuir, whose earlier name was Sheeplees.

As we walk in to Falkirk, the A803 Camelon Road is lined with large mansions, and, on the left, the attractive Dollar Park, named after Robert Dollar who left it to the town. He was a Falkirk Bairn who emigrated to Canada last century and made a fortune. There are plenty of flowers and mature trees, and the large glasshouses produce nearly ¼ million bedding plants each year for use in the District. Beside the pavement stands the war memorial. A plaque for the First World War starts 'Over eleven hundred Falkirk Bairns died...' – a horrific figure. Further on, left still, are the huge District Offices, Town Hall and Health Centre.

Continue on up West Bridge Street (Tanners' Brae locally) to a busy crossroads, an area with many good Victorian buildings. Just beyond the police station is the old Sheriff Court where we turn left, if heading to Falkirk Grahamston railway station or, straight on, for the pedestrianised High Street, Tourist Information Office, bus station and the remoter Falkirk High railway station.

Walking along to Grahamston station the road curves round a huge *Asda* complex. Keep on the left, passing, in turn, the St Xavier Roman Catholic Church (which shows concrete can be used creatively), the red sandstone library building and a car park. This is probably the easiest choice if returning to Linlithgow, but do have a look at the town first if possible.

If heading up the High Street turn in through an old arch to reach the solid Old Parish Church with its octagonal tower, and the site of one of the oldest historical tombs in Scotland, that of the Graeme who was killed at the Battle of Falkirk in 1298. This was rebuilt in 1771, and again in 1860 when the arched crown of Gothic ironwork was added. The church dates to 1810 though the tower is earlier and the site goes back to the start of historical time. The grounds were cleared of gravestones in 1962, except for a few historical ones, like Sir John de Graeme's. There are tombs to some victims of the 1746 Battle of Falkirk too: William Edmonstone and Munro of Foulis and his doctor brother. Foulis must have been a paragon; 'His death was universally regretted. Even by those who slew him'.

The pedestrian High Street becomes very 'identikit' in character, but note the Scots' penchant for baking. Every other shop is a bakery and the town has over thirty eating places so 'beans and pease' are still easily enough found. The Steeple, dominating the High Street, houses the Tourist Information Office which can help with accommodation, town maps, leaflets etc.

This is actually the third Tolbooth Steeple. The original was rebuilt in 1697, but a century later the demolition of adjoining property so undermined the foundations it had to be taken down as well. For eleven years there was no Steeple, but funds were raised to build the present 140 feet spire. The top thirty feet were rebuilt in 1927 after suffering a lightning strike. The weather cock went flying and masonry crashed everywhere, but the only fatality was a horse belonging to Mr (*Irn-Bru*) Barr. The Cross Well beside the Steeple dates to 1817, replacing one originally given to the town by the Livingstones of Callendar in 1681. The site of the Mercat Cross (and of the town's last public hanging in 1826) is marked out on the setts (cobbles). Tolbooth Street, behind the Steeple, makes the *Guinness Book of Records* as the shortest street in Britain. First left, walking on, is Wooers Street then, bearing off right is the large Cow Wynd which is the route to Falkirk High railway station. (Note that this station is as far out as the distance we've walked in from Rosebank.) For the bus station continue along the High Street, past the huge new Callendar Square complex and cross the motorable road at a pedestrian crossing. Turn right and the first opening on the left (about thirty yards on) leads into the bus station. A ten minute walk out along this street brings one to Callendar Park with its fine example of Roman wall and ditch, and its *château*.

The local museum is well worth a visit. There are fascinating displays and old photographs about the town, the Antonine Wall, the canals, Dunmore pottery and past industries. To find it, after crossing the road for the bus station, turn left and walk along to a roundabout. Across it, on the same line, is Orchard Street (narrow entrance) and the museum is half way down, on the left. Open 10.00–17.00 Monday–Saturday (lunch closed 12.30–13.30).

PRACTICAL INFORMATION: FALKIRK

Tourist Information Centre, The Steeple, High Street, 0324-20244 (Open all year.)
Telephone code for Falkirk numbers is 0324-

ACCOMMODATION: There is limited B & B accommodation in Falkirk and hotels tend to be glossy recent creations, designed for those travelling on expense accounts and somewhat overpriced for those on foot. I've listed what there is but the easy remedy is just to take a taxi to nearer B & Bs or catch a train or bus back to Linlithgow. There are two railway stations: Falkirk High just beside the west end of the canal tunnel (the railway, perforce, tunnels through the same hill) and Falkirk Grahamston, at the north side of the centre of the town. Both have frequent trains to Linlithgow. Falkirk High is on the main Glasgow–Edinbugh route, Grahamston has trains from Stirling, as well as Glasgow, heading for the capital. There is also a frequent bus service between Falkirk and Linlithgow (which passes some of the remote B & Bs) but ensure you catch the *direct* service. Taxis are available at train and bus stations and at Kirk Wynd, off the High Street beside the Steeple.

Reasonably priced accommodation: Union Inn, Camelon, -23578. Annescroft, 149 Mungalhead, -20468 (small but recommended).

Expensive: Friendly Hotel, Manor Street, -24066, Hotel Cladham, Kemper Avenue, -27241. Very expensive: Stakis Park Hotel, Camelon Road, -28331.

The following lie east of Falkirk and could be approached directly from the canal, continuing the walk next day – or simply take a bus, train or taxi back towards them if finishing the day in Falkirk.

Brightons: Chez Nous, Sunnyside Road, -715953, Lomond Bank, Redding Road, -713496, Reddingmuirhead: Mayfield, Shieldhill Road, -716551.

Other practical accommodation, using taxi, bus or train transport is listed below. Most of tomorrow's B & Bs would be within reasonable taxi distance.

Carronbridge: Lochend Farm, 0324-822778 (west), Denny: 70 Main Street, 0506-811291 (west). Larbert: 67 Burnhead Road, 0324-553168 (north-west), Coach House, Glenberrie, Larbert, 0324-552512 (north-west), Wester Carmuirs Farm, Larbert, 0324-812459 (north-west), Stenhousemuir: 1 Dunnotter Drive, 0324-556256 (north). Grangemouth: 63 Oswald Avenue, 0324-486349 (north-east), 55 Bo'ness Road, 0324-471301(north-east).

TAXI: Taxi services are numerous, showing how much the area uses this facility. (I only list some of the numbers!): -612221, -28000, -23999, -36000, -21335, -22100, -22133, -233380, -38000, -36060, -27000.

Falkirk Bus Station, Callendar Riggs 0324-23985. Linlithgow Bus Station, 85 High Street, 0506-842167.

MEALS: Limited range. Check with B & B if phoning ahead. Falkirk itself has several restaurants and chip shops abound in all the towns mentioned.

FALKIRK

to

CASTLECARY/ KILSYTH AREA

Bart 45 OSLR 65, 64
OSPF 405(NS 87/97), 404 (NS 67/77)

The first part of this day explores the best reaches of the Antonine Wall, the second follows the open country of the Forth and Clyde Canal. Accommodation at the end is scattered so do thorough homework, key the options onto the map and telephone to book the chosen B & B, and ensure an evening meal.

THE ANTONINE WALL

This great monument deserves to be better known. It has had a rough passage historically with roads, railways, canals, buildings, industry and agriculture all wrecking its course across 'the waist of Scotland'. Perhaps the worst damage was done in the eighteenth century. Before then several of the sites had extensive ruins, by the end of that century the 'convenient' stonework had been carried off to build houses, field walls, canal banks etc. An interest in historical remains came just fifty years too late.

The wall runs for thirty-seven miles, linking the River Forth near Bo'ness to the River Clyde at Old Kilpatrick. It generally commands the low ground facing north and had forts at regular intervals along its length. Some, like Rough Castle and Bar Hill, are still of interest as we'll see. The wall was built of turf, though on a stone base, so it has not survived very well, nor has what could be called the service road which ran along behind the wall, though this Military Way, as with Dere Street, is often indicated by the pockmarkings of quarries alongside. The best surviving feature has been the *vallum*, or ditch, which ran along in front of the wall – and we'll see the best length of that feature shortly. The main road north beyond the wall started at Camelon, just west of Falkirk and there are traces of Roman forts and camps angling across behind the Ochils to Perth and up to the north-east of Scotland – far beyond Hadrian's Wall which tends to be regarded as the Roman's northern boundary.

The Ditch/Wall/Military Way was constructed by Antoninus Pius *c.* AD 140 along the line of forts built by Agricola sixty years earlier. Ironically, the wall was then only occupied for about twenty years. Anne Robertson's *The Antonine Wall*, or the A4-sized booklet *The Wild Frontier* (see bibliography) are well worth carrying for these days along the Antonine Wall.

We pick up our route just south of the Union Inn at Tamfourhill Road. Almost at once, on the south side, there is a gate with a Historic Scotland sign for the *Watling Lodge* section of the Antonine Wall. This is the finest section of ditch on the wall, still showing the deep V nature of this defensive feature. With a wall overlooking the south side it was a formidable barrier. The soil dug out was always heaped up on the north side.

This beech-lined ditch is all too soon violently interrupted: a brick building sits across it, one of the outbuildings of Watling Lodge. Sadly, Watling Lodge appears to have been built on the main gateway/road through the Antonine Wall which led to Camelon, site of Roman forts and a Pictish town brutally levelled by Kenneth MacAlpine as he forged a single nation out of the Picts and Scots tribes. We perforce turn, right, back down onto Tamfourhill road (sign and gate). Turn left and when the road bends slightly there is a section of brick wall on the other side. Cut into the wood from the end of this wall and wander along through the wood following the line of the ditch until forced back onto the road again by two houses (and a nursing home) sitting on the wall. These houses have their own footbridges across the Roman ditch in order to reach their gardens!

Turn right along Tamfourhill Road. After a couple of minutes there is a crossroads, with a telephone box on the Mayfield Place corner, and we turn off into the wood again, just beyond the crossroads on a small footpath which angles off where a small stream appears from under the road. (If you arrive at a big boulder on the left side of the road you'll know you've overshot!) The road actually runs along on top of the Military Way.

Our path gradually draws away from the road to follow, more or less, beside the ditch as it climbs slightly through Tentfield Wood. After a barely-noticed ruined wall the path begins to descend again. It picks up the ruined wall line, crosses it and runs on past a pylon.

When the path comes out to an open area swing more *left*, through the birch scrub, towards a line of power poles and follow a path along under the wires to come out on a dirt road (part of the old workings – there is still open-cast coal mining just to the south). If you go astray here don't worry – if you simply head west you must come on the road and you know the line of the Roman ditch lies over to the right.

At the road turn right (north) until you find the ditch line again (the road cuts brutally across it) and follow along its north side, after negotiating the fence, about twenty yards before the pylon line which crosses the road. There are odd bits of track but the ditch itself on the left remains clear and deep-cut in places as it runs through the continuing woodland strip.

The area is overgrown in places too, then we come to what would be called 'gruffy ground' in Somerset. There's a grey spoil tip on the left as we drop to a tiny burn which is crossed by a causeway and so to an area of grey, cow foot-printed spoil with a marshy pool, on the left, in the line of the Roman ditch. A grassy track leads on. Keep left at a vague fork after 100 yards and wend on through pleasant oakwood. The open-cast mining

THE LILIA (DEFENSIVE PITS) AT ROUGH CASTLE ON THE ANTONINE WALL

THE ANTONINE WALL AT ROUGH CASTLE – LOOKING IN THE DIRECTION OF OUR WALK

(PHOTO: CAMBRIDGE UNIVERSITY COLLECTION; COPYRIGHT RESERVED)

can be seen over to the left but, on the right, the views are rather fine. There is a stile and an official sign for 'Rough Castle'.

For about a mile the walking is along what could pass for a golf course. Rough Castle lies on the left as we walk along, with the defensive ditches of the annex and small fort quite clear. We soon come on the north entrance causeway of the main fort. This crosses the ditch very plainly, but before invading the fort turn off at 45° and you come on a strange area of closely-packed pits. This is the *lilia*, dug as a booby trap against mounted raiders. With sharpened stakes set in the bottom of the pits and their presence disguised the pits would be a very effective way of breaking a charge.

Cross the causeway into the fort. There is nothing visible except vague shapes in the turf. It was excavated in 1909 but then the foundations were covered over again to preserve them. Objects found are in the Royal Scottish Museum, Edinburgh, where they are, with other Roman remains, given a room to themselves and make a fascinating display.

Walk west and you soon come on a steep drop to the Rowan Tree Burn with its very obvious defensive ramparts and a west gate with a track descending to a wooden bridge just as it did 1700 years ago. Go down by a pylon and cross a bridge in the hollow. The *vallum* runs very clearly and one can walk along the top of the south side bank, on what is actually the Roman wall.

To the left there is a car-turning circle and the car track goes out over a cattle grid to run along on top of the old Roman road. There are plenty of wet hollows where the road's foundation material was dug out.

The end of this fine bit of the Antonine Wall is marked by an official sign and a V gate onto the unsurfaced road. This time it is Bonnyside House which sits on the frontier. The road onwards is tarred from beside the gate into its grounds. There is a rise to a bridge over a railway track and this small rise opens up on a huge view. The dominant hills are Ben Vorlich and Stuc a' Chroin and, further left, the cone of Ben Ledi. At last the Campsies lie just ahead, but we can still see the Ochil scarp (and back to the Saline Hills in Fife): bulwarks against the Highlands.

Rough Castle was for one period the site of the Falkirk Tryst which had started near Polmont (after overtaking Crieff as the main market) and, about 1785, possibly because the new Forth and Clyde Canal made access difficult, it finally moved to Stenhousemuir. The whole traffic went over the Cauldstane Slap to West Linton, Romanno Bridge and Peebles, and some on by Minchmoor. We've walked a very historic route. The coming of the railways and changes in agricultural methods saw droving practically die out in the 1860s.

Industry, houses and more industry follows, none of it very bonny. When the road swings up left turn off right, down by derelict works where, unexpectedly, a cobbled road, a stream and a raised footpath all dive into a tunnel which goes under more works, the road, and the Forth and Clyde Canal! When we come out onto the road turn *left* to twist steeply up to the Forth and Clyde Canal, which we follow for most of today's route. We are on the outskirts of Bonnybridge here but it has little to lure us off-route.

The works across the canal were famous for their murals, but these are fading from years of neglect. A signpost indicates 'Castlecary Picnic site 2 ½' and this is our next towpath ramble. Considering the intense urban nature of the Denny–Larbert–Falkirk area to the north we have won through very easily. The Forth and Clyde Canal and the Antonine Wall will see us to Kilsyth, and most of the way to Milngavie. Not far along, on the right, is a yard with a collection of traction engines and the like. After about half a mile you may see a notice on the other side of the canal that says 'Dennyloanhead 1km' which is a bit confusing as this place lies to our right. Shortly after, though, down to the right there is a signpost saying 'Underpass to Antonine Wall'. This is an interesting enough length of

SEABEGS WOOD – ONE OF THE FINEST SECTIONS OF THE ANTONINE WALL AND DITCH

road/wall/ditch to go and have a look, and the underpass for pedestrians is a curiosity in its own right. Watch your head if you are over six foot in height. Seabegs Wood has been well restored, so provides a clear view of the frontier. The Military Way here is the best preserved length, the wall and ditch are clear and the upthrown ditch material forms an obvious rampart. There is a Historic Scotland explanatory notice.

Returning to the towpath we continue westwards. Underwood Lockhouse (Lock 17) gives a pleasant surprise – it is a pub (which also offers good food). The lock is in better condition than most. Castlecary is signed as one and a half miles, and we are onto our last Landranger map before we reach it. There are two more very sad and decayed locks (18 and 19). Wynford, Lock 20, a mile beyond the A80 is the 'summit' of the canal and, as the level does not drop till Maryhill (in Glasgow), we will not see another lock on our walk. The buzz of the A80 (which turns into M80) makes itself known as we approach the old Castlecary swing bridge, now fixed, with the A80 'bridge' barging across the canal beyond.

Arrowhead, *Sagittaria sagitifolia*, is a plant thriving in the canal here, and in several places back over the last few miles, yet is is not supposed to grow north of the Tyne. It will only grow in unpolluted waters which is something to commend the canal.

There is a largely-ignored picnic site across the road, but who on earth would want to picnic next to the noise, stink and sight of the A(M)80? (Planners should be compelled to experience their creations!) This squalid road has also flattened the canal into a culvert.

The Forth and Clyde Canal was a much tougher proposition than the Union Canal. There are forty locks for a start. The canal is thirty-five

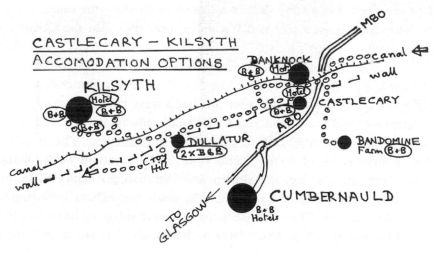

miles long, twenty-eight feet wide and eight feet deep. It took twenty-two years to complete. Five years were spent working along to Kirkintilloch, but the Glasgow end set problems of construction and finance. Money from the forfeited estates of the Jacobite rebels was eventually used to complete the work, and a puncheon of Forth water was ceremoniously poured into the Clyde in 1790. The earliest commercial canal in Scotland, it was a great feat for the period.

The only redeeming feature here is that the swing bridge for the largely abandoned old road is still in reasonable condition. The Forth and Clyde Canal had to have swing bridges to allow larger, sea-going vessels, with masts, to use the waterway. I rather miss the friendly arches of the Union Canal bridges.

If not going on to accommodation at Castlecary, Dullatur or Kilsyth this is where diversions are made for the two northern B & Bs and Bandominie Farm to the south.

The Gordon Arms Hotel, Banknock, is shown on the Landranger map (785794) and one takes the road north, climbing steeply up by the first fork left to the A803 at Haggs, left along the A803 and, once over the A80, the hotel is on the right: an opulent-looking place but quite modest in reality. Tel: 0324-8420237. Orchard Grove is at Auchineloch on the maps (767788) and is clearly signposted from the start of the drive to Orchard Farm. It is an opulent bungalow sited by a woodland pond. From Castlecary picnic site take the canal path under the A80 and on for three quarters of a mile to Wyndford Lock, then head up to the A803 and turn left or, much safer, continue along the towpath, until immediately below Auhineloch, and cut up the field to a gate – a line of power poles is a guide. Wynford Lock is in a sorry state and, like so much along the canal, can be unsightly from litter, a pity as it is a much nicer spot than the Castlecary picnic site.

The main route on from Castlecary picnic site has to cross the M80/A80, a road which the locals hate as it sliced their community in two, but it does show what a vital spot this has always been historically, and geographically. Roman road and wall, canal, railway and modern roads culminating in the M80/A80 all criss-cross at Castlecary. The auxiliary Roman fort was one of the few built of stone, and excavations yielded many coins, weapons, urns etc, and also an altar ingratiatingly dedicated to the god Mercury by the Sixth Legion. Castle, roads and railway have largely demolished the site. The sturdy keep that gave the village its name was the seat of the Baillie family, descendants of the Baliols. The Jacobites burned the castle in 1715 but it has been restored as a private house.

Cross the canal by the old swing bridge and continue up to meet a slip road off the A80. Turn left, but watch out for cars belting round from the right: they've been on motorway for miles and are often still travelling faster than is good for pedestrians. Turn right when the B816 is reached to cross the M80/A80. The road then curves left and leads on under the railway viaduct, (still the Edinburgh–Glasgow line). A quarter of a mile beyond, on the right, is the Castlecary House Hotel (0324-840233) which offers everything from a single room to an executive cottage and meals (and liquids) at most times of the day. Note the Historic Scotland sign at the entrance as this points to our onward route. ('Antonine Wall. Garnhall Hill, 250 yards.')

About a third of a mile further along the B816 a small road, on the right, heads for Garnhall, and on this is Wayside Lodge, Castlecary (Non-smokers B & B, 0324-840310). If staying there, next day just walk up this wee road to Garnhall and join the Antonine Wall route there.

Bandominie Farm (798770), south of Castlecary, is a delightful alternative. Having gone up onto the B816, instead of crossing the M80/A80, turn off left onto a minor road which leads to a T-junction. The wall across our bows marks the northern defences of the Roman fort of Castlecary, mentioned above.

Turn right at the T-junction. The road swings left round the fort side, with the A80 just to the right, and the railway crossing overhead. It then wends steadily up Castle Glen, and where it wiggles across another railway line (Glasgow–Stirling line) there is a glimpse of the actual castle of Castle Cary among the trees to the right.

The road pulls up onto more open country, passing Walton Farm, right, then the Bandominic drive is on the left. The farm sits high and has extensive views. At least one Land's End to John o' Groats walker had stayed there before I found this welcome haven. In the morning simply walk down again to cross the A80 – back on line again.

The continuation from Castlecary House Hotel is signposted. Just up from the hotel, as the road bends, there is a gate and deeply-worn steps beside it (official sign) which takes us into the field, the edge of which is then followed to curve up to the Antonine Wall at the top corner of the field, where there is another sign board. The ditch is very plain and we follow it along through several fields (note Garnhall has been demolished) to another sign board and a gate onto a small tarred road. Cross this road and the Roman road leads us on alongside an industrial estate, with the ditch to the right, backed by a line of trees. (Tollpark.) The easiest walking is along through the trees, but there are several unfriendly fences and no stiles. The field is deep grass. Cumbernauld Airfield lies over to the left.

At the end of the trees, beside a gate, there is an official sign for 'Antonine Wall, Tollpark'. The track continues beyond, a bit wet and grassy initially where the Roman ditch used to be, to reach the edge of Cumbernauld Airfield with its windsock etc. It then skirts along beside the airfield as a green track, becomes more of a footpath for a short overgrown stretch, then, from a gate by a wee burn, it is a perfect green track again. The ditch runs clearly all the way on our right. At weekends plenty of interesting old and small aircraft will be taking off or buzzing about overhead.

The green track swings back across the ditch, then runs along beside a wall with a grand view over the canal to the Kilsyth Hills. A couple of *shoogly* gates are crossed, the second lands us on a proper farm track at what was once Westerwood Farm, then a youth camp and (in 1990) a temporary club house for a new championship golf course – designed by Seve Ballesteros. The farm buildings sit in a corner of a Roman fort, the Roman entrance and farm entrance being on the same line. We keep on straight ahead. A notice board points out some local walks, our continuation being the 'Roman Walk' (yellow on the map). It leads straight on through the middle of the golf course and all side paths and tracks should be ignored.

A green gate leads into a woody section and the ditch on our left is still deeply-cut in places. The track dips. Note the brick-walled cutting to the left, the line of an old mineral line up to a disused quarry. As we walk on we can see its continuation along an embankment. The ditch keeps its deep V shape as it is now the course of a burn. Our track becomes tarmacadam just before it goes under the railway, then it swings left to follow along below the railway, being joined by another small road from a disused mine (just beyond a gate) and passes a farm, then Easter Dullatur House, before coming out onto a minor road at a bend with an official sign for 'Antonine Wall: Dullatur ½m'. We turn left for Dullatur House, or continue right on for West Dullatur Farm and Kilsyth.

For Dullatur House go under the railway bridge and then turn right along Victoria Terrace. This is overlooked by a row of houses. Turn left immediately beyond them to go up a steep lane which brings one to the bend of a road where one turns left and along to a junction/crossroads. Before reaching this cut across the grassy triangle, just past the tennis courts (right), to head along the small road (no name shown). Dullatur House is the fourth building on the right, a substantial white house, after some bungalows. If you are feeling stiff you might be tempted by the sauna!

Heading in for Kilsyth the road makes a couple of bends and then West Dullatur Farm is the first building on the left (there may not be a B & B sign), a comfortable establishment and the best placed of all.

In the Dullatur Moss a dead trooper was reputedly found still sitting in the saddle of the horse on which he'd fled from the Battle of Kilsyth. The bog had engulfed them. Baillie, the Covenanting general, nearly came to grief in the bog too, but struggled through to Castle Cary, then owned by a cousin.

Witchcraft and superstition lingered long in this area. Even last century there were known 'witches'. A sceptical farmer met one when carting along the canal bank and gave her a piece of his mind. She held up her fingers and muttered a curse before taking to the fields. The farmer laughed and plodded on. The sedate mare however suddenly went daft and plunged, cart, farmer and all, into the canal.

The road dips down to cross the canal at the Craigmarloch Bridge (737773), quite an important spot in the canal's lifetime. Dullatur Bog was still a morass when the canal was built, and even today the ground is wet all along the line of springs issuing from the slopes above. A mass exodus of frogs (tens of thousands of them!) was a sensation during the canal's construction. The local minister was not slow to draw Biblical comparisons.

ONE OF THE QUEENS AT THE BUNGALOW AT CRAIGMARLOCH – A SCENE HARD TO ENVISAGE TODAY (PHOTO: COURTESY STRATHKELVIN DISTRICT LIBRARIES)

From Victorian times to the demise of canal cruises Craigmarloch was a popular outing from Glasgow. Old photographs show 'The Bungalow' (restaurant and cafe) with several boats, the various 'Queens', in the basin. All buildings and signs of this past activity have gone. The basin is filled with reeds. The old bascule bridge has gone though the modern one has less height for craft to pass along the canal.

The large building (windows boarded up) lying north of the bridge is the old stabling block. It is built well back from the canal to avoid boggy ground – into which a first stable block sank. A quarry behind supplied stone for the canal. Coming down from Townhead (Banton) Reservoir is a burn/aqueduct which passes the stables to enter the canal fifty yards east of the bridge while, just west of the bridge, is an overflow from the canal, the canal being higher than the River Kelvin and the large alluvial plain stretching over towards Kilsyth. This aqueduct was the main water source for the Forth and Clyde Canal. (A lock spills 80,000 gallons of water every time it is used, so topping-up is essential). The aqueduct offers a short cut to Shawend Farm B & B (see below). The reservoir taps the Birkenburn Reservoir and Garrel Burn coming off the hills above Kilsyth. The battle symbol and date 1645 does not mark some aquatic fight. The battle predated the water catchment and during the construction work plenty of souvenirs were found.

Litter defiles this pleasant corner too. I actually saw a car pull in. A couple were eating carry-oot suppers. When finished they carefully laid the remains, plus their cans, on the ground outside their respective doors – and drove off. Do any other countries behave like this I wonder?

From the canal the road wiggles across the flat ground. There is a junction/crossroads and the road, sharply back to the left, is Coach Road (not named) with Mashobra (B & B) being about 400 metres along it on the right. The only sign at the junction points the way we have just come: 'Dullatur 1 ½ Cumbernauld 4'.

At the junction keep on, rightwards, if aiming for Shawend. The minor road makes a T-junction with a bit of the old A803. Turn right along the section blocked off by boulders (a 'No dumping' sign is much ignored!) to gain the A803 just 250 yards from Shawend Farm (B & B). An alternative route to the farm is to walk up by the aqueduct, but ensure all gates are shut, and no dogs, as there may be stock in the fields. Pick up the lade at the entrance to the attractive old stable block and go along the true right (south) side of the flow. This leads round a hill then, at a sluice and a walled-off burn, cross to the other side and continue up the bank to the bit of old road mentioned above. Note how the bridge over the burn/aqueduct has been altered. Just above the A803 the burn was used to drive a mill. The building is still a sawmill.

The two remaining accommodation options are up in Kilsyth itself, and to reach them it is best to walk along the towpath to the Auchinstarry Bridge.

North of the bridge a bit of parkland has been created out of the huge, derelict Auchinstarry Quarry. A large pond now fills the hollow under the basaltic whinstone cliffs. I've seen fishermen practising how to cast their lines here on a Sunday morning, and there seemed to be some polishing of the holds on obvious lines tempting the rock climber. Confirmation of this activity came in a circular I received mentioning a lecture on 'World Rock' with Duncan McCallum showing slides of exploits in 'Yosemite, Australia, Italy, France and Auchinstarry Quarry'. There is a basin on the south bank, just east of Auchinstarry Bridge, where Sunday afternoon cruises on *Gypsy* are offered.

Auchinstarry was where Kilsyth coal would be loaded onto canal boats to take it to Glasgow and even to Belfast, later the mineral lines all converged on Twechar and then railways completely took over from the canal. Auchinstarry quarry produced the whinstone *setts* that paved the

KILSYTH CHURCHYARD – THE WATCH HOUSE
(OVER THE TOMB DESCRIBED)

streets of Glasgow and dates back to the eighteenth century.

Follow the B802 into Kilsyth. The town sign bears the burgh's coat-of-arms, and just beyond there's an unusual watch house in the cemetery on the left. Under this watch house lies the Kilsyth family vault, of which more later. On entering the Kilsyth graveyard note the unusual lamb sculptures on stones to left and right, memorials to young girls and a change from the ubiquitous draped urn, which is even present on a cast iron 'stone'.

The road on into Kilsyth dips to a pedestrian crossing with playing fields left, then pulls up again. Have a look at the monument on the right. Erected to the memory of a minister who died in 1910, the language is as sugary as it comes, the extreme being to saddle poor Mr Jeffrey (he looks quite handsome in fact) with 'He wore the White Flower of a blameless life'. Kilsyth has a tradition of religious fervour dating back to Covenanting times but being most notable during religious revivals in mid-eighteenth and nineteenth centuries. There seem to be as many churches here as in Selkirk.

We pass another church on the right as we walk up to a roundabout. Follow the Glasgow–Edinburgh A803 road which dips to cross another valley bottom, passing a Methodist church and behind it, another rather fine church with a tower, the present parish church. To the north-east from the roundabout lies the old, original Kilsyth – worth a diversion.

At the T-junction the modern, roadside, expensive Coachman Hotel

A FINE EXAMPLE OF THE IRON WORK ON THE BRIDGES IN THE CENTRE OF KILSYTH

lies just 200 yards right. Left, along Glasgow Road, is Fairfield, a more homely B & B. A garage is passed, then there is a 'Safe Journey' greeting (on the back of the town name sign) and the blue B & B sign will be seen just past the first road, on the right.

Kilsyth has become a vast sprawl of modern houses, but still maintains a heart of historical interest and well worth seeing if passing within reasonable distance. The library (office hours roughly) on Burngreen usually has historical/local displays, and the green itself has a painted lady fountain (akin to the one in Tomintoul – or Kirkintilloch's Peel Park), a bandstand, bridge railings (each different) and even house signs (one a tortoise), all made of cast iron. Just off the green is the attractive Market Square and a Main/High Street which is being brought back to life.

Kilsyth has gone through hard times, even recently, when the mining industry finally petered out. The library has a display on this more recent history. An exhibition on the local temperance movement had a cutting from the local paper in 1923 (when the town went 'dry') pointing out that the sale of methylated spirits had increased by leaps and bounds!

Close to Shawend is Colzium Park and its mansion, which was given to Kilsyth in 1937. There is a local museum in Colzium House, open Wednesdays 14.00–17.00, 18.00–20.00, 0236-735077, which includes a display on the Battle of Kilsyth. A plinth below the house commemorates

THE UNFORTUNATE TITLING OF THE MONUMENT TO THE BATTLE OF KILSYTH AND THE MARQUIS OF MONTROSE

the battle, but boobs in ascribing the victory to the Duke (*sic*) of Montrose. (The Grahams only gained that title through supporting the 1707 sell-out, the local Livingston, Lord Kilsyth, fought its every clause.) The grounds are well-kept and full of interesting shrubs and trees (glorious in autumn colours). The old laundry has been restored and turned into a theatre, the Clock Theatre, after the clock above it which dates to 1863. Just up from the bridge, leading to the house, is a well-preserved example of an ice house. Townhead (Banton) Reservoir lies just below and to the east, and is the main 'feeder' for the Forth and Clyde Canal.

The Colzium factor, in 1739, was responsible for introducing the potato to Scotland. Robert Graham began experimenting with potatoes in his garden at Tamrawer (near Banton), and planted out crops above Kilsyth. An astute business man he bought up farms right across Scotland and planted potatoes. As they say, the rest is history.

To revert to earlier history, Kilsyth 1645 was the last of Montrose's victories in his *annus mirabilis*. When Montrose was in north-east Scotland Cromwell had inflicted a crushing defeat on the King's forces at Naseby and Montrose realised that however many Covenanting armies he defeated in the north, the result would be marginal. He had to move south. In the middle of August the two opposing forces found themselves face to face at Kilsyth.

Baillie had the larger force but was hampered by his serving a committee which included the Earls of Argyll, Elcho, Burleigh and Balcarres, who had all suffered under Montrose's highlanders. Montrose was encamped below the Campsies, the Covenanters were on a ridge above. Quite why Montrose had allowed his opponents the higher ground is not known but the ground between was not suitable for cavalry and Baillie was wary about a possible trap. His committee, however, felt they had caught Montrose at last and to leave him no chance of escape they began to shift their men across Montrose's front to occupy a dominant hill from which they would swoop down.

In a glen below the route a small force of Macleans occupied some houses and a small body from the Covenanters' column broke off to attack these, were repulsed and chased back. This sight was too much for Colkitto's men who charged after them. The clansmen swept through the column and, before long, the Covenanting army was in flight. Scotland belonged to Montrose, the King's Captain General. But south of the border there was no Montrose, and defeat at Philiphaugh was only a month away. He was to lose his wife and eldest son the same year. He was only thirty-eight when he was executed.

Five years after the battle Cromwell marched into Scotland and, following his 'crowning mercy' of victory at the Battle of Dunbar, he marched into the west. On the way he blew up the Livingston castle at Kilsyth.

The Livingston support for the Stewarts was to have a somewhat macabre continuation. The ill-fated Bonnie Dundee, who died in his moment of victory at the Battle of Killiecrankie (1689), had married Jean Cochrane, granddaughter of the Earl of Dundonald, and his widow then married William Livingston (later Viscount Kilsyth) with whom she went into exile. On a visit to Rotterdam in 1695 the couple were making a goodnight visit to their infant, asleep with her nurse, when the roof fell in and all but Livingston were killed. The bodies were embalmed and brought home to Kilsyth. In 1795 the vault was accidentally opened (perhaps by medical students after anatomical material!) and the bodies were found to be remarkably well preserved. They became a bit of a spectacle before the vault was closed again. Vandalism is not new. I found this in a book dated 1872 and visited the site in 1989, a year when an inspection showed the bodies were still preserved.

The (Old) *Statistical Account* (Vol 9 in the recent series of EP reprints) is very thorough on Kilsyth, and full of fascinating descriptions of work generally, and particular topics like the creation of a cut to take the Kelvin or the coming of the canal. Something none of the archaeologist sources mention is the *natural* defensive line across this neck of Scotland. A strong wall was not needed: between Antonine Wall and mountains all was water or bog (Camelon was a seaport!) so a large scale attack would be difficult to mount.

The minister describes the local climate as 'rather watery'. In 1733 the area was hit by a freak thunderstorm when three-inch hailstones wrought havoc and left the ground several inches in water. The burns came down off the hills in torrents and did a great deal of damage (twenty-ton boulders were trundled down) but, amazingly, no human life was lost. A woman and child had a fright when a bolt of lightening came down the chimney as they hugged the fire – and killed the cat at their feet.

PRACTICAL INFORMATION: KILSYTH AREA

Telephone codes are given along with the numbers.

ACCOMODATION, (In order of convenience): Castlecary, Banknock, Dullatur and Kilsyth, in order of convenience. When phoning check on evening meals. One or two places do not normally offer evening meals, but may oblige walkers who cannot simply jump in a car and drive into Kilsyth.

Castlecary: Wayside Lodge, 0324-840310, (784777), Castlecary House Hotel, 0324-840233, (787781), Bandominie Farm, 324-840284 (798770).

Banknock: Gordon Arms Hotel, 0324-840237 (785794), Orchard Grove, 0324-840146 (767788).

Dullatur: Wester Dullatur Farm, 0236-723218 (742772), Dullatur House, 0236-738855 (747767).

Kilsyth: Rural; Mashobra, Coach Road, 0236-822122 (732775), Williamswood , Shawend Farm 0236-823142 (742778). Urban; Fairfield, Glasgow Road, 0236-825745 (710780), Coachman Hotel, 0236-821649 (716781).

Within Taxi Range: Kirkintilloch: Broadcroft Hotel, 041-775-0398, 43 St Columba Drive, 041-776-0420, 37 Kilsyth Road, 041-775-0930, 19 Linsaybeg Road, Lenzie, 041-776-1989. Lennoxtown: Glazertbank Hotel, 0360-310790, Cumbernauld: 68 Lammermoor Drive, 0236-721307, Milton of Campsie: Ravenslee, Alton Holdings, 0360-311683, Kincaid House Hotel, 041-776-2226, Little Baldoran, 0360-311419.

TAXIS: Banknock; 0324-840047, -840880. Kilsyth; 0263-821707, -824100, -823959, 0821099, -822174. Kirkintilloch; 041-776-7889, -777-7711, -775-0100, -776-0055, -777-8811. Cumbernauld; 0236-736965, -725280, -722385, -727665, -738383, -729501, -722198, -720208.

MEALS: Limited. If booking B & B ahead try and ensure an evening meal as well. Otherwise it is just the old chip shop or bar supper.

KILSYTH

to

MILNGAVIE

Bart 45 OSLR 64
OSPF 404 (NS 67/77), 403 (NS 47/57)

A vintage mixture ends the walk, starting with Croy Hill and Bar Hill (superb atmosphere), giving the last miles of Forth and Clyde Canal and ending with a rich rural landscape. (The main crop seems to be the golf courses!) Our end at Milngavie is the portal to the north, and start of the West Highland Way, and I trust will whet the appetite for further journeys – maybe completing a personal Groats End Walk?

CROY HILL AND BAR HILL

The initial miles of today's walk will vary depending on where the night was spent but, wherever possible, take in the traverse of Croy Hill and Bar Hill which are among the highlights of the walk. If the weather is diabolical however, then the canal towpath gives a salvation alternative.

From Dullatur return to the little road leading to Kilsyth, and 100 yards past Wester Dullatur Farm there is an Historic Scotland sign for 'Croy Hill ¼ mile'. From Castlecary one simply catches up by following the described route along by Garnhall and Westerwood, which is also the best alternative from Banknock. From Orchard Grove cut down to the canal as soon as possible (the A803 is a busy commuter route), and on up from Wyndford Lock to join the route near Garnhall, or follow the canal along to the Craigmarloch Bridge, south-east of Kilsyth, and join in for Croy Hill.

THE STRONG LINE OF THE ROMAN WALL ON CROY HILL, WESTER DULLATUR FARM TOP LEFT
(PHOTO: CAMBRIDGE UNIVERSITY COLLECTION; COPYRIGHT RESERVED)

Backtracking to this bridge and on for Croy Hill is the best approach for those on the south-east side of Kilsyth. Those staying in central or western Kilsyth would be best joining in via the Auchinstarry Bridge and the track up Barr Hill. Dullatur starters should walk down to see Craigmarloch Bridge (only five minutes!) before heading off for Croy Hill.

Croy Hill is approached by the track signposted 'Croy Hill ¼ mile' (738772). This leads to a gate and then on past a big pylon. Keep left at a junction. The line of the Roman wall/ditch can be seen crossing in front of the next pylon, and we follow the track round to pick up its line. The railway will probably be heard if not seen – our last contact with this inter-city artery which passes south of Croy Hill in a deep, mile-long cutting. An alternative railway line, the Kelvin Valley Railway, wended along by the hills to the north, linked with the Kilsyth and Bonnybridge line at Kilsyth. John Thomas's *Forgotten Railways, Scotland* has plenty of interesting stories. Coal mining, on Croy Hill and Bar Hill, at Twechar, Shirva, St Flannan, Tintock, Cadder (all on our route), has vanished with almost no trace.

The path wends on up towards a clump of trees which marks the site of a Roman fort. Walk through the trees and on beyond. Nearing the top of Croy Hill there is no ditch, the rock being too hard even for the Roman soldiers to quarry and, later, the scarp by itself is an adequate defensive feature. On the east summit there is a big view as one would expect, but most eye-catching is the ditch which arcs across the side of a dip to the marginally higher western top. From there take a right fork of path to descend a spur (the line of the Roman wall) towards the north edge of Croy. On the descent to Croy the ditch is actually hewn out of solid rock. (It shows clearly looking back from Bar Hill.)

Croy is a rather sad town, for its mines closed in the early eighties and nothing has taken their place. Our path descends to skirt down by the north end of the town, through an area of waste ground that leads out to the B802 at Croy Tavern. Turn right along this to a T-junction where the B802 turns right for Kilsyth. After eighty yards there is a sign for Bar Hill, on the left.

Take this farm track (which runs up along the Roman line) to a gate leading into a cool deciduous wood. When an open green space is reached the track forks. (The green swathe, straight on up the forest ride, is the line of the Military Way.) Bear right for about forty yards and, as the track bends left, turn off right to follow a footpath up a bank where there's a sign for the Bar Hill Fort. Drop down to the obvious ditch line and follow a path along beside it, dipping and then climbing brutally upwards – the steepest ascent in days!

At the top end of the wood there is a marker post and, up left, the prominent trig point of Castle Hill, 155 metres, the highest part of the whole defensive system and, naturally, a superb viewpoint. On a clear day both Forth and Clyde can be seen, and the hills to the north are spread in fine array beyond the ever-expanding sprawl of Kilsyth.

Descend the far slope of Castle Hill. The path then swings left a bit, passing between two beech trees, to reach the grassy, cared-for site of the Roman fort of Bar Hill. A notice board explains the site: mostly the outline of the headquarters building, and a forty-three feet deep well that proved a 'treasure' for the archaeologists as the Romans not only dropped things into it accidentally or as votive offerings (tin coins), but when they left for good all kinds of objects were thrown in, even the winding gear of the well itself, an altar, weapons, tools, ballista balls, over twenty columns, bases and capitals from the headquarter building, pottery and much else – all to be preserved till dug out this century. Bar Hill is unusual in being sited back from the wall so the Military Way passes between fort and wall/ditch.

Another notice board, down a bit to the north-west, explains the

A SUPERB SECTION OF THE ANTONINE WALL DITCH ON BAR HILL

ruins of the separate bath house and latrines. Every fort had its bath house, laid out in roughly similar fashion. One entered a changing room, then a cold wash room before a series of ever-hotter bath rooms, the heat coming from under-floor and/or inter-wall ducts, the air being heated in a furnace at the end of the building. The toilet block would usually be sited downhill slightly so waste water could be channelled down to flush it. A trip to the loo was a somewhat sociable event with the room fitted with the optimum number of wooden seats ranged round the walls and lined over troughs. All very hygienic and organised though. Very Roman.

Leave Bar Hill Fort from the south-west corner where there is a gate onto a gravelly track, which leads down to a second gate onto a farm track at a big circular, covered water tank. Turn right and follow the curving track down to Twechar. A curve of the canal ahead is obvious and the road hugs its north bank. This road has been constructed on top of the old towpath, so there is no safe walking along that side. For the only time we will follow a short stretch of route on the south side of the canal.

The path comes out to Twechar (pronounced Tweech-ar) at the war memorial. Turn right and walk down towards the canal and, just before reaching it, turn left along the road leading to a housing scheme. Twechar is another mining village with no mines. The old housing scheme blocks with their square buildings and high chimneys have a certain character, now. Room and kitchen, outside loo and water pump and no electricity was the older reality.

ALONG THE FORTH AND CLYDE CANAL

Walk along the road parallel to the canal, passing a village store (right), and when the tarred road swings left keep on ahead on a track (largely dirt track) which runs along the backs of houses, with many garages. At a fork bear right. Shortly after there is another fork with a footpath, right, obviously going onto the canal bank. Do not take this but continue down the sunken gravel lane to its end at a stream where there is a footbridge. There are also several paths but ignore these and turn downstream to go through the tunnel under the canal. There is a date, 1771, above the arch at the north end.

There is a farm, Shirva, which must stand pretty well on the line of the wall. Very little of the wall remains visible from here westwards. Low ground or houses, roads etc have swallowed it up. Through much of time it was Graham's Dyke (or Grim's Dyke) rather than Antonine Wall (just as Hadrian's Wall was the Picts' Wall). Archaeology is a young science.

Once through the tunnel cut back up steps, on the right, to regain the familiar north bank of the canal. Turn right (west) along the towpath, a peaceful area and much more spacious than the Union Canal. The ruin is old canal stabling of the style we'll see, restored, at Glasgow Bridge. Odd garden escapes can be spotted, and there are even water lilies in the water. The presence of Kirkintilloch's suburbs is made obvious by the litter on banks and in the canal itself. A large pipe (Loch Lomond water!) crossing the waterway is covered in graffiti. A small road (four feet nine inches headroom!) passes below the canal and then there's a smaller pipe crossing. Houses lie to the right. The bold brick church on the south side is St Flannan's Roman Catholic church, well worth a visit as it's only five minutes walk from Hillhead Bridge and the airy, dramatic, modern interior is really beautiful.

'Kirky' (as locals abbreviate Kirkintilloch) will seem quite bustly after the quiet canal. A swing bridge (Hillhead Bridge) with iron tracery/finials forces the walker up to a road. Traffic! Cross carefully – or walk along through Hillhead for five minutes to see the beautiful interior of St Flannan's Church. From Hillhead Bridge continue along the canal bank. The Luggie Water passes underneath (as did an old railway line), then we go under a new concrete flyover of a bridge to debouch at a car park dominated by the red Victorian gothic of St Mary's Parish Church. The

THE FAIRY QUEEN *PASSING THROUGH THE ORIGINAL HILLHEAD BASCULE BRIDGE IN KIRKINTILLOCH (PHOTO: COURTESY STRATHKELVIN DISTRICT LIBRARIES)*

canal here, Townhead, is culverted under the busy Cowgate, and its banks were the most litter-strewn of the whole walk when we passed. (We had a wry smile at the name seen on one carton – the *Kirky Mahal*.)

By turning right, down the Cowgate, one can find all the services of the town. Note the well with the motto of the town over it: 'Ca' canny but ca' awa'. The centre is being drastically restored and has little character, but walk to the Cross at the far end to visit the Auld Kirk (1644) and Barony Chambers, interesting old buildings in themselves and the latter an award-winning museum containing displays on the town's major past industries: coal mining, iron works, shipbuilding and weaving. All have gone now, though there is still a soap factory in the town. There's also an evocative re-creation of a 'single end' in the museum. The building dates to 1815 when it replaced the old tolbooth. The top floor had a school, the middle floor acted as town hall and court room and, below, lay the gaol. The steeple's clock was known as the 'four faced liar' as each face tended to show a different time! The museum has an interesting range of local books etc, for sale. 041-775-1185.

Behind the Auld Kirk are commemorative gates leading into the Peel Park, where there is a fountain and bandstand (just like at Kilsyth), a good view to the Campsies, an excavated section of Wall foundation and the site of a castle *motte*. Walk down the park to Union Street and turn left back to the Cowgate. There's another red (St Ninian's Roman Catholic) church beside the Peel Park. Kirkintilloch, like Kilsyth, has plenty of churches, having the same history of religious revivals in the eighteenth and nineteenth centuries. South of the canal lies Townhead; the only interest there for us is a couple of coffee houses at the far end of the shops.

Kirkintilloch developed as a result of the canal coming. Two shipyards were sited there and industries developed as they could use the canal for transport. Passengers were a minor part of the commercial use of the canal. Glasgow traded with eastern Europe via the canal. Maryhill (Kelvinlock then) had the first registered Temperance Society in 1827, and Kirkintilloch was also a dry town for forty-seven years, 1921-68. (Not quite the position today!) Records still show that many of the accidents on the canal had drink/alcohol to blame – drunk in charge of a *swift*, *screw* or *gabbart* perhaps! Something like three million tons of goods and 200,000 passengers were being carried annually in mid-Victorian times.

From late Victorian times up until World War II cruising on the canal was popular (an alternative to sailing 'doon the waater'). The famous 'Queens' ran to the basin at Craigmarloch (Kilsyth) with its tearoom and putting green. A band and singing enlivened the evening run home to Glasgow. This is the image which lingers rather than the reality of the canals being, for 200 years, as vital to industrial transportation as are the motorways today.

Bonnie Prince Charlie's army passed through Kirkintilloch on the way to Falkirk. A shot was fired after the troops, who had to be quietly placated to stop them sacking the town. Edward I seized the castle, but Bishop Wishart paused in his building work on Glasgow Cathedral to help dislodge the English forces. Bruce gave the castle and lands to the Flemings, but they rebuilt the castle at Cumbernauld. The library (west of Peel Park) has a treasured burgh 'Court Book' (1658-94) which contains a range of historical information. In those days it was a crime in Kirky to be unemployed.

Kirkintilloch was early involved with railways, a line being built from the mines at Monkland in 1826 (horse drawn) to take coal by the canal to Edinburgh. Lines proliferated, and in 1840 another line went by Slamannan to the Union Canal at Causwayend. North of Kirkintilloch the line skirted the Campsies so you could travel to Aberfoyle, Balloch, Stirling etc – all gone now. A walkway has been created from Kirkintilloch to Lennoxtown and Strathblane using parts of the old line.

This book has had to use an odd compromise, giving heights in metres yet distance in miles – all thanks to the mess that we made of metrification – but change is not new. While browsing through *The Old Statistical Account* on Kirkintilloch I saw that the minister quoted measures (and money) which now mean nothing to us. 'A chalder of lime, consisting of 16 bolls, each of which contains 3 firlots is bought for 6s 8d.'

Kirkintilloch had one remarkable visitor in 1785: the Italian balloonist Lunardi took off from central Glasgow watched by a crowd put at 100,000. He landed north of Kirkintilloch which practically emptied as people streamed out to see this marvel. A mile or two from Lunardi's touch-down site is Antermony where a more remarkable traveller was born in 1691. John Bell, a doctor, went to serve the Czar Peter I in 1714. From there he went to Persia (Iran), and later right across Russia to China – a sixteen-month journey. After further journeys in Turkey and Persia he became a merchant in Constantinople. He retuned to Antermony about 1746, and wrote a book about his adventures.

Probably the town's most famous son was journalist, historian, politician, Secretary of State for Scotland, creator of the Highland Hydro industry, chairman of the Scottish Council of the Forestry Commission and the Scottish Tourist Board (among other things) – Tom Johnston, who was also a consummate politician and a member of Churchill's wartime cabinet. It was the war that led to his appointment as surely the best (some would say only) Secretary of State *for* Scotland and out of the war, with shortages and difficulties, the Hydro was created to tap the Highland water resource, a fairly assured renewable energy resource!

Back to the canal at Townhead Bridge – and off west again. It is difficult to envisage this area once had a busy shipbuilding industry but something like 150 boats (scows, puffers and the like) were built at the two yards, one sited where we still see a large boathouse, the other in a huge basin further back. The basin is now filled in. The present boathouse is the winter quarters for the charitable Seagull Trust boat, *Yarrow Seagull*. There's a landing stage on our side too, for summer cruises (see book by A.I. Bowman for the Kirky boatbuilding story).

A bend leads us round a bluff to pass St Ninian's High School and then we are in completely rural surroundings again. A black gritty path makes for easy walking along to Glasgow Bridge. A plaque on the wall below the bridge mentions it being opened in 1990 – the first of the culverts to be replaced once more with a bridge so canal navigation can be resumed. The Stables was just that in olden days. Its modern status as a pub may be welcome!

THE REINSTATED FORTH AND CLYDE CANAL HAS BROUGHT BACK LIFE TO THIS STRETCH AT GLASGOW BRIDGE

THE CAMPSIE FELLS FROM THE CANAL NEAR GLASGOW BRIDGE

The Stables is also a good restaurant and Glasgow Bridge is the base for two cruising restaurants, a tourist novelty which is a welcome addition to canal use: *The Barge* 0836-704287 and *Lady Margaret* 041-776-6996. On Sundays at 13.30 the Forth and Clyde Canal Society's *Ferry Queen No 8* makes a cruise on the canal and is also available for chartering.

Hungryside Bridge, next along, originally opened as a drawbridge (the original Glasgow Bridge was a swing bridge), and it is worth clambering up to have a look at the landscape on the north side. The canal is surprisingly high above the flat plain of the River Kelvin. The name Bogton just below us tells what it once was. To the north-west we look over the Balmore Haughs and the rolling lower slopes of the Campsies which will take us to Milngavie. The area north of the canal, between Kirky and Milngavie must have the heaviest concentration of golf courses in Britain (nine at least). Between Torrance and Kirky are some fine examples of oxbow lakes.

A well-made path takes us on a last half mile curve of canal to Cadder. A Roman fort site lies in the crook of the bend, the canal here cutting through the Roman wall line. Two modern railway accidents are connected with the Cadder stretch of the Edinburgh–Glasgow line. In 1973 fifty yards of track were ripped up during a high speed derailment, and ten

A HORSE-DRAWN SCOW ON THE CANAL AT CADDER IN PRE-MECHANICAL DAYS
(PHOTO: COURTESY STRATHKELVIN DISTRICT LIBRARIES)

years later passengers had to leap from the train as two coaches went on fire.

Don't overshoot the turn-off at Cadder. There is a car park by a landing stage as we come to tarred road and street lights. Here we turn first right to Cadder Church, marking the old *kirktown* of Cadder village which lay south-east in pre-canal days.

Glasgow's suburbs sprawl right out to Cadder now, but we keep to our rural route right to the end. There's a row of old canal workers' cottages across the canal and the attractive Cadder Bridge spans the canal, allowing access to Keir Golf Course which we'll be crossing beyond Cadder Church to reach the Kelvin. As soon as we turn right we come on Cadder church.

RURAL ENDING: CADDER TO MILNGAVIE

Cadder church dates back to the twelfth century, a tree-hidden, graveyard-knoll of a site which is straight out of *Tam o' Shanter*. There's a doll's house of a watchers' shelter (to foil body-snatchers), an iron coffin-carrier, and dozens of tumbled headstones and monuments. The iron fountain on the gable does not provide water. The present building dates to 1830.

In the eighteenth century the patronage row in the Church of Scotland involved a young lawyer who was an elder at Cadder Kirk, and whose family home at Huntershill has made the name Muir of Huntershill one to remember. He suggested the, to us quite innocuous, idea that everyone should have a vote, and for his stand on such principles he was to be thrown into a life which, if written as fiction, would sound overdone.

Arrested for sedition and then released on bail he went to France to try and plead with the Revolution leaders not to execute Louis XVI which would damage the cause of reform in Britain. The outbreak of war between Britain and France meant he was late back for his trial, so he was arrested and carried to Edinburgh in chains. In England he would probably soon have been free, but the grim Lord Braxfield sentenced him to fourteen years transportation, which was all too often a death sentence in disguise. Muir survived the horrendous voyage out to Australia and then escaped on an American ship which, after crossing the Pacific, was wrecked on the west coast of North America. He and one other survived though the latter soon died. Despite Red Indians he walked out of that situation only to be arrested by the Spanish authorities in Central America. He was sent to Spain, but that ship was wrecked too. Fished out of the sea he was taken to Cuba and then across the Atlantic to Cadiz where the ship was engaged in a ferocious battle with an English frigate. Muir fought for the Spaniards as the best of evils, was severely wounded, losing the sight of one eye. Put ashore he was eventually freed to travel to France where he lived out the rest of his short life, being only thirty-four when he died.

Patronage simply meant the local laird, not the congregation, appointed the minister, an issue that divided Scotland for a century until the system was abolished. In Kirkintilloch those who objected ('seceders') used to *walk* over the Campsies to church in Stirling each Sunday – a round trip of thirty-five miles !

The road on from Cadder Church is private (to vehicles), but is a pedestrian footpath to Balmore. It is a tarred road past Kirkton Cottage, and finally turns into the grounds of a large house, but the way on is now unsurfaced track which curves down, left, to cross Keir Golf Course. At a house the road swings left, but the right-of-way continues as a hedge-held footpath, on in the same line, starting between gate and the double garage of the house. At the end of the golf course a smaller footpath runs straight on up a bank – and there is the River Kelvin and the footbridge. The river was banked-up in 1770 to stop the periodic flooding of the valley. There were stepping stones originally, and some Victorian antiquarians were waxing enthusiastic about one which they proclaimed to be Roman – until a local lass pointed out it was just the cheese press from her farm. The District Council refloored the bridge in 1990.

Turn left once across the Kelvin footbridge, and then right along a farm track straight across the flat fields to Balmore, joining a small loop road off the A807. Immediately right is the Balmore Nursery and Tea Room and, 200 yards further on on the left, the Coach House Craft and Coffee shop (closed Mondays); these offer the last chance of refreshments before Milngavie.

Follow this loop road left to cross the A807 onto the small road signed for 'Glenorchard Road'. At a crossroads keep straight on along Golf Course Road, and follow this to the club house, a red-roofed, white-washed building which looks over a course which must be one of the most beautiful anywhere. Go along the lane behind the club house and down to a bridge over the Branziet Burn, which is then followed along the edge of the golf course. There is a sharp turn left (17th hole), and we stick to the burnside path until there is no option but to cross the burn again (telegraph pole), and on across the fairway to enter a gap in the trees left of the cottage ('Temple' on map) to then walk along its drive. Look left when about to cross the fairway as golfers may be driving off from a tee. The road exits through the far end of the golf course then turns left up to meet a quiet road at Baldernock Primary School (Fluchter).

Turn left along this country road, passing under a line of pylons, and take the right fork at the first junction. As height is gained there is a view down to the rim of Glasgow with its rectangular high-rise towers rather overwhelming the familiar shape of the spire of the university. The Red Road flats (thirty-five storeys) were, when built, the highest residential blocks in Europe. Our road twists up to a T-junction on a dangerously blind corner (a mirror helps motorists), where we turn right and then left at the war memorial cross outside Baldernock Parish Church ('Langbank' sign).

If the churchyard gate is locked there are steps up the wall. The church has an unusual layout, and has outside stairs to reach the balconies. A motto declares *Deo optimo maximo*! and is dated 1795 but many of the flat gravestones have earlier dates. The open hillside setting makes it a cheerful place compared to Cadder earlier on. The site dates back to the thirteenth century. There is also a watch house built in the days of the resurrectionists. Thomas Baird, of the Barrie and Baird Cairngorms tragedy on New Year's day 1928, is buried here.

If heading for Bankell Farm for B & B, keep on north and the farm road is first on the left. Next day reach Milngavie by crossing the busy A81 and on round Craigmaddie Reservoir – the A81 is worth avoiding on foot.

Being hit by a car on the last day would be inconvenient.

Take the road along the front of the church, passing a porticoed house, to drop steeply down to the cluster of buildings of the old mill, now turned into attractive houses. The building on the left has a goose weathervane. The lowest building is the mill itself (last used as a sawmill), and the wheel has been restored – make sure you see it if turning right at the junction for Milngavie, for the wheel is on the left of the building and can be missed. The mill appears on Timothy Pont's map of 1654. 'Kirktoun' is shown for Baldernock, Milngavie appears as 'Milgay' and Mugdock as 'Mukdack'. Standard spelling is a modern concept.

The road pulls up steeply from the mill; from the crest there is a good view to the Kilpatrick Hills then a dip again to a ford (footbridge if needed) over the Tinkers Burn, marked with a 'Milngavie' sign. The last stretch of our walk runs through the middle of woody golf courses. Some may prefer to walk the edge of these, on footpaths parallel to the road, but the road is quiet enough and the odd idiot motorist by the nature of his sins, will be heard well in advance. The hexagonal folly-like building off to the left is a doocot standing in the Dougalston Estate grounds, an estate

THE DOUGALSTON DOOCOT ('FOLLY TYPE')
ABOVE MILNGAVIE

created out of late eighteenth-century tobacco trade profits (turnover of £1.5 million, yet the Glassford cook received £6.50 per annum in wages!). The American War of Independence and war with France, plus Glassford's gambling propensities, brought that dream to an end, debts ran on for several generations and their Dougalston mansion, damaged by fire in 1830, soon became a ruin and was later demolished. The estate is now a golf course and only the doocot and the Factor's House survive from its affluent years.

North of Milngavie is the large sprawl of Mugdock Country Park which began with a gift of 350 acres from Sir Hugh Fraser and now runs to over 700 acres of woods, lochs and delightful landscape. There are several castles, the most historical being Mugdock Castle, early seat of the Lennox earls who sold it to the founder of the Graham of Montrose family. It was the home of the Great Marquis whose battle sites (victory at Kilsyth and defeat at Philiphaugh) have waymarked our route.

We finish with a steep brae (Baldernock Road) down into Milngavie, a prosperous middle-class suburb for mighty Glasgow. The parish church of St Paul's stands on the corner. After crossing Glasgow Road the rail and bus station will be seen on the left. If going into the town centre keep on the

WALKING ROUND THE CLOCK AT MILNGAVIE – THE END OF THE WALK (OR THE START OF THE WEST HIGHLAND WAY)

right-hand side of the road and follow the pedestrian path (there is also a underpass from the train/bus station) which leads to the cheery, continental-like central area, traffic-free with a pedestal clock and war memorial of a kneeling female, apparently pointing the way north. The town makes little contribution to meeting the visitor. There is no information centre or even a notice board, no current local guidebook, few B & B opportunities and even the West Highland Way's start is given minimal indication. Laid-back I think is the term to describe the end of our tramp from Borders to Highlands.

Maybe it is a bit late now to add a warning about the pronunciation of Milngavie. This is approximately *Mil-guy*, (which is how it used to be spelt), with the accent on the second syllable, which is uncommon in Scottish place names. At least you are not asking for tickets to Milngavie. I'm sure Acharacle is one of the less-used starting points of the *Ultimate Challenge* coast-to-coast backpacking event because nobody knows how to pronounce it.

Last century Milngavie grew from a country village on the banks of the Allander Water, into a busy town. (Population in 1775 was 200, in 1875 it was 2,000, in 1990 it was 12,000.) Life was linked with the river which gave power for textile, snuff and paper mills. There were extensive bleach works. Now it is the northern, outermost, fringe, *des-res* suburb of Glasgow, linked to the city by Bearsden and Maryhill. Bearsden, only a few minutes away by bus or train, has a Roman Bath House (see Appendix 1), which is worth seeing, either this evening or, if staying overnight, in the morning on the way into Glasgow. The Hunterian Museum in Glasgow has many of the finds from the Antonine Wall on display, and the friendly city is worth exploring too before heading off home.

In the thirties, boom years for 'heading to the country', six times as many trams ran from Glasgow to Milngavie on a Sunday as operated on weekdays. Now the last trams are in Glasgow's Transport Museum, but we continue the tradition of walking the 'higher lands and cleaner airs'. I trust Milngavie is no ending for our activities. Just a refreshment stop where we can rest our feet and dream of the next stages of adventure.

> *O, some grow old, and dream no more*
> *And some do dream by day, lad.*
> *And some put feet upon their dream*
> *And have a song to sing, lad.*

PRACTICAL INFORMATION: MILNGAVIE, BEARSDEN, GLASGOW

Telephone Code for Milngavie is 041-956-
Telephone Code for Bearsden is 041-942- (or 041-923)

ACCOMMODATION: Rough directions from the centre of Milngavie or from Bearsden are given. Milngavie: Black Bull Hotel, Main Street, -2291 (central but expensive), Barloch Guest House, 82 Strathblane Road, -1432 (north-east), Arnish, 14 Blane Drive, -1767 (north-east), Westview, 1 Dougalston Gardens South, -5973 (east). 93 Drumlin Drive, -1596 (south). 13 Craigdhu Avenue, -3439 (west), Fairways, 19 James Watt Road, -3262 (north-west), Banknell Farm, Strathblane Road, -1733 (two miles out and reached from Baldernock Church).

Bearsden: Burnbrae Hotel, Milngavie Road, -5951 (north-east – expensive). Kilmadinny Guest House, Milngavie Road, -943-1310 (north-east), 14 Rannoch Drive, -3557 (south-west), 28 Ballater Drive, -7530 (south), 11 Strathyre Gardens, -7443 (east), St Andrews College of Education, Duntocher Road, -943-1424 (west, open: Easter and June-September, 210 singles, 105 twins, evening meals).

CAMPING: Kilmadinny Riding Centre, Milngavie Road, Bearsden, 041-942-4404 (May-September).

MEALS: Milngavie has a large number of coffee houses, cafes and restaurants, plus hotel and bar meals so, whenever one arrives, there should be no lack of refreshments. Shops, banks, telephones are all available in the town centre.

ONWARD TRANSPORT: There is an excellent train and bus service from Milngavie to the centre of Glasgow. Three bus lines operate services and trains leave at ten minutes to the hour and twenty minutes past the hour. The last train is at 22.52. Hillfoot and Bearsden are the first stations down the line; either is convenient for visiting the Roman bath house or for reaching alternative accommodation (as listed).

Train enquiries: 041-204-2844.

Bus enquiries: 041-942-2291 or 041-332-9644.

OPTIONAL EXTRA DAY IN GLASGOW

Many of the finds from Bar Hill and elsewhere on the Antonine Wall are on display in the Hunterian Museum, 041-330-4421, at Glasgow University, the landmark building above the Kelvin. The museum is in the main building near the Visitor Centre, 041-330-5511. Glasgow's main Art Gallery and Museum lies just below the University at Kelvingrove – but really Glasgow is well-off for many visitor interests, and you can choose your own. Send for the annual Guide and 'What's On' to Glasgow Tourist Information Centre, 35 St Vincent Place, Gl 2ER, 041-204-4400. One day will prove quite inadequate to see the Hunterian Museum – and Art Gallery, Kelvingrove, the Botanic Gardens, Museum of Transport, Glasgow Cathedral, the Burrell Collection, the People's Palace, the Maritime Museum, the City Chambers, to name a few at random. Glasgow has a deserved reputation for its musical and theatrical life, and there are scores of good places to eat, besides which just being there can be fun for – even if you can't grasp the accent – the people are so friendly and welcoming.

ACCOMMODATION: Check with the Tourist Information Centre. There is a Grade I Youth Hostel, 11 Woodlands Terrace, 041-332-3004.

ONWARD TRAVEL: Train enquiries: 041-204-2844 (24 hrs) (Sleepers to London). Buchanan Street Bus Station: 041-332 9191 (Direct links to most cities). Glasgow Airport: 041-887-1111 (Regular flights to UK cities),

If having to return to Edinburgh (I'm not making any comparisons between the rival cities) there is an excellent fast, frequent train service, forty minutes travel time. We've come a long way since the 'speedy' canal service – or our own pedestrian crossing of Scotland. Glimpses of hills and canal bridges, viaducts and the Cauldstane Slap as we speed eastwards – memories already, to be enjoyed in turn.

Appendix 1

THE BEARSDEN ROMAN BATH HOUSE

This was discovered in 1973 during excavations for building flats, which now circle round the site on Roman Road. From Bearsden Station turn left, Station Road, left again, Drymen Road (A809) then first right, Roman Road. From Hillfoot Station go out on the west side by a pedestrian exit on Milngavie Road (A81). Roman Drive breaks off, diagonally, left, across the A8, and soon merges with Roman Road.

This was the communal bath house of a fort on the extreme fringe of the empire, yet even here facilities like a bath house and flush toilets were standard. (They also ate a balanced diet, and each unit had medical back-up.) Though only the foundations survive these give a clear plan of the lay-out and a display board provides an interesting explanation of the site. Most bath houses were built to pattern: an entrance hall-changing room, then a choice of cold room, hot dry room, and a series of increasingly hot steam rooms. The heat came from a furnace with the hot air fed through underfloor and wall cavity spaces. The toilets were often at a lower level, so all water could flow through to flush the effluent. The complex was usually on the outskirts of a fort or, as here, in an annex. Baths like this are still in use in Arab lands (I've used them in Morocco) and are the outcome of Roman influences.

One kilometre east of the bath house, along Boclair Road B8049 (the continuation of Roman Road across Milngavie Road, A81), in New Kilpatrick (or Hillfoot) cemetery are two short stretches of the Antonine Wall base, the best such to be seen. One is more or less straight ahead, running north to south, the other is at the far east side, running east to west, the wall making a sharp bend between. Culverts can be seen and one bit has been stepped for greater stability. The Antonine Wall was basically a turf wall, but good stone foundations like this were laid first.

Objects discovered at Bearsden are held at the Hunterian Museum in the University of Glasgow. There is a Roman Room with permanent displays, temporary exhibitions and school facilities, well worth taking in before heading off home. Glasgow deserves an extra day. It was not made European City of Culture in 1990 without good reason.

Appendix 2

UPDATING OF INFORMATION

There is always a continuous changing of the practical information concerning B & Bs, timetables, state of paths, opening hours of castles, shops, museums and so on. While the information in this guide is as comprehensive and accurate as possible there will be changes which will invalidate points of detail: a B & B may close, or a very useful youth hostel open. To assist those planning a crossing I've made an Information Sheet which will be updated each year. The usefulness of this is obvious, but to be as thorough as possible could I ask those who have followed this route to report *any* changes they have encountered, so the information can be passed on. This will be sifted in the autumn and the updated Information Sheet made available for early December, ready for the Christmas holiday dreaming of next summer's activities!

To obtain a copy please enclose a SAE and ten second class postage stamps: send to Scottish Mountain Holidays, P to H, 21 Carlin Craig, Kinghorn, Fife, KY3 9RX.

Appendix 3

COUNTRYSIDE COMFORT AND BEHAVIOUR

> I should feel it as a sort of sacrilege to prefer, or even to compare anything to the Firth of Clyde. But one great difference between the sources of its beauty and that of Scavaig was forcibly impressed upon me. How much does Clyde owe to human association, to culture, to seats, to villages, to towns, to vessels! The peculiarity of the interest in Scavaig arose from the total absence of all human interference. The scene would have been the same had man not existed.

So wrote Lord Cockburn in *Circuit Journeys,* describing a visit to Skye in 1841. The same duality in the attractiveness of scenery still applies today: Scavaig and Tweed, Cairngorms and Clyde; we like them for such different, such opposite, reasons. In our Peninnes To Highlands walk we have some of the wild and lonely, even if it is not quite Scavaig, and we have a great deal more of the other landscape where people live and work and leave their mark on all we see about us. Because it is a peopled landscape we need perhaps to be reminded of countryside behaviour. The Country Code is a charter of freedom, not a restriction. Some care and thought can avoid most 'situations' from developing.

BEFORE LEAVING HOME

Ensure competence in basic navigational skills. Descending the Coquet instead of the Kale is not just inconvenient - it could be disastrous.

Plan within your capabilities. Tired people are far more accident-prone.

Learn something of elementary First Aid and prepare a small field kit. Acquire adequate waterproofs, comfy boots and emergency items.

If going alone organise some system of phoning home or to someone acting as base. If you break a leg on the Moorfoots it is nice to know someone will be worried sooner rather than later and send out an SOS on your behalf. Know the distress signal.

Read-up about the areas being visited. The curious traveller is usually the happiest traveller. Buy all the maps you need and prepare by reading through this book *with* the maps.

ALONG THE WAY

Close all gates. There is nothing calculated to annoy farmers more than having to round up strayed livestock. Don't go over walls, or through fences or hedges - there are few places without gates or stiles on our route.

Leave livestock, crops, and machinery alone.

Guard against all risk of fires. There is no need to light a fire of any kind. A lighter is safer than matches if you do use a stove.

Dump your litter in bins not in the countryside. You'll see some bad sights – so don't add to them. Poly bags can mean death to a grazing cow, broken glass is wicked for both man and beast, and drink cans an insufferable eyesore.

Leave wildlife alone. Collect memories not eggs or flowers. 'Lost' creatures are rare; parents will soon find their young unless some helpful person has carried them off!

Walk quietly in the countryside. Nature goes unobtrusively and you'll see far more if you are not clad in garish colours and walking with a ghetto blaster. (I joke not - I've met one on top of the Eildons!) While most of this trip is on rights-of-way or other established walking routes it is still running through a farmed and used landscape so treat it with respect. Local people's livelihood depends on this countryside. There is no wilderness.

Dogs are best left at home. In prime sheep/farming country they need strict control so neither dog nor owner can relax much. In the lambing season (March-May) dogs are particularly unwelcome.

Be extra careful when walking on roads, however quiet these appear. Manic drivers are no respecters of pedestrians.

Make local contacts. Rural people are still sociable and a 'crack' will often be welcomed. Use the Tourist Information Offices and bookshops along the way to widen knowledge and enrich one's experience. Those met in bars, cafes or overnight stops are often a fund of information. They may even find *us* interesting!

Keeping a record of some kind is usually rewarding - if not always at the time. I've seen some remarkable 'creations' of notes, photos, postcards, drawings or in the case of one girl, a bound collection of all her letters home to her absent husband. In later years these are great souvenirs.

AND AFTERWARDS?

Start preparing for the next trip.

Appendix 4

FACTS AND FIGURES, MAPS COVERING THE ROUTE

Below is a rough estimate of distances and heights for the trip. As a practical guide for time needed allow three miles per hour plus one minute for every ten metres of height gained. These figures apply to the full day's possibilities and not to any shorter, easier alternatives. Anomalies come in as the Broxburn or Kilsyth endings can be plus or minus five miles (eight kilometres) depending on where accommodation is found, but this does not influence the eventual total of about 170 miles (250 kilometres) and 4,560 metres (14,800 feet) of ascent.

Also listed are the maps which cover the route. *Bart* is Bartholemew's 1:100,000 series, *OSLR* is the Ordnance Survey's 1:50,000 series and *OSPF* is the Ordnance Survey's 1:25,000 series.

DAY ONE: Byrness to Jedburgh
> 20 miles/31 kilometres,   770 metres of ascent
> Bart 41 OSLR 80,74   OSPF 498 (NT 60/70),
> 486 (NT 61/71), 474 (NT 62/72).

DAY TWO: Jedburgh Day
> 1.5miles/2 kilometres,   70 metres
> Accumulative, 21.5miles/33 kilometres, 840 metres
> Bart 41   OSLR 74   OSPF 474 (NT 62/72).

DAY THREE: Jedburgh to Melrose
> 20 miles/31 kilometres, 500 metres
> Accumulative, 41.5miles/64 kilometres, 1,340 metres
> Bart 41   OSLR 74,73   OSPF 474 (NT 62/72),
> 462 (NT 63/73), 461 (NT43/53).

DAY FOUR: Eildons and Melrose
> 5.5miles/9 kilometres, 450 metres
> Accumulative 47 miles/73 kilometres,   1,790 metres
> Bart 41   OSLR 73   OSPF 461 (NT 43/53).

DAY FIVE: Melrose to Selkirk
  10 miles/16 kilometres, 270 metres
  Accumulative 57 miles/89 kilometres, 2,060 metres
  Bart 41   OSLR 73   OSPF 461 (NT 43/53),
  473 (NT 42/52).

DAY SIX: Selkirk to Innerleithen
  14.5 miles/23 kilometres, 685 metres
  Accumulative 71.5 miles/112 kilometres, 2,745 metres
  Bart 41   OSLR 73   OSPF 473 (NT 42/52),
  461 (NT 43/53), 460 (NT 23/33).

DAY SEVEN: Innerleithen to Peebles
  12 miles/18 kilometres, 780 metres
  Accumulative 83.5 miles/130 kilometres, 3,525 metres
  Bart 41   OSLR 73   OSPF 460 (NT 23/33),
  448 (NT 24/34).

DAY EIGHT: Peebles to West Linton
  14.5 miles/22 kilometres, 370 metres
  Accumulative 98 miles/152 kilometres, 3,895 metres
  Bart 41 OSLR 73,72   OSPF 448 (NT 24/34),
  447 (NT 04/14), 433 (NT 05/15).

DAY NINE: West Linton to Broxburn
  18 miles/27 kilometres,   230 metres
  Accumulative 116 miles/179 kilometres, 4,125 metres
  Bart 45   OSLR 65   OSPF 433 (NT 05/15),
  419 (NT 06/16), 406 (NT 07/17).

DAY TEN: Broxburn to Linlithgow
  10 miles/16 kilometres, 55 metres
  Accumulative 126 miles/195 kilometres, 4,180 metres
  Bart 45   OSLR 65   OSPF 406 (NT 07/17),
  405 (NT 87/97).

DAY ELEVEN: Linlithgow to Falkirk
  9 miles/14 kilometres, 30 metres
  Accumulative 135 miles/209 kilometres, 4,210 metres
  Bart 45   OSLR 65   OSPF 405 (NT 87/97).

DAY TWELVE: Falkirk to Kilsyth
  10 miles/16 kilometres, 130 metres
  Accumulative 145 miles/225 kilometres, 4,340 metres
  Bart 45   OSLR 65,64   OSPF 405 (NS 87/97),
  404 (NS 67/77).

DAY THIRTEEN: Kilsyth to Milngavie
14 miles/21 kilometres, 220 metres
Accumulative 169 miles/246 kilometres, 4,560 metres/ 14,800 feet
Bart 45 OSLR 64   OSPF 404 (NS 67/77),
403 (NS 47/57).

Quick map check:
Bartholemew: 41,45
Landranger: 64, 65, 72, 74, 80
Pathfinder: 403, 404, 405, 419, 433, 447, 448, 460, 461, 462,
473, 474, 486, 498.

Bibliography

There is an enormous literature on the Borders so the list here is very much a limited personal selection, mostly of books in print or readily available, but also including some older classics which can always be ordered from one's home library. I've also included books (just a few to satisfy the curious traveller) on some of the topics or individual places mentioned along the route. All the Tourist Information Offices carry town maps and local booklets, and I've mentioned bookshops where these exist. Glasgow and Edinburgh have many big bookshops so there is the chance of loading up after the walk. Reading, to me, is very much part and parcel of enjoying a walk through new territory; I hope it is one of your delights.

Aitken, R. : *The West Highland Way*. HMSO/CCS. 3rd ed. 1990.
Allan, R. & Candlish, I.: *The Scottish Borderland*. BCLA 1988.
Allen, G. H.: *From Land's End to John o' Groats*. London 1905 (In 16 days!)
Anderson, H.: *Innerleithen & Traquair, Ancient & Modern*. Bognor Press 1984. (Booklet)
Anderson, R.: *A History of Kilsyth*. Duncan. 1901.
Andrew, K.: *The Southern Upland Way* (Eastern Section): CCS/HMSO 1984.
Andrew, K. & Thrippleton, A.: *The Southern Uplands*. SMC 1976.
Anton, P.: *Kilsyth, A Parish History*. John Smith. 1843 *et seq* (Quite absorbing.)
Antonine Wall, The. HMSO 1969. (An archaeological map.)

Baldernock, Profile of a Parish. Baldernock Amenity Society. 1974.
Baldwin, J.R.: *Exploring Scotland's Heritage, Lothian & Borders*. HMSO 1985. (Indispensable handbook to sites)
Banks, F.R.: *The Borders*. Batsford. 1977.
Barron, E.M.: *The Scottish War of Independence*. 2nd edition. Inverness. 1934.
Barrow, G.W.S.: *Robert Bruce*. EUP. 1988.
Barnett, T.R.: *Border By-Ways & Lothian Lore*. Grant. 1943.
Bell, A.S. (edit): *The Scottish Antiquarian Tradition*. John Donald. 1981. (Has an essay on the Earl of Buchan)
Bell, J.: *A Journey from St Petersburg to Peking 1719-22*. (Edit J. L. Stevenson) EUP. 1966.
Bewley, C.: *Muir of Huntershill*. OUP. 1981.
Bingham, C.: *The Stewart Kingdom of Scotland 1371-1603*. Weidenfeld & Nicolson. 1974.
Bonser, K.J.: *The Drovers*. Country Book Club. 1970. (The English aspect.)
Borland, R.: *Border Raids and Reivers*. Scott. 1910.
Bower, J.: *Description of the Abbey of Melrose*. Edinburgh. 1822.
Bowman, A.I.: *Kirkintilloch Shipbuilding*. Strathkelvin Dist. Pubs. 1983.

: *Swifts & Queens: Passenger Transport on Forth & Clyde Canal.* Strathkelvin Dist. Pubs. 1984.

Breeze, D.J.: *The Northern Frontiers of Roman Britain.* Batsford. 1982.

Brotchie, T.C.F.: *Some Sylvan Scenes Near Glasgow.* Glasgow. 1910 *et seq.*

Brown, H.M.: *Hamish's Groats End Walk.* Paladin 1983 *et seq.*

Brown, J.: *Horae Subsecivae.* (3 vols) 1882 *et seq.*

Brown, J.L. & Lawson, I.C.: *History of Peebles 1850-1990.* Mainstream. 1990.

Brown, J.W.: *Enquiry into the Life and Legend of Michael Scot.* Douglas. 1897.

Bryce, M.R.L.: *Memoir of John Veitch* . Blackwood. 1896.

Buchan. J.: *Sir Walter Scott.* Cassell. 1932.

Buchan, J.W.: *History of Peeblshire* (3 vols) Glasgow. 1925. (exhaustiv.)

Buchan, J.W.: *John Buchan.* Canongate. 1978. (Biography of the writer/politician.)

Burritt, E.: *A Walk from London to John o' Groats.* London. 1864.

Cameron, A. (edit): *Poetry of the Scottish Borders.* Albyn Press. n.d.

Ceram, C.W.: *Gods, Graves & Scholars.* Gollancz. 1952 *et seq.* (World-wide archaeology.)

Chalmers, J. and Storey, D.: *One Hundred Hill Walks Around Edinburgh.* Mainstream. 1990.

Chambers, W.: *History of Peeblshire.* W. & W. Chambers. 1864.

Clarke, D.V., Breeze, D.J., Mackay G.: *The Romans in Scotland.* National Museum HMSO. 1980. (Pictures of treasured finds.)

Clavering, M.: *From the Border Hills.* Nelson. 1953.

Cockburn, Lord: *Circuit Journeys.* (1888). James Thin. 1975.

Companion for Canal Passengers Betwixt Edinburgh and Glasgow. Edinburgh. 1823.   Reprinted LUCS booklet 1981.

Craig Brown, T.: *History of Selkirkshire.* Douglas. 1886.

Crockett, W.S.: *The Scott Country.* Black. 1930.

: *In Praise of Tweed.* Selkirk. 1899. (Anthology of Victorian poetry.)

Cruden, S.: *Scottish Castles.* Spur Books. 1981.

: *Scottish Abbeys.* HMS0. 1960.

Curle, J.: *A Roman Frontier Post and Its People.* Maclehose. 1911. (Large tome on Newstead excavations.)

Daiches, D.: *Sir Walter Scott and His World.* Thames and Hudson. 1971.

Devine, T.M.: *The Tobacco Lords.* John Donald. 1975.

Dixon, D.D.: *Upper Coquetdale.* Newcastle. 1903.

Douglas, Sir G.: *A History of the Border Counties.* Blackwood. 1899.:(edit) *Scottish Fairy and Folk Tales.* 1896. E.P. Publishing edit. 1977.

Dobson, T.: *Reminiscences of Innerleithen and Traquair.* Smail, Innerleithen. 1896.

Douglas-Home H.: *The Birdman.* Collins. 1977.

Edlin, H.L.: *Forests of Central and Southern Scotland.* HMSO. 1969.

Elder, M.: *Tell the Towers Thereof.* Hale. 1956.

Fawcett, R.: *Scottish Mediaeval Churches.* HMSO. 1985.
(Lavishly illustrated p.b.)

Feachem , R.: *Guide to Prehistoric Scotland.* Batsford. 1977 *et seq.*
        : *The North Britons, The Prehistory of a Border People.* Hutchinson.
    1965.

Fenwick, H.: *Scotland's Abbeys and Cathedrals.* Hale. 1978.

Ferguson, J.: *Linlithgow Palace. Its History and Traditions.* (369pp)
Oliver and Boyd. 1910.

Finlay, I.: *The Lothians.* Collins. 1960.

Fisher, A.: *William Wallace.* John Donald. 1986.

Fox, E. W.: *2,000 Miles on Foot.* London. 1911. (In France and Britain.)

Fraser, A.: *Mary Queen of Scots.* Panther. 1970 *et seq.*

Fraser, G.M.: *The Steel Bonnets.* Collins Havrill. 1989. (History of
Border reivers)

Gifford, D.: *James Hogg.* Ramsay Head. 1976.

Gilbert, J.M. (edit): *Flower of the Forest.* Selkirk Common Good Fund.
1985. (Selkirk history)

Gillespie, R.: *Round about Falkirk.* Glasgow. 1879.

Grant, W.:*Pentland Days and Country Ways.* Nelson. n.d.
        : *Tweeddale.* Oliver & Boyd. 1948.
        : *The Call of the Pentlands.* Grant. 1927.

Green, R.L.: *Andrew Lang.* Ward. 1946.

Greig, D.C.: *The South of Scotland.* British Regional Geology. 1980.

Haldane, A.R.B.: *The Drove Roads of Scotland.* David & Charles.
1973 *et seq.* (The classic work on droving.)

Hanson, W.H. & Maxwell, G.S.: *Rome's North-West Frontier:
The Antonine Wall.* E.U.P. 1983.

Hendrie, W.F.: *Discovering West Lothian.* John Donald. 1986. (Useful.)
        : *Linlithgow, Six Hundred Years a Royal Burgh.* John Donald. 1989.

Historic Buildings and Monuments, current booklets on *Jedburgh, Dryburgh*
and *Melrose Abbey.* HMSO. (Available at sites)

Hogg, James: *Selected Stories and Sketches.* (edit D. Mack) Scottish
Academic Press. 1982.

Horne, J. (edit): *Kirkintilloch.* Kirkintilloch. 1910.

Hume, J.R.: *The Industrial Archaeology of Scotland: 1. The Lowlands and
Borders.* Batsford. 1976.

Hutchison, J.: *Weavers, Miners and the Open Book.* Cumbernauld.
1986.(240pp history of Kilsyth.)

Jeffrey, A.: *History and Antiquities of Roxburghshire.* (4 vols)
Jedburgh. 1864.

Johnston, T.: *Old Kirkintilloch.* Kirkintilloch. 1937.

: *Memories*. Collins. 1952.

Johnstone, Anne: *The Wild Frontier*. Mowbray House Press. 1986. (The best introduction to the Roman Wall, well-illustrated, large-format, 40pp.)

Keppie, L.: *Scotland's Roman Remains*. John Donald. 1986. (Excellent.)

: *Roman Distance Slabs from the Antonine Wall*. Hunterian Museum. 1979. (Illustrated booklet)

Lang, A. & J.: *Highways and Byways in the Border*. Macmillan. 1923.

Lang, J.: *A Land of Romance. The Border, Its History and Legend*. Jack. n.d. (large book.)

Lang, T.: *The Border Counties*. (Queen's Scotland) Hodder. 1957.

Lawson, L. *A History of Falkirk*. Falkirk. 1975.

Lees, I.C.: *The Campsies and the Land of Lennox*. Blackie. 1933.

Leslie, R.H.: *Steam on the Waverley Route*. Bradford Burton. n.d. (c. 1970)

Lindsay, J.: *The Canals of Scotland*. David & Charles. 1968. (Standard work.)

Lindsay, M.: *The Lowlands of Scotland; Glasgow and the North*. Hale. 1953.

: *The Lowlands of Scotland; Edinburgh and the South*. Hale. 1977.

: *The Castles of Scotland*. Constable. 1986.

: *The Eye is Delighted*. Muller. 1971. (Romantic Travellers in Scotland.)

Lochhead, M.: *Portrait of the Scott Country*. Hale. 1976.

: *Magic and Witchcraft of the Borders*. Hale. 1984. (Classic stories retold.)

Love, D.: *Scottish Kirkyards*. Hale. 1989.

McCall, H.B.: *History and Antiquities of Mid Calder*. Cameron. 1894.

Macdonald, A.: *Linlithgow in Pictures*. A. & C. Black. 1932.

: *Place Names of West Lothian*. Oliver & Boyd. 1941.

Macdonald, G.: *The Roman Wall in Scotland*. 2nd edit. Clarendon Press. (Big tome.) 1934.

Macdonald, H.: *Rambles Round Glasgow*. Smith. 1910.

McLean, A.P.: *This Magnificent Line*. Lang Syne. 1986. (Booklet on Edinburgh-Glasgow railway line.)

MacLeod, D.: *Land of Tweed*. Blackwood. 1983.

Mackie, R.L.: *King James IV of Scotland*. Oliver & Boyd. 1958.

McWilliam, C: *The Buildings of Scotland: Lothian*. Penguin. 1980. (Exhaustive.)

Manuel, D.G.: *Dryburgh Abbey*. (500pp) Blackwood. 1922.

Margary, I.D.: *Roman Roads in Britain*. Baker. 1973.

Martin, D.: *The Story of Kirkintilloch*. Strathkelvin Dist. Pubs. 1980.

: *The Monkland and Kirkintilloch Railway*. Strathkelvin Dist. (1976.)

: *The Forth and Clyde Canal: A Kirkintilloch View*. Strathkelvin Dist. (1977.)

Massey, A.: *The Edinburgh & Glasgow Union Canal*. Falkirk Museums. 1983.

Maxwell, G.S.: *The Romans in Scotland*. J. Thin/Mercat Press. 1989.

Maxwell, H.: *The Story of the Tweed*. Nisbet. 1909.

Maylard, A.E.: *Walks in and Around Peebles*. 4th ed. Peebles. c.1940.

Millman, R.N.: *The Making of the Scottish Landscape*. Batsford. 1975.

Mitchell, A.: *A Field Guide to the Trees of Britain and Northern Europe*. Collins. 1974 *et seq*.

Moir, D.G.: *Scottish Hill Tracks*. (Southern Scotland) Bartholomew. 1975.

    : *Pentland Walks*. Bartholomew. 1977.

    : *Lothian Walks*. Elliot. 1939.

Morwood, W.: *Traveller in a Vanished Landscape*. Gentry Books. 1973. (Biography of David Douglas)

Mullay, A.J.: *Rails Across the Border*. Patrick Stephen. 1990.

Murray, R.: *The Birds of the Borders*. SOC. 1986.

Naylor, J.: *From John o' Groats to Land's End*. Caxton. 1916.

Nelson, J.: *Highland Bridges*. AUP. 1990. (Interesting explanations about bridges in general)

New, A.: *A Guide to the Abbeys of Scotland*. Constable. 1988.

New History of Scotland (8 vols). Edward Arnold. (Published through the 80s, this thorough paperback history, by different authors, is the best currently available.)

Nicolaisen, W.F.H.: *Scottish Place Names*. Batsford. 1976.

Nimmo, W.: *The History of Stirlingshire*. (2 vols) London. 1880. (Exhaustive)

Ogilvie, W.H.: *The Border Poems*. Hood. Hawick. 1959.

    : *A Clean Wind Blowing*. Constable. 1930.

Ordnance Survey: Special 2.5 Inch map of Antonine Wall, after being long out of print, is being reissued.

Parkinson, D. (edit): *The Eildon Hills*. SWT. 1987. (Best current booklet)

Parry, M.L. & Slater, T.R.: *The Making of the Scottish Countryside*. Croom Helm. 1980.

Paterson, I.: *West Linton. A Brief Historical Guide*. Edinburgh. c.1989. (Stocked locally)

Peel, J.H.B.: *Along the Pennine Way*. David and Charles. 1979.

Powell, M.N.: *Linlithgow, A Brief Architectural and Historical Guide*. Linlithgow Civic Trust. 1976.

Pratt, E.A.: *Scottish Canals & Waterways*. Selwyn & Blount. 1922.

Proceedings of the Society of Antiquaries Scotland: These annual tomes are an invaluable record of research and exploration. Some articles (often exhaustive) on subjects or places of interest along our route are:

1898-99 The Gifford Stones, West Linton; 1902-03 Castlecary excavations;

1904-05 Rough Castle excavations; 1905-06 Bar Hill excavations; 1911-12
Cappuck excavations; 1911-1912 Ancient Bridges of Scotland; 1912-13
Roads and Bridges in Early Scottish History;   1914-15 The Most
Ancient Bridges in Britain; 1923-24 Ancient Border Highways: Minchmoor
Road;   1930-31 The Romanno Terraces;   1931-32 and 1936-37 Croy
Hill;   1938-39 Cultivation Terraces in SE Scotland; 1955-56 The
Arthurian Legend in Scotland; 1960-61 Green Knowe Platform Settlement.

Reid, J.M.: *Traveller Extraordinary*. Eye. Spottiswoode. (Biography of James
Bruce.)
Reith, J.: *Life of Dr John Leyden*. Galashiels. n.d. (Victorian.)
Ridpath, G.: *Border History*. (1848) Mercat Press. 1979.
(Readable old tome.)
Robertson, A.S.: *The Antonine Wall*. Glasgow Archaeological Soc.
(revised edit) 1990. (The best field guide to carry)
Royal Commission on the Ancient and Historical Monuments of Scotland, The.:
Large-size volumes, covering the country, county by county, and detailing
everything of interest. *Roxburghshire* (2 vols) 1956, *Selkirkshire* 1957,
Peebleshire (2 vols) 1967, *Midlothian & West Lothian* 1929, *Stirlingshire* (2
vols) 1963.
Sandison, B.: *The Hillwalker's Guide to Scotland*. Unwin Hyman. 1988.
Scott, R.M.: *Robert the Bruce*. Hutchinson. 1982.(Canongate p.b. 1988.)
Scott, T.: *Tales of Sir William Wallace*. Wright. 1981.
Scott, Sir W.: *Minstrelsy of the Scottish Border*. 1802 *et seq*. (Latest I know is
    Edit. A. Noyes, Mercat Press 1979)
        : *Heart of Midlothian, St Ronan's Well, The Black Dwarf, Old Mortality*
    are novels with a Borders or local setting.
        : *Tales of a Grandfather*. 1828 *et seq*.
Scottish Wildlife Trust: *The Eildon Hills*. 1976. (Leaflet)
Selkirk, J.B.: *The Complete Poems*. Selkirk. 1938.
Sissons, J.B.: *The Evolution of Scotland's Scenery*. Oliver & Boyd. 1967.
Skene, W.F.: *Arthur and the Britons in Wales and Scotland*. (Edit D. Bryce)
Llanerch Enterprises. 1988.
Skinner, B.C.: *Union Canal: A Report*. LUCS. 1977.
Smith, Alexander: *Dreamthorp*. Routledge. n.d. (Titular essay in mid-
Victorian collection – on Linlithgow.)
Smith, T.G.: *Milngavie & District*. 1878.
(Old) Statistical Account of Scotland: Edit John Sinclair 1791-99 and
reprinted in 1980s by EP Publishing by areas; our route is covered by Vol 2
Lothians, Vol 3 *Eastern Borders*, Vol 9 *Dunbartonshire, Stirlingshire and
Clackmannanshire*.
Steel, D. & J.: *David Steel's Border Country*. Weidenfeld & Nicholson. 1985.
Stevenson, J.B.: *Exploring Scotland's Heritage, The Clyde Estuary and Central
Region*. HMSO. 1985.

Thackrah, J.R.: *The River Tweed*. Dalton. 1980.

Thom, V.M.: *Birds in Scotland*. Poyser. 1986. (Current best study)

Thomas, John: *Regional History of the Railways of Great Britain: Vol 6 Scotland, The Lowlands and the Borders*. David and Charles. 1981 revised edition.

: *Forgotten Railways: Scotland*. David & Charles. 1981.

Tough, D.I.W.: *The Last Years of a Frontier*. (1928) Sandhill Press. 1987.

Tranter, N.: *Portrait of the Lothians*. Hale. 1979.

: *Portrait of the Border Country*. Hale. 1978. (A readable survey.)

: *The Queen's Scotland: The Heartlands*. Hodder. 1971. (Includes Stirlingshire.)

: *The Fortified House in Scotland, Vol 1 South-East Scotland, Vol 2 Central Scotland*. J. Thin/Mercat Press. 1962, 1982.

: *The Bruce Trilogy*. Coronet. 1988. (Fictionalised history.)

: *Montrose*. Coronet. 1987. (Ditto, but an excellent introduction to making the past live.)

: *Cheviot Chase*. Ward Lock. 1952. (a modern ballad of a novel)

Veitch, J.: *History and Poetry of the Scottish Border* (2 vols. Blackwood. 1893.)

Wainwright, A : *Pennine Way Companion*. Westmorland Gazette. 1968 *et seq.*

Waldie, G.: *A History of the Town and Palace of Linlithgow*. Linlithgow. 1897. (1982 p.b. reprint)

: *Walks Along the Northern Roman Wall*. Linlithgow. 1883 and 1913.

Walker, A.: *The Big Walk*. Prentice-Hall. 1961. (The *Butlin* mobs, end to end.)

Walker, G.: *Thomas Johnstone*. Manchester UP. 1988.

Walton, J.: (edit) *The Border*. HMSO. 1962. (Forest Parks guide.)

Watson, G.: *The Border Reivers*. Sandhill Press. 1988.

Watson, J.: *Jedburgh Abbey*. Douglas. 1894.

Watson, T.: *Kirkintilloch: Town and Parish*. John Smith. 1894. (Standard history.)

White, J.T.: *The Scottish Border and Northumberland*. Eyre Methuen. 1973.

Whittle, T.: *The Plant Hunters*. Heinemann. 1970.

Williams, D.: *A Guide to the Southern Uplands Way*. Constable. 1989.

Williamson, A.G.: *Twixt Forth and Clyde*. London. 1944.

Willsher, B.: *Understanding Scottish Graveyards*. Chambers. 1985.

Willsher, B. and Hunter, D.: *Stones*. Canongate. 1978. (18th century gravestones)

Wilson, J.M.: *Tales of the Borders*. 1834 *et seq.* (Large, classic collection)

Wordsworth, D.: *Recollections of a Tour Made in Scotland*. Edinburgh. 1874 *et seq.*

Wright, C.J.: *The Pennine Way*. Constable. 1975 *et seq.*